S. Prakash Sethi and Dow Votaw, *editors*

THE PRENTICE-HALL SERIES
IN ECONOMIC INSTITUTIONS AND SOCIAL SYSTEMS

American
Business Values
in Transition

American Business Values in Transition

Gerald F. Cavanagh
Wayne State University

PRENTICE-HALL, INC., *Englewood Cliffs, New Jersey*

Library of Congress Cataloging in Publication Data

CAVANAGH, GERALD F
  American business values in transition.

  (The Prentice-Hall series in economic institutions
and social systems)
  Includes bibliographical references and index.
  1. United States—Commerce. 2. Industry—Social
aspects—United States 3. Business ethics. I. Title.
HF5343.C38   338'.0973   75-38745
ISBN 0-13-024141-5
ISBN 0-13-024133-4 pbk.

Printed in the United States of America

10 9 8 7 6 5 4

PRENTICE-HALL INTERNATIONAL, INC., *London*
PRENTICE-HALL OF AUSTRALIA PTY. LIMITED, *Sydney*
PRENTICE-HALL OF CANADA, LTD., *Toronto*
PRENTICE-HALL OF INDIA PRIVATE LIMITED, *New Delhi*
PRENTICE-HALL OF JAPAN, INC., *Tokyo*
PRENTICE-HALL OF SOUTHEAST ASIA PTE. LTD., *Singapore*

Contents

Foreword

After having been a part of the curriculum in many schools of business for twenty years or more, the field now vaguely described as "business and society" seems at last to be coming into focus. A common core of interest has begun to evolve and to give promise of providing the integrating concepts of teaching and research that have been so conspicuous by their absence in the past. Evidence of this long delayed crystallization can be found in new course descriptions and outlines, in the research interests of those working in the field, and in the proceedings of conferences convened for the purpose of examining the proper content and parameters of this important area of practical, as well as academic, concern. The field and its integrating theme appear very clearly, as suggested above, to be the complex, dynamic, two-way relationship between the economic institutions of our society, with which most schools of business are primarily concerned, and the social systems in which those institutions now operate and are likely to operate in the future.

It would be incorrect and misleading to suggest that the interaction between business and society has not been a part of the business school curriculum in the past. In one form or another, this interaction has played an important role in business and society courses for many years. There are, however, several basic differences between what has been done in the past and the new rallying point we now see evolving. The old, and still dominant, approach has been very narrow in its emphasis and in its boundaries and has all too often been limited to little more than an instructor's own specialty in such areas as social control, business and government, or antitrust. Even where an instructor's narrow predispositions are not present, the "social" side of the relationship is often viewed as being static, or relatively so, and external to the current decision or situational context; and the primary goals of the course are those of explaining the phenomenon of business to the students and of analyzing the requirements of business-like, efficient, or responsible behavior in a rather loose social sense. Furthermore, the emphasis is almost wholly the private, large, and industrial aspects of the economic sector, with little, if any, attention devoted to the public, small, or nonindustrial variables.

The flaws in the approach are obvious, and changes are already beginning to take place. What appears to be evolving, and what we believe should be evolving, is a much greater interest in the dynamics of the whole system. What is needed is a systematic analysis of the effects (noneconomic as well as economic) of business on other institutions and on the social system, and of the effects of changes in other institutions and in the social system on the economic sector. Most important, perhaps, the stage should be set for an understanding of the basic assumptions, attitudes, values, concepts, and ideologies that underlie a particular arrangement of economic institutions and social systems and of how changes in these assumptions affect the arrangements and the interactions among the various parts of the whole system.

Two other points ought also to be made here. *First*, although most schools of business do not behave as though it were so, they are actually engaged in training the managers of tomorrow and not the managers of today. As the relationships between economic institutions and their social environment become more intimate and as each part of the whole system becomes more sensitive and more responsive to changes in the other parts, how much more important it is going to be for the manager to understand the dynamics of the system as a whole than it is for him to know what the momentary conformation happened to be when he was in school. It seems to us, further, that one of the manifestations of an industrially mature society will be the economic sector's diminishing importance and, as a consequence, a reversal of the flow of influence from the economic sector to society as a whole. The manager of the future will need to be more sensitive to changes in society than he ever was in the past. His training will have to include a very different congeries of tools and ingredients than it now does.

Second, we think note should be taken of some evidence now beginning to accumulate that suggests that in the future schools of business may come to play the same sort of influential role in the profession of management that schools of law and medicine now play in theirs. If this change should come about, it will become ever more important that managers, during their period of formal education, be provided with those conceptual and analytical tools that best meet the needs of their profession and of the society as a whole. If present forecasts prove to be accurate and "continuing education" becomes a much more important aspect of higher education than it is now, among the first academic institutions to be profoundly affected will be the schools of business. The influence of the schools upon the profession of management will become more immediate and the need for pragmatic training in the interactions between economic institutions and social systems greatly enhanced.

While there is no great disagreement on these general issues, it would be a mistake to assume that there is consensus on the details. We believe that this series takes into account both the agreement on some of the broader points and the lack of consensus on many of the more specific aspects of the changes taking place in the environmental field. For example, there are people who believe that comments like those made above dictate the integration of social materials in all parts of the business curriculum rather than their use in specialized courses devoted to the field; there are many who feel that the bulk of such work should be done in specialized courses; there are many views in the area between these two extremes. We feel that this series is designed in such a way that it can cater to business school curricula of all varieties.

We visualize this series evolving in a set of concentric circles starting at the core and expanding outward. The innermost circle consists of those books that provide much of the basic material that is usually included in the introductory courses in "business and society," including the institutional role of large corporations; government interaction with business; business ideology and values; methodological approaches to measuring the social impact of business activities; corporations and political activities; and the influence of corporate management on the formulation of public policy.

The next circle is made up of books that deal with the impact of corporate activities in specific functional areas. The issues covered here include marketing and social conflict; accounting, accountability, and the public interest; corporate personnel policies and individual rights; and computers and invasion of privacy.

The outermost circle consists of books that are either interdisciplinary or cross-cultural in nature or both. Here we are concerned with the synergistic effect of various economic activities on the society as a whole. On one dimension we are concerned with issues such as how technology gets introduced into society; the economic effects of various types of social welfare programs; how various social activities like health, sanitation, mass transit, and public education are affected by the actions of business; and the social consequences of zero economic growth or population growth. On another level, studies will include comparison between corporate behavior in different social systems.

The concentric circles are not intended to be mutually exclusive, nor do they reflect a certain order of priority in the nature of problems or publication schedule. They are simply a convenient arrangement for thinking about the relationships among various problem areas.

In addition to their role as part of the training provided by collegiate schools of business and management and other social science disciplines, most of the volumes in this series are also of use and interest to managers and to the general public. The basic purpose of the series is to help provide a better understanding of the relationship between our economic institutions and the broader social system, and it is obvious that the need which the series hopes to satisfy is not confined to students of business and management or for that matter even to students. The ultimate goal, we suppose, is not just better corporate social policy but better public policy as well, in the formation of which all citizens participate. Consequently, we have urged the authors of these volumes to keep in mind the broad, in addition to the narrow, targets and to couch their work in language, content, and style that meet both kinds of requirements.

S. Prakash Sethi
Dow Votaw

University of California
Berkeley, California

Preface

This book will examine the values, ideals, and ideology upon which our American business system is built. Business, the corporation, and work are so central in our society that they, in turn, have a profound influence on personal values, attitudes, and life styles.

The purpose of this book is (1) to aid the individual in clarifying and formulating personal values, as they touch on both career and personal life, and (2) to aid business managers in determining corporate policy, and to help all citizens in clarifying their attitudes toward corporate and public policy. This book will therefore examine the value foundation upon which the business system of production and exchange has been built. Some of these values have shifted in recent years, and the modifications have had considerable influence on the corporation and the manager. These rifts and shifts in values, and their effect on the business system, will be examined in the following chapters.

It is the conviction of the author that we Americans must honestly face these shifts in values. Hence the challenges to the system and the inadequacies of traditional values will be presented straightforwardly and strongly. It is only in coping with these challenges that we can hope to reformulate our values and better structure our business system. And although this book will present many of the contemporary criticisms and challenges to business, it is written with the conviction that business—along with initiative and creativity in the private sector—is vital to the well-being of a developed society. The survival and health of both business and citizens depend on intelligent, perceptive, and energetic responses to these newly recognized values.

It would be too presumptuous to attempt here to construct a more adequate business ideology. Nevertheless, various chapters will focus on crucial issues out of which personal and institutional values and goals will be fashioned. The building blocks of a new ideology are here. Chapter 5 is the core, and in many ways the real beginning, of the book. One could begin reading there. It focuses on the contemporary situation, with special attention to current challenges to the traditional business ideology, along with some of the corporate responses. Chapter 3 examines the individual person within the organization with the aid of the behavioral sciences. It looks at the effect on life styles and the conflict in values that stem from pragmatism and the success ethic. Chapter 4 presents the Marxist position, which remains the most accurate indictment of and the most successful alternative to free enterprise.

Chapters 1 and 2 are a historical overview of the persons, problems, and events that have brought us to where we are. Chapter 1 also offers some definitions, along with an attempt to articulate some of the traditional values of Americans. Chapter 6, the last, summarizes inadequacies, underscores the importance of values and ideology, and then goes on to examine trends and project future shifts in values.

This book is the result of many years of stimulating and happy association with colleagues: fellow faculty, business people, experienced students, and brother members of the Society of Jesus. The manuscript has received invaluable constructive criticisms from the editors, Prakash Sethi and Dow Votaw. Margaret Betz, Michael Lavelle, and John Maurer also read the manuscript and provided important suggestions on content, style, and organization. My co-author in an earlier research project, Theodore Purcell, also read the latter chapters and added important qualifications and references, and Henry Wirtenberger and Joseph Daoust provided helpful critiques. Prentice-Hall's editors have been superb in shepherding the manuscript through to completion; I especially thank Earl Kivett, Maureen Wilson, and Jeannine Ciliotta.

Painstaking typing and checking of references was done by Linda Flack and Catherine Grisdela; and for this and other support, I am indebted to Dean Victor Doherty and Wayne State University's School of Business Administration. Finally, mature graduate students here, who have for some years faced management responsibilities, have provided significant inputs, emphases, and qualifications to the final manuscript.

Gerald F. Cavanagh

American
Business Values
in Transition

CHAPTER ONE

Values and Ideology in American Life

Probe the earth and see where your main roots are.

Henry David Thoreau

Values undergird, and sometimes determine, the important decisions that any individual makes. Whether these values are acknowledged or implicit, they are there; moreover, they have a profound influence on our lives and actions. To be aware of and to probe one's values allows a person to have greater control over those values, and hence over her or his own life and actions. To deny the importance of values is blind and obtuse.

Americans have some values that are rather unique; others we possess in common with other peoples. Here we will briefly examine our traditional American values and ideals in historical and critical overview. Before plunging into history, let us try to clarify what we mean by values, ideals, and ideology.

For the present, let us say that *values* are the criteria upon which important choices are made. These criteria are not merely objective, but contain a heavy affective component. Values are not only in the head, but are real and active enough in the person to actually influence decisions and actions. An *ideology* is a constellation of values that have been integrated into a fairly comprehensive, coherent, and motivating statement of purpose. As is true of values, an ideology is not merely a theoretical statement of position and purpose; it contains considerable motivating force. It is the rationale for life and action. It is the response one gives to oneself and to others on questions of purpose and meaning. An ideology embodies accepted *ideals,* the long-range goals an individual or a society holds out for itself. Hence ideals can significantly influence values. Ideals are sometimes distant, whereas values affect actions. Unless ideals are integrated into an ideology, they generally do not have much influence on actions and choices.

EARLY AMERICANS AND ENTERPRISE

The immigrants who came to the New World risked their lives and their fortunes in the hope of finding freedom and new opportunities. They came to a land that seemed to have limitless natural resources—timber, coal, much good farming land. Clearing the land was back-breaking, but it was good, fertile acreage that could be handed on to one's children. The changing climate encouraged work: it was brisk and invigorating; and the winters, when there would be no fruits or crops, demanded that settlers plan ahead and save something from the harvest. Two wide oceans provided natural defenses that until rather recently allowed the New World to focus on its own needs and development without much fear of foreign intrusions.

All these natural characteristics affected the values and ideology of the people. But when the settlers came, they brought with them values and ideals that heavily influenced these attitudes. Most of the early American immigrants were religious people. In fact, many of those who came to the colonies did so largely because of religious persecution in their native country; they sought a land where they could live and pray as conscience dictated. The men and women who settled along the coasts came from Europe, and so brought with them the religion that predominated there—Christianity. Of these groups, the Puritans, who came very early, have probably had the most profound influence on early American values and ideology.

The Puritans fled Europe so that they might freely follow their anthihierarchical religious faith and practices. To these men and women, who came well before the American Revolution, their work or their "calling" was an essential part of their total world view. To us today, the Puritan ideal is a delicate, even mysterious, paradox. It is succinctly described by the Puritan preacher John Cotton (1584-1652):

> There is another combination of virtues strangely mixed in every lively, holy Christian: and that is, diligence in worldly businesses, and yet deadness to the world. Such a mystery as none can read but they that know it.[1]

The Puritan plunged into his work with a dedication that could only come because it was his "calling." In John Cotton's words, "First, faith draws the heart of a Christian to live in some warrantable calling . . . though it be of an hired servant."[2] His worship of God was not shown in hymn singing, colorful religious services, or sterile monasticism; his worship was a simple, reverent prayer. Moreover, the Puritan's prayer was not separated

[1]Perry Miller, *The American Puritans* (Garden City, N.Y.: Doubleday, 1956), p. 171.
[2]*Ibid.,* p. 173.

from his work, for work was his most effective means of giving glory to God. So his work was disciplined and clear-eyed, because ". . . when he serves man, he serves the Lord; he doth the work set before him and he doth it sincerely and faithfully so as he may give account for it."[3] This early Puritan ideology strengthened the emerging social order by giving importance to every type of work. Again in John Cotton's words, "[faith] encourageth a man in his calling to the most homeliest and difficultest and most dangerous things his calling can lead and expose himself to."[4] Self-discipline was also important, for the Puritan was not to be caught up in his own success or failure. He was an ascetic in the world; although in it, he was detached from it.

Two generations later, Cotton Mather (1663-1728) was born into the same family of erudition and clerical leadership. Like his grandfather, Mather held that "A Christian has two callings: a general calling 'to serve the Lord Jesus Christ,' and a particular calling which was his work or his business. Both of these callings are essential if the Christian is to achieve salvation. Neither can be overemphasized. The Puritan divine says, 'Contemplation of the good means nothing without accomplishment of the good. A man must not only be pious; he must be useful' "[5] The Puritan businessman fully integrated his work with his worship. Often he would mention God in his invoices, thanking him for a profit, or accepting losses for his greater glory. Moreover, the individual determined his calling, and his work was generally done individually. In the same fashion, he achieved salvation individually.

American Puritans did not invent this position; they took the theology of Martin Luther and John Calvin, and spelled out in some detail the implications for the businessman. The businessman in turn, eager for some justification of the efforts to which he devoted most of his waking hours, happily received the Puritan preacher's words. So there began the mutual understanding and support between preacher and businessman that became a hallmark of New World society.

Benjamin Franklin's Way to Wealth

In the pre-Revolutionary period, Benjamin Franklin accepted the work values of the Puritans, shifted them from a religious to a secular foundation, and restated them for Americans. Franklin, especially in *Poor Richard's Almanack,* was prolific, mundane, incisive, and widely influential. Many of his homely bits of advice have become embedded in our lan-

[3]John Cotton in *ibid.,* p.176.
[4]*Ibid.,* p. 177.
[5]A. Whitney Griswold, "Two Puritans on Prosperity," in *Benjamin Franklin and the American Character,* ed. Charles L. Sanford (Boston: D. C. Heath, 1955), p. 41.

guage; they now belong to us all. Looking back over twenty-five years of his *Almanack,* Franklin brought together his writings on the world of work and of business and published them in 1758 as the essay "The Way to Wealth."

> God helps them that helps themselves. . . . Diligence is the mother of good luck, as Poor Richard says, and God gives all things to industry. Then plough deep, while sluggards sleep, and you shall have corn to sell and to keep, says Poor Dick. Work while it is called today, for you know not how much you may be hindered tomorrow. . . . Be ashamed to catch yourself idle. . . . When there is so much to be done for your- self, your family, your country, and your gracious king, be up at peep of day; . . . 'Tis true that much is to be done, and perhaps you are weak handed, but stick to it steadily, and you will see great effects, for constant dropping wears away stones . . . and little strokes fell great Oaks.[6]

In his own simple way, Franklin focuses on the importance of saving and the need for capital when he urges: "A man may, if he knows not how to save as he gets, keep his nose all his life to the grindstone. . . . If you would be wealthy, think of saving as well as of getting."[7] It must have been immensely satisfying to Franklin's early American contemporaries to see him supporting the same values and justification for their work as did their ministers. He provided a rationale for work and a purpose for life; at the same time, he buttressed the existing social order.

Franklin's writings were best sellers in his day and have exerted a tre- mendous influence up to the present. In his *Almanack,* his *Autobiography,* and in his very life Franklin embodied the Puritan virtues. Here was a man who was eminently successful as an inventor, statesman, diplomat, and bus- inessman, and who espoused the same virtues as did the Puritan ministers. Although some aristocrats of his own day, such as John Adams, resented Franklin's popular wisdom, he was popular with the people. Harvard- educated John Adams was a New England patrician: brilliant and coura- geous, but also haughty and stubborn. Adams conceded that Franklin was a genius, wit, politician, and humorist, but questioned his greatness as a phi- losopher, moralist, or statesman.[8] In spite of Adams' petty quarrels with Franklin, history shows Franklin to have had greater influence on values. Thomas Jefferson agreed with the hard-working, individualistic ideals of Franklin, although Jefferson, who wrote the *Declaration of Independence* in the same year (1776) that Adam Smith wrote his *Wealth of Nations,* was

---

[6]Benjamin Franklin, *The Autobiography and Other Writings* (New York: New American Library, 1961), p. 190.

[7]*Ibid.,* p. 192.

[8]For this essay, see John Adams, "An Exaggerated Reputation," in Sanford, *op. cit.,* pp. 22-26.

convinced that these virtues could best be fostered, and the new nation grow best, as an agricultural society.[9] Jefferson felt that as long as a man had his own land to till and crops to care for, the economy would thrive and men would be happier.

At this time more than 80 percent of the American work force were farmers, and if Jefferson had had his way, that is how it would have remained. Jefferson was opposed to the industrialization he had seen in England. He would rather import finished manufactured goods than undergo the undesirable changes manufacturing inevitably brings: urbanization, landless workers, banking. In an agricultural society, where work and initiative immediately pay off for the individual, and for the society as a whole, government intervention could be kept to an absolute minimum. It could only retard the natural forces of growth and encumber society with additional overhead, regulations, and bureaucracy. In Jefferson's own oft-quoted words, "That government is best which governs least." The ambivalent feelings toward and even fear of industry appeared early, for industry spawns cities. An agrarian society is simpler; duties and rewards are more easily seen and measured. Early Americans were therefore not always favorably disposed toward industry or the cities.

The American Frontier

The continuing westward expansion served to keep alive the simpler, measurable agrarian values. The effect of this westward movement and the frontier on the American character was spelled out by Fredrick Jackson Turner[10] just before the turn of this century. To successive waves of hunters, traders, ranchers, and finally farmers, there were always new lands to conquer. It seemed to be a world without limits. The Indians were not settled, and there were few of them to offer resistance. For the brave and hearty immigrant, it was worth taking great risks, whether in moving or in building. Success meant wealth; failure, the chance to try again somewhere else.

The new territories demanded the strenuous effort of clearing the land. The first farmers faced the immense task of pulling out trees and building their homes and barns. Nevertheless, the rewards were also great: they would have homes, incomes, and could pass on those farms to future generations. The rewards were clear, tangible, and permanent, and they gave settlers incentive and zest. The land is measurable and unambiguous. It is

---

[9] Arthur M. Schlesinger, "Ideas and Economic Development," in *Paths of American Thought,* ed. Arthur M. Schlesinger, Jr., and Morton White (Boston: Houghton Mifflin, 1963), pp. 108-9.
[10] *The Frontier in American History* (New York: Holt, 1920).

open to human effort; if one works harder, one will be able to produce more.

Turner himself sums up how the effect of the frontier has given the American intellect its striking characteristics:

> That coarseness and strength combined with acuteness and inquisitiveness; that practical, inventive turn of mind, quick to find expedients; that masterful grasp of material things, lacking in the artistic but powerful to effect great ends; that restless, nervous energy; that dominant individualism, working for good and for evil, and withal that buoyancy and exuberance which comes with freedom—these are traits of the frontier or traits called out elsewhere because of the existence of the frontier.[11]

Turner's thesis has been widely quoted and has had a great influence on thinkers and men of affairs. President John F. Kennedy's New Frontier was an attempt to tap that vision again, and the energy, initiative, and sense of accomplishment that comes with it. Perhaps there was a new frontier in the 1960s; clearly, profound new challenges face Americans today. The question then becomes whether Americans will respond to those challenges with something of the same task-orientation, energy, creativity, and determination as did their forebears.

Tocqueville's View of Americans

As anyone who has lived in another culture for any length of time knows, the peculiar characteristics of that culture stand out in bold relief to the foreigner. In that same process, of course, one is also far better able to recognize the unique qualities of one's own culture. A people's characteristic values and ideology can best be understood in comparison with another culture. Thus a perceptive foreign visitor often is able to describe the values and characteristics of the host people with considerable insight. Because of this, Alexis de Tocqueville remains one of the best commentators on the American character.

A young French lawyer, Alexis de Tocqueville came to the United States in 1831 to observe and learn from the people. His reflections, *Democracy in America,* were written for the French, but they attained instant success not only in France, but in England and the United States as well. Published in English translation in 1838, the work was immediately praised for its insight and lack of bias, and it is still regarded almost 140 years later as one of the finest commentaries on American life. Tocqueville tried to understand Americans on their own terms. The well-known leader of English liberal-

[11]*Ibid.,* p. 37.

ism, John Stuart Mill, reviewed Tocqueville's work and was deeply impressed with it.[12]

On arriving, Tocqueville noted the physical expanse of the new country: "The inhabitants of the U.S. constitute a great civilized people, which fortune has placed in the midst of an uncivilized country."[13] It was this same combination, of course, which was to help give rise to the independence, resourcefulness, and frontier spirit of which Fredrick Jackson Turner was later to write. Tocqueville noticed that, preoccupied by the great task to be accomplished, Americans tend to value facts more than consistent ideals, that which works more than the beauty of a comprehensive ideological system. He characterized the American "philosophical method," the American method of reflection and learning, as "to evade the bondage of system and habit, of family maxims, class opinions, and, in some degree, of national prejudices." Americans accept tradition only as a starting point, the existing situation only "as a lesson to be used in doing otherwise and in doing better."[14] Each individual seeks to understand for himself. All these characteristics Tocqueville summed up as an individualism of thought: ". . . each American appeals only to the individual effort of his own understanding." This mentality shows that what we today call the generation gap is no new thing: ". . . every man there readily loses all traces of the ideas of his forefathers or takes no care about them."[15] Looking back on recent United States' history, we see that the exaggerated stability that characterized the 1950s and early 1960s was actually a temporary interlude, and by American standards it was precarious and unreal.

Tocqueville saw Americans as hard working and individualistic. The only rationale they might have for their actions and attitudes is enlightened self-interest. They are not inclined to reverence for tradition, philosophy, or even much reflection. He focused on the same favorable attitude toward work that has been attributed to the Puritan, the immigrant, and the frontier settler. Americans see work "as the necessary, natural, and honest condition of human existence."[16] Labor is not only not dishonorable, it is held in honor among the people. Even the rich man feels it his obligation to take up some sort of worthwhile work, whether this work be private or some sort of public business.

When Americans were asked *why* they work, act, and think as they do, Tocqueville reported that they gave a rather consistent response:

[12]For the substance of the review, see the Introduction to *Democracy in America,* tr. Henry Reeve (New York: Knopf, 1946), pp. xxix-xl.

[13]*Ibid.,* Vol. 1, p. 422.

[14]*Ibid.,* Vol. II, p. 3.

[15]*Ibid.,* Vol. II, p. 4.

[16]*Ibid.,* Vol. II, p. 152.

> The Americans . . . are fond of explaining almost all the actions of
> their lives by the principle of self-interest rightly understood; they
> show with complacency how an enlightened regard for themselves
> constantly prompts them to assist one another and inclines them will-
> ingly to sacrifice a portion of their time and property to the welfare of
> the state.[17]

Although not unique to America, by the time of Tocqueville's visit enlightened self-interest had taken firm root here. The coming of Social Darwinism in the generation following the publication of *Democracy in
America* was to make the self-interest doctrine even more popular, as we
shall see later.

With remarkable insight, Tocqueville underscored both the strengths and
the weaknesses of this philosophy. The principle of self-interest is not a
lofty goal, but it is clear and certain. It does not demand much of a person,
yet observing it does produce results. It is not difficult to understand for all
sorts and classes of people. As a principle of human life, self-interest builds
on man's infirmities:

> By its admirable conformity to human weaknesses it easily obtains
> great dominion; nor is that dominion precarious, since the principle
> checks one personal interest by another, and uses, to direct the pas-
> sions, the very same instrument that excites them.[18]

The principle of enlightened self-interest produces no great acts of
self-sacrifice, but it encourages a daily discipline of self-denial. By itself
self-interest cannot make a man good and virtuous, and hence can hardly
serve as a cornerstone of morality. Nevertheless, said Tocqueville, "it disciplines large numbers of people in habits of regularity, temperance, moder-
ation, foresight, self-command."

Enlightened self-interest is closely related to individualism. Tocqueville's
work was the first to discuss individualism and, in fact, the first to bring the
word into the English language. It is characteristic of Americans that individualism was not a common word among them, even though it so well described some of their salient attitudes and values. People develop a vocabu-
lary for those things of concern to them, those things they therefore want to
discuss. Americans were not then, nor are they now, a very reflective
people. Tocqueville suggested that there is probably no other civilized
country in which less attention is paid to reflection and philosophy than the
United States.

Tocqueville described individualism as a mature and calm feeling, which
disposes each member of the community "to sever himself from the mass of

[17]*Ibid.,* Vol. II, p. 122.
[18]*Ibid.,* Vol. II, pp. 122-23.

his fellows and to draw apart with his family and his friends.'' Each individual retreats to his own familiar turf, and thus ''leaves society at large to itself.'' The Frenchman contrasted individualism and selfishness, and he found both seriously deficient:

> Selfishness originates in blind instinct; individualism proceeds from erroneous judgment more than from depraved feelings; it originates as much in deficiencies of mind as in perversity of heart.
>
> Selfishness blights the germ of all virtue; individualism, at first, only saps the virtues of public life; but in the long run it attacks and destroys all others and is at length absorbed in downright selfishness.[19]

Tocqueville quite early pinpointed possibly the most serious weakness of free enterprise. Enlightened self-interest and individualism narrow one's perspective. They encourage one to think less of public responsibilities, and they lead eventually and almost inevitably to selfishness. He almost sounded like a contemporary critic reflecting on the weaknesses of the corporate executive or the bureaucrat. Tocqueville's sensitive assessment of the American character—its impatience with tradition, reflection, and abstract ideals; its task-orientation and individualism; its self-interest leading to selfishness—still stands as one of the great social commentaries. Later observers often used Tocqueville as a starting point, but few have done a better overall appraisal than he.

Recent Foreign Views

Another Frenchman, writing in the 1950s, attempted to probe the basic values of the American people. He found that he

> . . . admires unreservedly the Americans' courage, energy and generosity as individuals, the way they work together as a harmonious team, and the healthy social atmosphere which on the whole they have managed to create and maintain.[20]

He sees these characteristics as not only a cause of prosperity in this country, but also an effect. He finds other tendencies much less attractive:

> . . . to subordinate the spiritual and artistic values to that of material success. Their impatience and restlessness, their cult of speed, and the breathless pace of their lives.[21]

---

[19]*Ibid.,* Vol. II, p. 98.

[20]William E. Rappard, *The Secret of American Prosperity,* tr. Kenneth A. J. Kickson (New York: Greenberg, 1955), p. 123.

[21]*Ibid.*

These tendencies, both the attractive and the unattractive, describe the attitudes that support the great economic prosperity of the United States. They underlie the passion for productivity and efficiency and the spirit of competition, which in turn contribute to the traditional measures of economic success.

Underscoring these same work-oriented yet approachable qualities of the American is the work of a European scientist, the French Jesuit palaeontologist Pierre Teilhard de Chardin, who spent many years in the United States. Teilhard had a sympathetic view of the American character in spite of his own penchant for reflection and asceticism. Writing from an expedition where he was working with Americans in the Gobi Desert, Teilhard says:

> People here are inclined to treat the Americans as a joke, but the more I see of them the more I admire their ability to work and get things done, and the kinder and more approachable I find them. . . . In my own branch of science it's the Americans who are showing us how we must set to work on the earth if we are to read its secret and make ourselves its masters.[22]

Granting an American's ability to get a job done, that orientation to action is also the source of much criticism. Many foreigners see Americans as shallow and materialistic—more wedded to things than to goals, more inclined to do than to reflect. An Englishman gives his impression of American shallowness by pointing to "a general preoccupation with trivia—I mean Coke machines, launderettes . . . laxatives and baseball." He sees being caught up in superficialities as "the American attempt to exclude the bigger reality—reflection and looking to larger goals."[23]

On the other hand, Jacques Maritain, a shrewd interpreter of medieval European philosophy and contemporary humanism, defends Americans against the charge of being excessively materialistic. Maritain speaks of the people among whom he spent the last decades of his life:

> I would say that the accusation of materialism, technocratic inhumanity, etc., appears especially unfair. . . . Of course, here [America] as elsewhere in the world, industrial civilization entails the temptation of materialist technocratism. But this country, which seems at first glance more threatened by such a temptation because it is more industrialized, has, in reality, a better chance of overcoming it, because from the very start the American effort is directed toward the good of man, the humble dignity of man in each one of us.[24]

[22]*Letters from a Traveller,* tr. Rene Hague, Violet Hammersley, Barbara Wall, and Noel Lindsay (New York: Harper & Row, 1962), p. 106.

[23]Robert Robinson, quoted in *U.S.A.: The Permanent Revolution,* by the editors of *Fortune* (Englewood Cliffs, N.J.: Prentice-Hall, 1951), p. 220.

[24]*Reflections on America* (New York: Scribner's, 1958), pp. 89-90.

Maritain articulately summarizes the national characteristic that foreign
and domestic observers view as being basic to American survival and
growth not only as an economy, but as a people: the attitude toward every
man and woman. It is this characteristic, a combination of humaneness and
pragmatism, that may be the best foundation for the solution of future
dilemmas.

Foreign social commentators, then, have felt the pulse of America and
pointed to elements in our national character that make us simultaneously
proud and humble. It is essential that we be aware of these characteristics if
we are to make any intelligent assessment of our national character. It is
even more important if we expect to have any influence on our own values
and the values of our nation.

Social Darwinism and Herbert Spencer

Herbert Spencer (1820-1903) proposed a harsh "survival of the fittest"
philosophy. The bright and able contribute most to society, and so are to be
encouraged and rewarded. The poor, the weak, and the handicapped
demand more than they contribute, and so should not be supported but
rather allowed to die a natural death. Contact with harsh and demanding
reality is a maturing experience that should not be diluted by well-intentioned
but in reality destructive charities and handouts. If "natural" principles
were followed, evolution and the survival of the fittest in the competition of
human life would be the result. Spencer did not set out to examine any
particular society and its values; rather, his critique was proposed as
"culture-free." According to Spencer, it applied to all people for it was
derived from basic, organic principles of growth and development. Spencer
applied to society the same principles that Charles Darwin saw in biological
life—hence the name, Social Darwinism.

The events of the latter half of the nineteenth century had a profound impact on attitudes. The Industrial Revolution, the growth of cities, and the
beginning of the concept of evolution shook the foundations of life and
thought. Speaking of evolution, the contemporary American historian
Richard Hofstadter has said: "Many scientific discoveries affect ways of
living more profoundly than evolution did; but none have had a greater
impact on ways of thinking and believing."[25]

Spencer, William Graham Sumner, and others who became prophets of
the new evolutionary social ideology were impressed with the suffering of
the poor, but they nevertheless felt that progress in an industrial society
could come only through long hours of work, saving, self-discipline, and
even the death of the less able. Rather than considering this a tragedy, they
were convinced that through this process of natural selection, those of

[25]Richard Hofstadter, *Social Darwinism in American Thought* (New York: Braziller, 1959),
p. 3.

greater talent, intelligence, and ability would survive and be successful. The physically and mentally handicapped, unable to compete successfully, would be less apt to survive. It would obviously be a mistake for the government to provide assistance to these handicapped and deficient persons. That would allow them to stay alive, and worse, to reproduce, and so transmit their deficiencies to future generations.

Any attempt to minister to the needs of the poor or needy is misguided on several counts. It keeps alive those who are less able. It diverts the attention and abilities of able people who would be better off pursuing more profitable careers. And finally, it insulates the less able from a sobering contact with harsh reality and poverty, an opportunity that might have jerked them from their complacency and encouraged them to work harder to better themselves. Although it might be painful to the weak in the short run, the overall good of society in the long run demands that these less fit individuals not be supported or encouraged. According to Spencer, society improves because of the survival of the fittest:

> The poverty of the incapable, the distresses that come upon the imprudent, the starvation of the idle, and those shoulderings aside of the weak by the strong, which leave so many "in shallows and in miseries," are the decrees of a large, farseeing benevolence. . . . Under the natural order of things society is constantly excreting its unhealthy, imbecile, slow, vacillating, faithless members.[26]

It is especially clear in primitive societies that the strongest and cleverest survive best. But this is a natural process, and so it occurs in civilized societies, too. People would be wise to prepare themselves and their children for this struggle.

Society as a whole will benefit from this struggle for survival. Since the most intellectually and physically fit survive, the race will improve. Given a difficult and demanding environment, over several generations the ideal man will develop. There should therefore be little state interference in this natural selection process. The state must not regulate industry, impose tariffs, give subsidies, establish a church, regulate entry into the professions, operate schools, or run the mail service. Most especially, the government must not provide for the poor, improve sanitation, or look to the health needs of the less able.[27]

Herbert Spencer's philosophy was far more popular in the United States than in his native England. His praise of the strong, clever, and aggressive individual coincided with the spirit of the times. Further, his theory of inevitable progress was received enthusiastically in a country already marked with general optimism. Spencer's thinking provided both a rational

[26]Herbert Spencer, *Social Statics* (London: Appleton, 1850), pp. 323-26, 353.
[27]See Donald Fleming, "Social Darwinism," in Schlesinger and White, *op. cit.,* pp. 124-25.

foundation for already existing attitudes and a justification for many public and private practices. In the last third of the nineteenth century, Spencer was a leader of thought, a thinker to be reckoned with, and a hero to many in the United States.

The personal attributes Spencer extolled are what we currently call "middle-class virtues." They focused on the hearty, adaptable individual in a hostile climate: careful planning ahead, hard work, loyalty and responsibility to family, and individual self-sufficiency. And as radical as they may have seemed to his contemporaries, Spencer's theories were actually quite conservative in overtone. Spencer saw great good in the way things were; there was no need to change or to plan ahead on a national or local level. Since natural processes will inevitably produce the best people and the best society, any sort of government or even private intervention in the process will only hurt society in the long run. Citizens must repress their feelings of pity for the poor, and must allow natural processes to work themselves out. Although Spencer's theories challenged all the established theologies of the time and were thus opposed by many churchmen, his position seemed a natural extension of the traditional Puritan ethic and especially its secularized counterpart, as expressed by Benjamin Franklin. It is thus no surprise that Spencer's theories were enthusiastically received by the business community of his day, but we will wait until the next chapter to examine their implications for business in greater detail.

Social commentators and intellectual historians have provided us with considerable insight into our own origins and character. Examining their commentaries has enabled us better to grasp our own root values, those values that provide the foundation for our current business ideology. The physical environment, combined with the attitudes and values of the people who came to the New World, has given the United States a unique world position: rich and abundant farmland, protected east and west borders, and the frontier, coupled with the Puritan ethic. (This ethic, more on the history of attitudes toward business, and the development of the contemporary American business creed will be discussed in the next chapter.)

THE FUNCTION OF IDEOLOGY

An ideology is a coherent, systematic, and moving statement of basic values and purpose. It is a constellation of values generally held by a group, and those in the group tend to support one another in that ideology. An ideology seeks and provides some systematic answers to these questions: What are we about? Why are we doing this? How can I explain my life and my society to myself and to others?

Ideologies possess certain common features. They are selective in the issues they treat and in the supporting evidence and argument they use.

They are straightforward and uncomplicated, even when the actual material is quite complicated. Their content is limited to what is publicly acceptable. Finally, although ideologies are answers to questions and hence address the intellect, they nevertheless do so in a manner that also engages the emotions. They can inspire and motivate men to cooperate and even undergo great hardship for the sake of a compelling goal.

The positive effect of an ideology is that it gives a people direction, coherence, norms, criteria, and motivation. It can bring clarity and assurance to the mind, and hence vigor and enthusiasm to life and work. These are great advantages, especially to a society troubled by doubts and by lessened confidence in institutions and inadequate leadership. A group possessing an ideology is thus given meaning, direction, and drive. Nations and peoples have left their mark on history, whether for good or ill, almost to the extent to which they have fashioned for themselves a comprehensive and compelling ideology—for example, ancient Rome, Victorian England, and Nazi Germany.

Almost everything that we do of any substance flows from an often implicit ideology, from raising children to going to work, from conducting foreign policy to meeting neighbors. Even a position that ideologies are unnecessary, or demeaning, or oppressive is in itself an ideology. Subgroups within a society, even the Rotary Club, possess some sort of constellation of values, however limited or narrow. Generally the more embracing a group, a movement, or a state, the more complete will be its ideology.

On the other hand, ideology has some disadvantages. It can rigidify. It tends to lock persons and systems into classes, roles, and expectations, as ironically often happens with contemporary Marxists. A doctrinaire ideology can cause fanaticism, intransigence, and uncompromising attitudes. It can impede progress and cause anxieties for those in the group who find difficulties with the ideology, often those who are the most innovative and talented. The group as a whole then tends to expend a great deal of effort on defending its position instead of looking to the future.

Ideology is actually a term of abuse for traditional Marxists. To them, it is the rationalization of privilege by the upper classes. These classes use ideology to justify the arrangements associated with their own positions and interests by claiming that they are essential for the good of the country and for mankind. Marx calls this "collective illusion," another tool of oppression of the ruling classes. He makes the excellent point that this sort of ideology mistakes the contingent and historical situation for a permanent and natural one.

An ideology is an explication of values. It is a spelling out of attitudes, feelings, and goals. Without an explicit ideology, a nation or group is left without clearly stated purposes, and hence without consensus or the drive that comes from purpose. When an ideology is spelled out, it can be examined, challenged, and altered as conditions change and new needs arise. It is then in the open for all to accept or reject as they see fit. When an ideology is not explicit, it is sometimes claimed that there is no ideology; but this is hardly true. The ideology is merely implicit, unspoken, and hence unexamined. This is a precarious position for any society, since probing questions can thus cause confusion and chaos.

There are a number of new pressures to spell out our national values and the ideology in which they are embedded. These pressures also apply to the rationale for our business activities, which is the subject of this book. Demands for an exposition of our ideology come from a variety of sources:

1. Younger people are asking of their parents, teachers, and national leaders "What are we about?" "What are our goals?" "Why?"
2. As we as a nation become better educated, and hence more reflective, we are more likely to expect informed, thoughtful, explicit statements of purpose and ideals.
3. As population increases and we live closer together, we find that what one does often infringes on others. For example, building a new expressway, polluting rivers, or moving a plant or office all infringe on others' rights. As managers, citizens, or government officials, we need criteria for making such decisions; and criteria require some explicit goals. Otherwise, "decisions " are often made on crass and unexamined immediate criteria, or by means of the "conventional wisdom," which is often not wisdom at all.

There is a need for answering these questions. Some consensus is necessary on large public issues. In addition, each person is challenged to work out his or her own answers to basic value questions, to formulate his or her own constellation of values. The agreed-on values, especially those that touch on public life and issues, can be called an ideology. As such, they can provide direction and verve. And an awareness of the dangers in ideology—for example, that it may be a mask for privilege or that it may rigidify—should better enable us to avoid these pitfalls.

Origin and Impact of Ideology

A continuing dispute pits those who say that an ideology comes after the fact as a rationalization of reality against those who maintain that an already-existing ideology has a powerful influence on the world. These positions are reconciled by Berger and Luckman:

It is correct to say that theories are concocted in order to legitimate already existing social institutions. But it also happens that social institutions are changed in order to bring them into conformity with already existing theories, that is, to make them more "legitimate."[28]

[28]Peter L. Berger and Thomas Luckman, *The Social Construction of Reality* (Garden City, N.Y.: Doubleday Anchor, 1967), p. 128.

An ideology as a rationalization of the existing order obviously tends to defend the status quo. An ideology based on ideals that aim to change that status quo into something that is viewed as better is often called utopian. To Americans, "utopian" has an idealistic, pie-in-the-sky, pejorative connotation. Here we will use it as a descriptive term only.

Karl Mannheim in his classic *Ideology and Utopia*[29] says that a state of mind is utopian if it has some elements that transcend reality as it exists. In addition, when these elements pass over into conduct, they "tend to shatter, either partially or wholly, the order of things prevailing at the time." In other words, ideas and ideals that tend to change reality can be called utopian. According to Mannheim, ideologies become utopian when groups begin to act on them and to challenge the existing order.

Many utopias of today become the realities of tomorrow. Indeed, one definition of utopia is that it is merely premature truths. The principles of democracy and freedom were utopian in the minds of those who founded the United States. Their notions of representation and individual rights were ideals which, when they were written into documents and acted upon, challenged the status quo, shattered the existing order, and even caused a revolution. Looking back over this same period of rising aspirations, especially in the Western world, Mannheim calls the prevailing ideology of freedom a utopia:

> The utopia of the ascendant bourgeoisie was the idea of "freedom." It was in part a real utopia, i.e., it contained elements oriented towards the realization of a new social order and which were instrumental in disintegrating the previously existing social order and which, after their realization, did in part become translated into reality. Freedom in the sense of bursting asunder the bonds of the static, guild, and caste order, in the sense of freedom of thought and opinion, in the sense of political freedom and freedom of the unhampered development of the personality became . . . a realizable possibility.[30]

Generalizing, Mannheim points out that any nation or group which wants to translate its ideals into reality must formulate an ideology that builds on the existing values, needs, and aspirations of the people. This utopian ideology may then catch the imagination of the people and be the inspiration for change. For every utopian ideology that eventually becomes reality, there are dozens that never get beyond the stage of ideas. They may have caused some upset and discord in society, and their adherents are often 'considered fanatical.

There are a number of dangers inherent in any ideology in addition to

---

[29]Karl Manheim, *Ideology and Utopia,* tr. Louis Wirth and Edward Shils (New York: Harcourt, Brace & World, 1936), p. 192. Quoted with permission.

[30]*Ibid.,* p. 203.

those pointed out earlier. Those of being closed to facts and of fanaticism are highlighted by Mannheim: "Nothing is more removed from actual events than the closed rational system. Under certain circumstances, nothing contains more irrational drive than a fully self-contained intellectualistic world view."[31] Those who feel they are well adjusted to the current state of affairs have little incentive to theorize, according to Mannheim.[32] These conservatives are happy with their situation, and so they defend the status quo. He points out that people do little theorizing about situations in which they find themselves as long as they are content. They tend to regard their current situation as part of the natural order of things; the way things are is the way they ought to be. As long as that current state is unquestioned, there is little impetus for conservatives to reflect on the situation. They tend to emphasize practical "how to do it" concerns—the means of coping within existing structures. It is only in the face of challenges to the status quo that conservatives do much reflecting. So the reflection and therefore the ideology of conservatives are generally not as profound or comprehensive as those of the challengers. It thus happens that the "most recent antagonist dictates the tempo and the form of the battle."[33]

Challenge Brings Understanding

A valuable by-product of this type of challenge and reformulation of goals and ideologies is that the society is compelled to examine itself. This sort of unmasking and examination of ideology can result in self-clarification for society as a whole. A society with a weak ideology, or one in which ideology is unimportant, can generally be characterized as stable, complacent, and content with its inherited laws, customs, and ideals. At the very end of his chapter on the utopian mentality, Mannheim paints a sad, even desperate, picture of a society or a people without a utopian ideology:

> The disappearance of utopia brings about a static state of affairs in which man himself becomes no more than a thing. We would be faced then with the greatest paradox imaginable, namely, that man, who has achieved the highest degree of rational mastery of existence, left without any ideals, becomes a mere creature of impulses. Thus, after a long, tortuous, but heroic development, just at the highest stage of awareness, when history is ceasing to be blind fate, and is becoming more and more man's own creation, with the relinquishment of utopias, man would lose his will to shape history and therewith his ability to understand it.[34]

[31]*Ibid.*, p. 219.
[32]*Ibid.*, p. 229.
[33]*Ibid.*, p. 231.
[34]*Ibid.*, pp. 262-63.

Mannheim presents an impersonal, alienating, and frightening prospect of a world without utopias—without ideals or engaging goals.

On the other hand, injustices can also be perpetrated in the name of an irrational but compelling ideology. Any strong, moving ideology risks being gross, oversimplified, and even unjust. Mannheim's own Germany a few years later was to undergo a revolution in the name of "Aryan superiority" and the "master race." Nevertheless, without ideals worked into some sort of ideology, little new can be accomplished on any significant scale. People cease to question themselves and their society. They lose their direction and their enthusiasm for life. Hitler's ideology was a reaction to such a vacuum.

Suspicion of Ideology

Probably a majority of Americans share with Arthur Schlesinger, Jr., an abiding distrust of ideology. In an attempt to outline what has caused the rapid economic development of the United States, Schlesinger acknowledges the physical advantages of the continent. But he points out that the fertile lands and natural resources were there for the Indians, too, but were never exploited.[35] Schlesinger maintains that the most important element in the success story of the United States was the spirit of the settlers. He contends that this spirit manifested itself in three important ways. The first was a faith in education; investment in people through education results in increases in productivity. A second factor encouraging development was the commitment to self-government and representative institutions. Democracy was important for releasing man's talents and energies.

The third uniquely favorable element in the American spirit, and probably the most important one according to Schlesinger, is a rejection of ideology: "America has had the good fortune not to be an ideological society."[36] Schlesinger defines ideology to be "a body of systematic and rigid dogma by which people seek to understand the world—and to preserve or transform it." Many Americans, with Schlesinger as a spokesman, feel that ideology constricts and distracts man from the reality around him. They would not allow ideology to "falsify reality, imprison experience, or narrow the spectrum of choice."[37] This is part of an attitude that encourages innovation and experiment, part of the dominant empirical and pragmatic American approach.

The principal difficulty with an ideology is that it is a partial depiction of reality. Certain elements are emphasized and others neglected. When decisions are made, they can thus be biased or even wrong. The Communist

[35]See "Epilogue: The One Against the Many," in Schlesinger and White, *op. cit.,* pp. 531-38.

[36]*Ibid.,* p. 532.

[37]*Ibid.,* p. 533.

states, for example, often do not tolerate positions that depart from the official ideology. The dominant American philosophy, pragmatism, is not heavily theoretical. It will be discussed in more detail in the next chapter, but suffice it for now to point out that pragmatism stays close to the facts; to simplify, it holds "that which works is true."

Schlesinger rightly rejects rigid dogma that would subjugate man and facts to an ideology. Americans have achieved much success in being flexible, open, and risk-taking in a pluralistic society. He is, however, too quick and cavalier in his rejection of ideology. His definition of ideology as "a body of systematic and rigid dogma" better enables him to do this, since it embodies the undesirable properties he seeks to reject. Furthermore, he seems to miss the essential point that value judgments are being made constantly, and these value judgments, along with the world view in which they are embedded, are in fact an ideology. It only obscures understanding to deny this.

Schlesinger may not like ideology, but his own position is an ideology in its own right. It is an ideology that values freedom, laissez-faire, and selective nonintervention. Moreover, that freedom is especially for me and mine. It does not apply to the American Indians who, in spite of the fact that they did not "exploit" their lands as Schlesinger would have liked, were pushed off those lands. The Indians did not have the freedom to decide how they would use their lands. This sort of double standard calls for government intervention to preserve *my* freedom and prerogatives; it calls for nonintervention when government regulations restrict my freedom, or the freedom of my organization. Schlesinger is consistent in using this same ideology in international relations. He supports the balance of power in the expectation that each nation will pursue its own self-interest; and he rejects any sort of moralism or altruism as a basis for policy between nations.

There is a typically American implied faith that, if each person or group uses its talents and intelligence to pursue its own long-term self-interest, it will work out most favorably for all. By any definition, this is an ideology. Its long-run effectiveness is questioned by blacks, Chicanos, American Indians and others in the United States and around the world whose freedom and best interests have not automatically been served.

Values in American Life

Individualism and enlightened self-interest are still basic to the value systems of most Americans. Moreover, these values affect entire life styles, not merely work attitudes. Indeed, whenever predominant American values are listed, it is remarkable how many of them support work attitudes and are directly related to individualism and enlightened self-interest. The current serious challenge to some of these values will be discussed later in the book. Here, let us make some attempt to indicate what these prevalent, traditional American values are.[38]

Achievement and Success. American culture has been and still is characterized by a stress on individual achievement. Horatio Alger, who rose from rags to riches, has become a legend. The American myth says that anyone who works hard enough can succeed in what he or she sets out to do. Moreover, if we meet a successful person, we are much more impressed if he or she did not inherit wealth. Someone who was born poor and then worked hard to obtain what he or she has is much more an idol for the young. In fact, it is a bit embarrassing to us to be reminded that several of our recent Presidents were born into wealthy families. This achievement and success ideal is, of course, best manifested in business. Achievement motivation is especially strong among executives and managers.[39]

Achievement implies that what is achieved has value. Success makes less reference to the ultimate goals of society. For example, a professional criminal who does his job extremely well is sometimes admired for his "success" in developing his abilities. On the other hand, the Watergate exposures and "White House horrors" are examples of a situation in which the legitimate work of getting the President reelected was accomplished through illegal and immoral means. Not only was it not successfully done, but it could not have been an achievement.

Money and wealth are valued for the comforts they can bring, but even more because they are the symbols of having "made it." It is a measure to the man himself and to the world around him of his own personal worth. Because these virtues developed in the westward expansion and the building of railroads and industry, there comes a correlative respect for size. Large homes, automobiles, and businesses are respected; they are signals of success.

Activity and Work. An extraordinary devotion to work on the part of both the unskilled worker and the executive has provided most of the wealth we now enjoy in the United States. That activity and work is respected not only because it has resulted in immense wealth, but also for its own sake—"The Devil finds idle hands." In the United States a person's self-respect is severely undermined when he or she is without work. Americans have traditionally not valued leisure for its own sake; it was valued if afterward a person could work better. It is *re*-creation; and it, too, has a pur-

---

[38]For a basic work in this area, and one to which the author is indebted, see the chapter "Values in American Society," in Robin M. Williams, Jr., *American Society: A Sociological Interpretation,* 3rd ed. (New York: Knopf, 1970), pp. 438-504.

[39]There is, of course, a great amount of literature on this, and the issue will be discussed in greater detail in Chapter 3. For now, see W. Lloyd Warner and James Abegglen's chapter "Success, Failure and Personality," in their classic, *Big Business Leaders in America* (New York: Atheneum, 1963), pp. 84-107.

pose. Task orientation has become a compulsion for which Americans are frequently criticized.

Workers in a shop know that even though the job is well in hand, or ahead of the daily quota, they had best appear busy to their boss, and especially to their boss's boss. Relaxing at the work station is rarely accepted. "Busyness" is a virtue in its own right. To call a person lazy is a serious criticism, especially because it is something over which that person seems to have control. Americans value the active virtues; they set out to shape and control their own lives and their world. They heed the biblical injunction "to subdue the world."

Efficiency and Practicality.   Closely related to the foregoing cultural values are efficiency and practicality, which refer more to the method of working and acting. We have earlier seen how Tocqueville was much impressed with American ingenuity and ability to "get the job done." Americans are often criticized for an overemphasis on technique, with little reference to goals.[40] These critics say that engineers and accountants run our society, and their values are at best instrumental and thus means. They may know how to accomplish a specific task, but rarely give any thought as to whether it is a good thing to do. A practical person, focusing on efficiency, assumes the basic worth of the task and the social order itself. A practical orientation demands only short-range adjustments to immediate situations.

The American is known as one who can quickly and effectively search out the best way to accomplish the task. He or she is active in the search for solutions, and is rarely contemplative. To call an American "impractical" would be a severe criticism. Characteristically, the best-known American philosophers, such as Dewey, Peirce, and William James, are not idealists or absolutists, but rather relativists and pragmatists.

Moral Orientation and Humanitarianism.   Although Americans are eminently practical, they still see the world in moral terms. Conduct of self and of others is constantly judged: honest, impractical, "a comer," lazy. Even our foreign policy is filled with righteous terms, such as Manifest Destiny, and "to protect the world for freedom."

Basic honesty and frankness are also part of our moral and humanitarian value orientation. President Gerald Ford brought a refreshing honesty and straightforwardness to the White House; Americans generally respect those values. Foreign commentators are often surprised at how open and straightforward they find Americans to be. However, the same highly moral person can quickly become quite cynical when his or her moral code is found to be superficial, inapplicable, or too idealistic. American charities, along with

[40]For a superb statement of this position, see Jacques Ellul, *The Technological Society* (New York: Knopf, 1964).

our social legislation since the 1930s, are examples of humanitarian attitudes. Increasing social security, minimum wage levels, and the extent of medical coverage are all examples of the attempt to take care of the less fortunate.

Freedom.   As a prime value in American life, freedom is obvious to the most obtuse observer. In addition, it is probably the most spoken about of American values. The individual has freedom to operate in the Social Darwinian world in which the fittest survive best, as we have seen earlier. He may freely move; change jobs; choose a home, friends, or a marriage partner. Freedom is the bedrock value not only of our laissez-faire, free enterprise economic system, but for most of the rest of American life. Freedom has been touted alike by the Founding Fathers and the members of the local Rotary. American individualism is, of course, possible only when freedom is the foundation value.

The value of freedom has inspired the women's movement and other liberation movements. Cultural norms that tie certain persons to predetermined roles and expectations can be oppressive. Freedom urges the elimination of these one sided and unjust bonds. Defense of freedom is a foundation of American foreign policy, and freedom is the cornerstone of the U.S. Chamber of Commerce and the John Birch Society's defense of the American business system—*free* enterprise. As we have pointed out earlier, this freedom is primarily for me and mine, foreign policy protestations notwithstanding. Freedom as a value so permeates business ideology that it will come up frequently in subsequent chapters.

Equality.   The American emphasis on equality goes back to early constitutional statements: *All men* are created equal. Citizens of the new world witnessed the elimination of indentured servitude, imprisonment for debt, primogeniture, slavery, and property requirements for voting and public office. New immigrants were able to acquire land and a free public education, and women and minorities have gained many important human rights.

New arrivals and observers have often remarked on the unusual informality, frankness, and lack of status consciousness in our interpersonal relations. Such open and direct relations can endure over a long period only if they are supported by basic notions of the equality and importance of individual persons. But it became clear quite early that the value of freedom often ran counter to that of equality. When people pursued freedom in the rugged individualist climate in which the fittest survive, it resulted in some becoming rich and others remaining poor. An attempt at resolving this conflict is in the distinction that our ideals call for equality of opportunity, but not equality of result. Varying talents will also influence what a person can achieve.

Of all the government and corporate policies that have been developed to bring about better equality of opportunity in the workplace, none meets more opposition than "preferential treatment." In order to equalize past practices that were clearly discriminatory, many would contend that when equally qualified black and white persons are presented for promotion, the black should be chosen. Ironically, both the reason for the practice (to equalize past discrimination) and the major objections to it (reverse discrimination) stem from the American ideal of equality, especially equality of opportunity.[41]

Patriotism. Every society has a sense of the greater value of its own people. Anthropologists tell us how in primitive societies the ordinary rules of respect for another's person and property do not apply to "outsiders." They apply only to the members of one's own tribe. On a contemporary national scale, this mentality seems to be supported when during warfare we not only have less respect for lives of the "enemy," but sometimes rate our successes on the basis of how many of the "enemy" were killed. Racism, too, stems from these same parochial values.

In the United States our loyalties in the early days of the republic were with local cities (Boston, Philadelphia) and then with the states; finally, after several national efforts (especially the two world wars), our loyalties now lie primarily with the nation-state. Our attitudes toward Communist states and "un-American" activities find their roots in nationalism and loyalty to America.

Material Comfort. Americans generally place high value on the luxurious automobile, the ample home in the suburbs, and a good meal. The fact that these things are material comforts and that they are clearly highly valued does not in itself indicate *why* they are valued. Underlying reasons may range from a simple symbol of achievement and success (moving to a larger home is a visible mark that I am moving up with the firm), to a hedonistic gratification in its own right.

The rise in popularity of spectator sports, packaged tours, the film, television, and alcohol all indicate a greater passivity on the part of people. There seems to be less active participation in favor of watching and being entertained. The drug culture and chemically induced pleasure seem to take this tendency just one more step. Seeking pleasure coincides with a decline in the Puritan ethic values of self-denial and asceticism.

External Conformity. Probably the most common criticism Europeans have leveled at Americans is the one of a vast uniformity in speech, housing, dress, recreation, and general attitudes. Observers point to a certain flatness, to homogeneity, to lack of dissent and challenge. Although we have since gone through a brief period in the late 1960s of racial and student dis-

---

[41]See the detailed discussion of this complex question in Theodore V. Purcell and Gerald F. Cavanagh, *Blacks in the Industrial World: Issues for the Manager* (New York: Free Press, 1972), esp. Chap. 10, "Equal Versus Preferential Treatment," pp. 275-93.

sent, many feel that to a large extent we now have returned to our more traditional complacent attitudes.

To American rugged individualists, these criticisms seemed harsh, unfair, and untrue. But on closer examination, our individualism is largely a rejection of state interference and restrictions on personal and economic activity. The war protesters who spoke out at some personal risk were not called individualists, but rather dissidents.

Rationality and Measurement.   This value is probably best exemplified in approaching a problem. A person is to be objective, gather the facts first, and not be unduly influenced by bias or emotions. The "scientific method," which embodies this approach, is the model for problem solving. If elements of the solution can be measured—whether length, time, or intelligence—that will make the solution more rational and objective.

The value of science is demonstrated in its intelligent use in mastering the external environment. This value orientation is compatible with a culture that does not value emotion, tends to deny frustration, and looks on the world as open to effort and eventual control.

Optimism and the Inevitability of Progress

The frontier, seemingly unlimited natural resources, and an immigrant people who were willing to work hard all combined to provide an atmosphere of great optimism. Any job could be accomplished, if only one put one's mind to it. The result of this combination of effort was growth: industrial, economic, urban. Growth has been so characteristic of the last two centuries that for most Americans it is inconceivable to think that growth and thus progress are not inevitable.

The optimistic euphoria that had enveloped the American people has only recently begun to dissipate. It is only in the last few years that the possibility of continued growth has been challenged and that we have been asked to rethink what we mean by progress. We had defined progress largely in economic terms. As long as gross national product and sales were increasing, this spelled progress. The possibility of a more stable economy, the necessity of rethinking what "progress" is, and what impact these changes will have on business and business ideology will be discussed in greater detail in Chapters 5 and 6.

THE NECESSITY OF AN IDEOLOGY FOR BUSINESS

An ideology, or some statement of goals and principles, is necessary for any social system. It is especially necessary for business in the wake of current challenges and criticisms. Without some rationale, it will become impossible for business either to defend itself against these attacks or to evaluate challenges and suggest new policies. In the future, as in the past, ideology will give business acceptance and thus whatever stature and power it may have.

Without an ideology, the corporation risks losing its privileged position in the United States, and perhaps even its legitimacy. In 1958, Adolph A. Berle put the issue strongly:

> Whenever there is a question of power there is a question of legitimacy. As things stand now, these instrumentalities of tremendous power have the slenderest claim of legitimacy. This is probably a transitory period. They must find some claim of legitimacy, which also means finding a field of responsibility and a field of accountability. Legitimacy, responsibility and accountability are essential to any power system if it is to endure.[42]

The transitory period of which he spoke is still with us.

Notice how Berle links legitimacy, responsibility, and accountability. It is precisely in clarifying these basic issues that the corporation is on weak ground. Without rehearsing the entire classic position of Berle and Means,[43] suffice it to say that the corporation is responsible to no one. Management, often with little legitimacy and less ownership, unilaterally makes decisions. Stockholders have no real control over the corporation. The board of directors is elected from a slate that has been chosen by management. The annual meeting of stockholders is a public relations effort, with the stockholders exercising no real power. If a stockholder does not vote, the abstention is counted as support for management.

The board of directors has no universal and clearly defined role. It is usually as active and effective as the chief executive wants it to be. And there are not many chief executives who want a strong board that might intervene. The board of directors is generally nominated by management, so its members are often dependent on the approval of management for continued tenure. If they are "inside" directors, there will probably be conflicts of interest, and thus they lack objectivity. If they are "outside," they serve only part time. One principal difficulty is that they have very little time to devote to the affairs of the corporations of which they are directors; indeed, a member of the Ling-Temco-Voughts' board, investment banker Gustave L. Levy, is on the boards of twenty-three corporations.[44]

Eugene V. Rostow, then dean of Yale's Law School, even coined a word

[42]*Economic Power and the Free Society* (New York: Fund for the Republic, 1958), p. 16.

[43]Adolf A. Berle, Jr., and Gardiner C. Means, *The Modern Corporation and Private Property* (New York: Macmillan, 1932).

[44]"The Board: It's Obsolete Unless Overhauled," *Business Week,* May 22, 1971, p. 56. Quoted with permission.

to describe this lack of responsibility in the corporation—*endocratic:* responsible to no one.[45] Management is also self-perpetuating, its members designate their own successors, and even new board members. Corporate management controls the firm, and thus is under no one else's control. After publishing a special report on the need to overhaul the role of the corporate board of directors, *Business Week* editorialized:

> If the corporate management is to survive in anything like its present form, directors will have to take on new responsibilities. They must make sure that corporate goals are consistent with the larger goals of U.S. society. And they must monitor management to see that it pursues these goals effectively, including the basic objectives of earning a reasonable income and keeping the company out of the bankruptcy courts.[46]

Ensuring that corporate goals are consistent with the goals of the larger society demands something more in the way of corporate purpose than merely enlightened self-interest. The last two generations of research on the power and legitimacy of the corporation, plus the more recent social demands on the firm, raise basic and serious questions about the role, purpose, and responsibilities of the corporation. Any response to these new questions and needs demands some clearer notions on the even more basic issue of the ideology of the corporation—its goals, rationale, responsibilities; its very reason for existence.

Without a basic ideology that is clear, consistent, and effective, these gnawing questions will continue to arise and we will be incapable of answering them. In any social system, this sort of situation is not stable. Indeed, it is probably true that much of the current loss of respect for business, the corporation, and the business person stems from an inability to respond in more than a defensive or perfunctory fashion to these very real questions. Without an ideology, business risks, and perhaps is already in the process of, losing its privileged position in American society and possibly even its legitimacy.

SUMMARY AND CONCLUSIONS

This first chapter has set the general scene and defined terms. It has examined major values and ideals in American life, and some of the elements of physical environment and personal character that have

---

[45]"To Whom and for What Ends Is Corporate Management Responsible?" in *The Corporation in Modern Society,* ed. Edward S. Mason (Cambridge, Mass.: Harvard University Press, 1959), p. 57.

[46]"The Board. . .," *op. cit.,* p. 90.

contributed to the development of those values. The vast expanse of virgin land was a challenge to the righteous, task-oriented Puritans. Their theology supported their work ethic: self-denial, hard work, thrift, early rising. Furthermore, the favorable results of these efforts indicated that the individual was saved. Benjamin Franklin, while not a Puritan, found this work ethic attractive, and he presented a secularized version to his contemporaries.

Educated Europeans who have visited us over the last century and a half have noted an honesty, frankness, and directness in Americans. They have found us to be pragmatic and practical and to have little time for unproductive theorizing. Freedom is a value that has been institutionalized in our Constitution and laws, and that remains predominant.

With this data as background, we then reflected on what an ideology is, what its function is, and some of its effects. An attempt was then made to spell out the main values in American life. This more general examination of American values and ideology has been necessary in order to mark out the turf where we will find business values. Business values exist in a larger context; and in this case, we already see how remarkably well the larger society's ideals support business ideology. Nevertheless, the very legitimacy of the corporation and business itself is being questioned. Moreover, it is increasingly clear that there can be no adequate response to these questions without some attempt at working out a purpose and an ideology for the business firm that coincides better with what the larger society expects of its business institutions.

The values of the American Puritan—hard work, saving, regular habits, diligence, and avoidance of sensuality—perhaps best characterize the American work ethic. These values have since come to be known as the Protestant ethic. It, and the conditions that led to these values, will be discussed in the next chapter.

CHAPTER TWO

Historical Roots
of the Business System

**In the past the man has been first; in the future
the system must be first.**

Frederick Winslow Taylor

We are a product of our past. No matter how rapidly society changes, current attitudes have their roots in history. History encompasses such diverse elements as the physical spread of our cities and the energetic, entre-preneurial attitudes of earlier generations of Americans. The past is indeed prologue. Where we go and what we do in the future is very much influenced by past values and attitudes. Whether we view the present as part of an organic development from what has gone before or as a rejection of it, that past has an immense influence. An inherited pragmatic faith in technology undergirds the conviction of many that we can readily overcome problems such as the energy crisis. On the other hand, a new concern for interpersonal relations and for the environment stems partly from a disenchantment with the attitudes of hard-nosed, efficiency-oriented earlier generations. It is impossible to understand current values and what the future will bring without some knowledge of the path we have taken to get where we are.

QUESTIONING THE PAST

Members of industrialized societies are generally more questioning of their everyday behavior than those of more traditional societies. They feel a more acute need to understand underlying values and attitudes for several reasons, the most basic of which is that change has taken place so rapidly in societies like those of the United States, Europe, and Japan that new explanations are needed for current activities and behavior. The traditional values and ideology that were sufficient in relatively unchanging societies are no longer applicable in these transitional, dynamic nations. The second reason is that a higher level of formal education encourages people to be more questioning and reflective. Third, and more immediate, the many choices that people face in industrialized societies—choosing a career, a style of life; whether or not to marry and have children—encourage them to examine the criteria on which they base these decisions.

The fourth and last reason why greater understanding of basic values and goals is necessary is the fact that in industrialized societies, actions and rights are more often in conflict. The desire for efficiency and the right to work collide in the person of the unemployed. The desire to produce at lowest cost conflicts with the air and water pollution that result. The resolution of these conflicts requires clarification of goals, principles, and criteria. Moreover, this inquiry is no mere academic venture; it is the foundation from which will rise public policy and legislation, and eventually a type of society and style of life.

People are beginning to ask the most basic questions of all: Why work? What is the value of work? Further, what is the value of business? Granted that if I want a car or a refrigerator, it must be produced and I must have some legitimate means of obtaining it for my own uses. But if I can obtain it in some lawful fashion without working, why not? Or, to pose the question in another way, is it acceptable to work only enough to stay alive? If I have a spouse and two children, why not obtain just enough to keep ourselves happy? Why should I try to accumulate more wealth than I actually need? Such basic questions are complex and difficult, yet people are asking them with increasing frequency. All over the world, people are inquiring into the value of work for themselves, and are questioning the goals of the entire business system. Some satisfying responses are essential for a happy people and a successful society.

Of course these questions are not new, but now they are being asked by more people and with greater urgency. In earlier and more traditional societies, they were largely academic or philosophical questions, asked by the wealthy and leisured, not by the ordinary citizen. The ordinary worker's life was largely determined at birth. If that person's father was a shoemaker or a baker, he would become one too, and use the tools, workshop, and home that had belonged to the family for generations. There was rarely any question of whether the person *would* work, or at what occupation. There was little choice. There was also little regret or frustration because there was no alternative. Heredity, custom, and geography determined one's life: "To ask men in such economically undeveloped traditional societies why they work is similar to asking them why they try to stay alive."[1] Furthermore, for the average person, there was little leisure in which to question the value of work.

[1] Sigmund Nosow and William H. Form, *Man, Work and Society* (New York: Basic Books, 1962), p.9.

The business system, and especially its rapid growth, is almost wholly dependent on people's attitudes toward work. Earlier generations did not much question it. Indeed, as we have seen and will examine in further detail, the American Puritan ethic supported tireless work and thus economic growth. Now the business system itself and attitudes toward it are even more dependent on people's assessment of the place and importance of work in their lives. Let us first look to our roots.

LISTENING TO OUR FOREFATHERS

Change has taken place very rapidly in the United States almost from its beginning as a nation. Its people are almost all immigrants from other lands, mostly from Europe. All the Founding Fathers were heavily influenced by European thinkers such as John Locke, Rousseau, and Adam Smith on such issues as the value of work, business, and private property. Although there were and are alternate strains of thought in the East, these values had little impact on the West. Hence we will limit ourselves largely to Western attitudes and philosophies on these practical issues.

Throughout most of recorded history, work has been an integrating force for the individual. It was a basic binding strand for the fabric of the social system, the family, and the city. It gave stability and meaning to people and their relations. A clear change, however, emerged with industrialization. Changes in work such as division of labor, mass production, and "scientific management" were introduced. And the individual worker had increasing choice as to the type and location of the work he or she might do. It is ironic that just when individuals began to be able to choose work and so look for greater satisfaction from their jobs, that work became more fragmented, repetitive, and less able to provide pride of accomplishment and workmanship.

The Ancient Greek Attitude Toward Business and Work

The ancient Greeks thought of work and commerce as demeaning to a citizen. At best, it was a burdensome task required if one was to survive. The meager legitimacy and value accorded to work was not because it had any value in itself, but because it was a necessary evil. There are two limitations to our knowledge of ancient attitudes toward work. First, most of our information comes from written sources whose authors were generally not from the working class; they were citizens and hence men of leisure. Second, most of the work was done by slaves under grueling, dirty, and very difficult conditions. These slaves were uneducated and often prisoners of war from other cultures.

Plato speaks of work as if it were a temptation to be avoided because it hinders a person's ability to live and to contemplate. In his *Laws,* Plato speaks for himself and his fellow citizens when he urges, "If a native stray from the pursuit of goodness into some trade or craft, they shall correct him by reproach and degradation until he be brought back again into the straight course."[2] Citizens of ancient Athens thought of work as something not worthy of a citizen. Plato, however, reveals the extent to which his contemporaries' attitudes are based on the accidental conditions under which work was done as he cuts to the heart of their disenchantment and even revulsion with work:

> . . . suppose the very best of men could be compelled—the fancy will sound ludicrous, I know, but I must give it utterance—suppose they could be compelled to take for a time to inn-keeping, or retail trade or some such calling; or suppose, for that matter, that some unavoidable destiny were to drive the best women into such professions: then we should discover that all are humane and beneficient occupations; if they were only conducted on the principles of strict integrity, we should respect them as we do the vocation of mother and nurse.[3]

Even under conditions of general disapproval, Plato recognizes that most of the objections to work are not basic to work itself. In fact, these occupations are in themselves "humane and beneficient."

Plato's pupil Aristotle is more severe in his condemnation of the life of the worker or tradesperson. To him, such a life is irksome and beneath the dignity of a citizen:

> . . . the citizens must not lead the life of mechanics or tradesmen, for such a life is ignoble, and inimical to virtue. Neither must they be husbandmen, since leisure is necessary both for the development of virtue and the performance of political duties.[4]

From his observations, Aristotle found crafts, trade, or business detrimental to health and character. Much of the work was done in cramped and unhealthy surroundings, and it was necessary to have daily dealings with the rude, the unprincipled, and the unethical. So industrial and commercial life was thought to begin by robbing the body of its health and to end by degrading the character. Moreover, whether those who followed a trade or craft should even be admitted to citizenship was a problem for Aristotle. This sort of work was generally done by slaves, and many contemporary

---

[2] Plato, *The Laws of Plato,* tr. A. E. Taylor (London: Dent, 1934), 847B, p. 235.
[3] *Ibid.,* 918B-E, p. 311.
[4] Aristotle, "Politics," in *Basic Works of Aristotle,* ed. Richard McKeon (New York: Random House, 1941), p. 1141.

states did not admit the laborer and the skilled worker to citizenship. "Even in states which admitted the industrial and commercial classes to power, popular sentiment held trade and industry cheap."[5]

Aristotle speaks of two types of business and trade activity, and his distinction goes to the root of a difficulty that perplexes many to the present day: the difference between careful management of goods and what often seems to be merely selfish profit orientation. He approves of the first, but disapproves of the second. *Oeconomia,* from which our word *economics* derives, is literally "household management." It includes careful and intelligent use not only of the household but of all one's property and resources. On the other hand, *chrematistike* is the use of skill and goods to achieve a profit. This term described the city traders who were few in number compared with the farmers and craftsmen. The trader often resorted to deceptive practices, and it seemed to Aristotle and scores of generations that followed him that this sort of person really contributed little or nothing to society. Aristotle's objections are not unlike those of Marx: the trader adds no value to a good. His service as a middleman does not enhance the good in question. Not surprisingly, then, Aristotle approved of *oeconomia,* but disapproved of *chrematistike.*[6]

Plato and Aristotle generally agree in their objections to the pursuit of a career in trade or a craft, although Aristotle raises these objections more strongly: (1) The practice of business or a craft deprives a person of the leisure necessary to contemplate the good, the true, and the beautiful. (2) It hinders proper physical, intellectual, and moral development. (3) It is "illiberal" because it is done for pay. (4) It is less perfect because its end is outside of itself.

Work in the Bible

Unlike the Greeks, who had slaves, the ancient Hebrews could not remain aloof from work; it was an integral part of their lives. They saw work as necessary, but also as a hardship. Even the painful aspect of work had its self-inflicted cause in man's original sin. This gave reason, integrity, and even verve to what for most other cultures was only something to be endured. On the positive side, the Hebrews pointed to the commands of God in Genesis that man was to cultivate the world and subdue it (Genesis, 2:15). Work was still drudgery for the Hebrews, but it was better integrated into their lives and had greater meaning for them. The God of the Hebrews is close to his people. He is often pictured as one who labors: a vine dresser (Ezekiel, 15:6), a pottery maker (Genesis, 2:7), a soldier (Isaiah, 27:1).

[5] W. L. Newman, *Politics of Aristotle,* Vol. I (Oxford: Clarendon Press, 1887), p. 98.

[6] Robert L. Heilbroner makes this same distinction in his *The Making of Economic Society* (Englewood Cliffs, N.J.: Prentice-Hall, 1972), p. 39.

Christianity built on the Hebraic tradition with regard to work, trade, and commerce. The new religion itself had working class origins. Jesus was a carpenter (Mark, 6:3) and Paul, a tentmaker (Acts, 18:2). The Apostles, all working men, were mostly fishermen. They were not from the priestly class. The Gospels caution against an excessive and exclusive concern with work and the things of this world (Matthew, 6:24-34), but they also make clear that work is a serious responsibility for the Christian (Luke, 12:41-49). Furthermore, in the often-quoted parable of the talents (Matthew, 25:14-30), the servant who has intelligently and profitably invested his money and his efforts is the one who is given additional rewards.

But the unique contribution of Christianity to the value of work is that it is done also out of love and concern for one's brothers and sisters. Work is necessary "not only to earn one's living, asking alms of no man, but above all so that the goods of fortune may be shared with one's needy brothers."[7] In investigating the foundations of industrial civilization, John U. Nef points to this new concept of love preached by Jesus Christ and presented in the New Testament. He finds it ". . . a peculiarly generous concept of charity, of the opportunity we have to give ourselves to others here and now, insofar as we love our neighbors for God."[8] Through the ages and in our own time people who call themselves Christian most often fall far short of these ideals. Nevertheless, Nef is convinced that as a foundation for work and business values, especially in its emphasis on love of neighbor, Christianity was an important step forward.

In the early centuries of the Christian era, the most important commentator was Augustine. He approved of handicraft, farming, and commerce on a small scale. But in any selling, no more than a "just price" can be asked; asking interest on the use of money is immoral. Those who have wealth should prize it as a trust from God. After their own modest needs are met, they should give the rest to the poor.[9] As early as the fifth century, Augustine held that work was obligatory for monks. During later centuries in the monasteries, especially among the Benedictines, a new work ethic developed.

Monastic Business

Benedictine monasteries have been credited as being "perhaps the original founders of capitalism."[10] The Benedictine Rule, as embodied in tens of thousands of monasteries throughout Europe, brought a much more

---

[7] Adriano Tilgher, "Work Through the Ages," in Nosow and Form, *op. cit.,* p. 13.

[8] *Cultural Foundations of Industrial Civilization* (Cambridge, Eng.: Cambridge University Press, 1958), p. 89.

[9] Tilgher, *op. cit.,* pp. 14-15.

[10] Lewis Mumford, *Techniques and Civilizations* (New York: Harcourt, Brace, 1934), p. 14.

positive attitude toward production and work. For the monks, work was not merely a curse, and manual work not merely degradation. These men looked on work as an opportunity to build, to grow and develop as a person and a community. They chose to work together, and they were among the first voluntarily to cooperate in all tasks. Since the men often worked in groups and varied their occupations, they found it helpful to work by the clock. They would begin and end their work together. They standardized tasks, so that any one of the monks could handle the work.

Living and working as a cooperative community helped to stimulate the use of various labor-saving devices. When in 1115 Bernard of Clairvaux led a band of monks to found a new monastery, one of his prime requisites for a new site was that it have a rapidly moving stream that could be harnessed by the monks to help them do their work. Bernard himself provides us with a description of his famous abbey at Clairvaux, and he provides considerable detail on the mechanical devices that are geared to waterwheels to make the work of the brothers easier.[11]

The monastery is built at the base of a mountain and literally over a fast-moving stream to make best use of the waterpower. The river is guided by "works laboriously constructed" by the monks so that the water may be of the greatest help to their efforts. The water thus "passes and repasses the many workshops of the abbey." In one instance, the water is channeled so that it "passes on at once to drive the wheels of a mill." In moving these wheels, "it grinds the meal under the weight of the mill-stones, and separates the fine from the coarse by a sieve." The river's waters are also harnessed to raise and drop hammers for the traditional fulling of cloth and to help the shoemaker in his chores. The waters are then split into smaller streams where they help "to cook the food, sift the grain, to drive the wheels and hammers, to damp, wash, soak and so to soften, objects; everywhere it stands ready to offer its help." The monks also constructed an elaborate irrigation apparatus to water the fields. Recall that all this happened in the 1100s, six centuries before the Industrial Revolution.

A century later the great Christian theologian of the Middle Ages, Thomas Aquinas, provided a rationale for work. He spelled out clearly and in some detail the reasons why it seemed to him that manual labor was necessary for all: (1) to obtain food, (2) to remove idleness, (3) to curb concupiscence, and (4) to provide for almsgiving.[12] Although Aquinas saw clearly that work was not only necessary but also of considerable value, there was still an element here of work being a burden, something to endure for the sake of some leisure.

---

[11] Bernard of Clairvaux, *Patrologiae Latinae, ed Migne* (Paris: Garnier, 1879), Vol. CLXXXV, pp. 570-74. A translation of much of this is in *Life and Works of St. Bernard,* by Samuel J. Eales (London: Burns & Oates, n.d.), Vol. II, pp. 460-67. The quoted words that follow are those of Bernard himself.

[12] Thomas Aquinas, *Summa Theologica,* II-II, qu. 87, art. 3.

Work, however, was not a burden for the monks; it was a vehicle of love and service. When setting up a new monastery, the monks would deliberately choose a site far from existing civilization. They did this both because it would be a better locale for prayer and because they deliberately set out to communicate their new view of the value of work as it is rooted in charity. Benedict and Bernard expected their monks to work in the fields and the shops, whether they were sons of aristocrats or of serfs. According to Lynn White, Jr., historian of technology and industry, this provision

> . . . marks a revolutionary reversal of the traditional attitude toward labor; it is a high peak along the watershed separating the modern from the ancient world. The Benedictine monks regarded manual labor not as a mere regrettable necessity of their corporate life but rather as an integral and spiritually valuable part of their discipline. During the Middle Ages the general reverence for the laboring monks did much to increase the prestige of labor and the self-respect of the laborer. Moreover, since the days of St. Benedict every major form of Western asceticism has held that "to labor is to pray," until in its final development under the Puritans, work in one's "calling" became not only the prime moral necessity but also the chief means of serving and praising God.[13]

The monks lived together and lived thriftily, and that enabled them to invest in productive machinery like that described above to aid them in their work. This is why some call the monks the first capitalists. Their resources and inventiveness combined and resulted in division of labor, interchangeable work, a clock-regulated work day, and ingenious labor-saving equipment—all of which added up to considerably greater productivity. They used the additional time that was then available for their common life and prayer. A few hundred years later, this same love-centered ethic was brought to the cities and marketplaces of seventeenth-century France by an eminent group of saints, artists, poets, and theologians. John U. Nef maintains that it was this unique emphasis on the centrality of love for one's brothers and sisters, especially as embodied in women, that made industrial society and its requirement of cooperation and hard work possible.[14] More specifically, he shows that the law of love and its vision as carried out by women were two of the greatest impetuses to the sort of civilization that makes industrialized society possible.

By 1700, Christianity, with its central love ethic, had helped to provide many of the elements necessary for the development of business and com-

---

[13] Lynn Whyte, Jr., "Dynamo and Virgin Reconsidered," *American Scholar,* 27 (Spring 1958), 188. Quoted with permission.

[14] See John U. Nef, *Cultural Foundations of Industrial Civilization,* cited above, note 8, and also his briefer *Civilization, Industrial Society and Love* (Santa Barbara, Calif.: Fund for the Republic, 1961).

merce. As we have seen, work began to be looked on as something of value; it provided self-discipline and an integrating force in a person's life. Christianity helped the individual to focus on the value of the product of work; if the same thing could be produced more easily, this was good—especially when it enabled one to help one's own family and neighbors. The importance of quantity and a new consciousness of time developed first in the monastery, and then spread to the larger society. In its otherworldly theology, however, Christianity thwarted the coming of capitalism. According to this theology, the purpose of life on earth was not merely to build up material goods. This attitude led to suspicion of those who would lend money to others and charge them for the use of it. Even as late as the sixteenth century, theologians condemned the opening of state banks.[15] Lending money at interest in the Christian tradition was the sin of usury.

In Christian society, work and industry were much more respected than they had been in aristocratic Greece or Rome. The average citizen had many reasons to do tasks well, and there were no slaves to do them for him. In addition, a person's trade or craft gave meaning and integrity to life. But it was the Protestant Reformation that provided the impetus for the development of attitudes that would propel Western society toward rapid economic growth.

From Luther and Calvin to the Protestant Ethic

It is Protestantism that eventually established hard work as central to a Christian life. Martin Luther (1483-1546), the initiator of this new movement, ironically intensely disliked the commerce and economic individualism of his day. Luther was appalled at the regal high living of the popes and the local merchants and princes. The sharp contrast between the ideals of Christianity and what he actually found around him motivated Luther to push for reform. He called for a return to a simple, hard-working peasant life; this would bring sufficient prosperity for all. A person should earn a living and not make an excessive profit.

Luther saw a number of Christian institutions as actually encouraging idleness: the mendicant friars glorifying begging, the many religious holidays, and the monasteries' support of some who did not work. Idleness is unnatural, according to Luther; charity should be given only to those who cannot work. His original contribution was in emphasizing the importance of one's profession. The best way to serve God was to do the work of one's profession as well as one can. Thus Luther healed what had been a breach between worship and work. As long as work was done in obedience to God

[15] Lewis Mumford, *The Myth of the Machine* (New York: Harcourt, Brace & World, 1966), p. 279.

and in service to one's fellows, every type of work had equal value in God's eyes.

Luther held that a person's salvation is achieved solely through faith in God; good works do not affect salvation. Moreover, all legitimate human activities are acts of worship, no one more than another. Since formal prayer and worship, and especially the monastic life of prayer, are no more valuable than tilling the fields, Protestantism released all human energies for the world of work. The farmer, the smith, and the baker all do work that is quite as honorable as that of the priest. Although the life of the simple worker is better, Luther concedes that

> Trade is permissible, provided that it is confined to the exchange of necessaries, and that the seller demands no more than will compensate him for his labor and risk. The unforgivable sins are idleness and covetousness, for they destroy the unity of the body of which Christians are members.[16]

Luther was vehement in preaching against lending at interest, yet paradoxically his denial of all religious authority eventually set economic life free from strictures on usury. This denial left business and commerce to develop their own life and laws independent of existing moral authority. Capitalism thus set up its own norms of right and wrong; it became a life set apart from and beyond the competence of the Church.

Luther's insistence on investing everyday life with the same value as worship and on breaking the system of canon law and religious authority eventually resulted in profound changes in economic and social life. The elaborate prescribed relationships with neighbor, family, and Church were swept away. Although they were encumbering and limiting, they also provided roots, personal relationships, and a meaning for life. Secular interests, work, and business now formed another world, one rather unconnected with the religious and moral values that had until this time governed all aspects of life.

The most important influence on what we now call the Protestant ethic was that of John Calvin (1509-1564), who followed Luther as a reformer of Christianity. Calvin and his followers did not idealize the peasant as did Luther, but accepted urban life as they found it. As Tawney puts it, "Like early Christianity and modern socialism, Calvinism was largely an urban movement."[17] Calvin's central theological notion, which distinguishes his position from that of Luther and of Catholicism, is predestination. God is infinite, absolute, and supreme; he is totally above and beyond man. There is no way of grasping or understanding God and his ways. In his infinite

---

[16]R. H. Tawney, *Religion and the Rise of Capitalism* (New York: Mentor, 1947), p. 83.

[17]*Ibid.,* p. 92.

power and wisdom, God has determined that it is fitting for his glory if only a small number of men and women be saved. Moreover, there is absolutely nothing a person can do to influence his or her own salvation; from all eternity God has freely predetermined it. A person lives to glorify God, and the major way a person glorifies God is in his or her very life. If a person bends every talent and energy in work, and achieves success, this may be an indication that he or she is one of the saved. Although these individual efforts cannot directly affect or ensure salvation, if successful, they do glorify God and may thus be a sign that the person is numbered among the elect. Probably even more motivating was the conviction that if a person was idle, disliked work, or was not successful, these were most likely signs that that individual was not among the saved.

Calvin taught that all must work, and must never cease working. Profits earned must not be hoarded, but must be invested in new works. Investment and resulting profit and wealth are thus encouraged: "With the new creed comes a new man, strong-willed, active, austere, hard-working from religious conviction. Idleness, luxury, prodigality, everything which softens the soul, is shunned as a deadly sin." [18] Calvin proposed a unique paradox. Deny the world; live as an ascetic in the world, because it cannot guarantee your salvation. Yet remember that your one duty is to glorify God, and the best way of doing that is by being a success at your chosen work, your calling. It is a precarious balance, difficult to achieve and even more difficult to maintain.

Calvin and Luther shared a concern for hard work and successful pursuit of one's "calling." The Protestant ethic, however, stems more directly from Calvin's teachings because he did not continue to condemn trade and urban commerce as Luther had. Calvin not only urged hard work at one's occupation, but also held that successful trade and commerce was but another way of glorifying God.

Weber and the Protestant Ethic.   Before leaving the influence of the Reformation on business ideology, let us look at the summary of that influence drawn up some two hundred years later by the sociologist Max Weber in *The Protestant Ethic and the Spirit of Capitalism.* It is ironic that Max Weber, a German, cites no other person more often as an example of the Protestant ethic than Benjamin Franklin, an American (we have examined Franklin's attitudes in Chapter 1).

Weber begins his analysis by noting that "business leaders and owners of Capital, as well as the higher grades of skilled labor, and even more the higher technically and commercially trained personnel of modern enterprises, are overwhelmingly Protestant." He goes on to compare the Catho-

---

[18] Tilgher, *op. cit.,* p. 19.

lic and the Protestant: "The Catholic is quieter, having less of the acquisitive impulse; he prefers a life of the greatest possible security, even with a smaller income, to a life of risk and excitement, even though it may bring the chance of gaining honor and riches."[19] In trying to determine the reason why Protestants seem to be more successful, Weber examines the roots of the theology of Luther and Calvin, as we have done above. He notes that Reformation theology encouraged individuals to look on their work more seriously. Life demanded sobriety, self-discipline, diligence, and above all, planning ahead and saving. A person's attention to the life of this world was serious in the extreme. In addition to having its own rewards, success was a reflection of God's glory, and hence a hint as to whether that person was saved or not. It was therefore incumbent on all to be successful. Moreover, they had the means to achieve that success: "In practice this means that God helps those who help themselves. Thus the Calvinist . . . himself creates his own salvation, or, as would be more correct, the conviction of it."[20]

An asceticism adequate to achieve the goal flowed from the Calvinistic ethic: "Waste of time is thus the first and in principle the deadliest of sins." On the same theme, the Calvinist asceticism "turned with all its force against one thing: the spontaneous enjoyment of life and all it had to offer." On the positive side, in the Calvinist and Puritan churches Weber finds ". . . the continually repeated, often almost passionate preaching of hard, continuous bodily or mental labor."[21] But Weber observes that even in his day, "The people filled with the spirit of capitalism today tend to be indifferent, if not hostile, to the Church." Then it most often happens that the pursuit of business and a career takes on the vehemence and all-embracing aspects of active religion; "business with its necessary work becomes a necessary part of their lives." But this is what is "so irrational about this sort of life, where a man exists for the sake of his business, instead of the reverse." The Protestant ethic changed history. Contrary to the ethical convictions of centuries, "money-making became an end in itself to which people were bound, as a calling."[22]

In his last chapter Weber quotes both John Wesley and John Calvin when they point out a paradox. It is religion that makes man careful, hard-working, frugal; and this, in turn, enables him to build up wealth. "But as riches increase, so will pride, anger, and love of the world," in Wesley's words. Speaking of those on the lower end of that same economic ladder, Weber quotes Calvin: ". . . only when the people, i.e., the mass of

---

[19] Max Weber, *The Protestant Ethic and the Spirit of Capitalism,* tr. Talcott Parsons (New York: Scribner's, 1958), pp. 35-41. Quoted with permission.

[20] *Ibid.,* p. 145.

[21] *Ibid.,* pp. 157-66.

[22] *Ibid.,* pp. 70-73.

laborers and craftsmen, were poor did they remain obedient to God."[23] Therein lies a paradox, and the men who themselves are most responsible for the Protestant ethic foresee it. Their religion demands hard work and saving, and this provides wealth. But wealth brings pride, luxury, and lack of will. It is therefore a highly unstable ethic, in part because its religious foundations tend to dissolve. But as we have seen in Benjamin Franklin and many others, the ethic can take on a secular life of its own. It can perhaps continue with other, changed though not less vital, sources of vision and motivation. It remains for us to ascertain precisely what this new secular vision and new motivation will be.

The Protestant ethic urges planning ahead, sobriety, diligence, and self-control for the individual. It promises a material reward; and in its religious strand, a good chance of salvation. Moreover, the Protestant ethic serves an additional, and psychologically perhaps more important, purpose. It assures the successful and wealthy that their wealth is deserved. They have property because they have worked for it, and so have a right to it. As Weber himself has observed, the wealthy man is not satisfied in knowing that he is fortunate:

> Beyond this, he needs to know that he has a *right* to his good fortune. He wants to be convinced that he "deserves" it, and above all, that he deserves it in comparison with others. He wishes to be allowed the belief that the less fortunate also merely experience their due.[24]

Thus the Protestant ethic not only provides a set of directions on how to succeed and a motivation for doing do, but also attempts to legitimate the wealth that is acquired. The successful person says, "Anyone who was willing to work as hard as I did could have done as well, so it is therefore clear that I deserve the wealth I have."

John Locke and the Right to Private Property

John Locke had a considerable influence on the Founding Fathers and through them on the American Constitution. He and Jean Jacques Rousseau also influenced the French Revolution and most of the subsequent

[23] *Ibid.,* pp. 175-77. Some reject the attempt to link economic success with religious faith. They maintain that there are more plausible explanations for commercial success, such as "special education, family relationships and alien status." See Kurt Samuelson, *Religion and Economic Action,* tr. E. G. French (New York: Basic Books, 1961), p. 154. Nevertheless, the fact that Weber's theses are so widely accepted make it a theory to be reckoned with. Whatever the causal relationships, religious values and economic development are there to be observed, and they have had a marked influence on one another.

[24] Max Weber, "The Social Psychology of World Religions," in *Max Weber: Essays in Sociology,* ed. H. H. Gerth and C. Wright Mills (New York: Oxford University Press, 1946), p. 271.

efforts to move toward more democratic governments. The Oxford-educated Locke (1632-1704) was both a philosopher and a politician. He was a practical man, having served various government figures of his day, and his philosophy showed a great concern for political and social questions.

Locke was concerned with various natural rights, but the right to which he devoted most of his energy was the right to private property.[25] Locke held that an individual has a right to self-preservation, and so has a right to those things that are required for this purpose. Individuals require property so that they may feed and clothe their families and themselves. A person's labor is what confers primary title to property. If individuals settle on land and work it, they therefore deserve title to it. Locke's ideal was America, where there was unlimited property available for anyone who was willing to clear it and work it.

Locke has been criticized for overemphasizing the rights of private property and thus catering to the interests of his landowning patrons, and this may be true. But he did not allow for a person's amassing wealth without limit. Whatever is beyond what the individual can use is not by right his; it belongs to others, and should be shared with them.

Rousseau's Social Contract

Jean Jacques Rousseau (1712-1778) shared with other members of the French Enlightenment a distrust of contemporary society and its institutions. He saw that society, and even Enlightenment ideals such as reason, culture, and progress, as having created unhealthy competition, self-interest, pseudosophistication, and a destruction of the "simple society" he valued. He saw that society as unjust, effete, and dominated by the rich and by civil and Church authorities. According to Rousseau, "Man was born free and everywhere he is in chains." Man's original state in nature is free; and although some form of society is necessary, freedom, reverence, family life, and the ordinary person must be central to it.

The *Social Contract* is an attempt to achieve the necessary activities, associations, and states required in a civilized society without losing basic individual rights. A citizen's duty of obedience cannot be founded simply on the possession of power by those in authority. To be legitimate, it must rest on some sort of freely given consensus.[26] Rousseau's distrust of society's insti-

---

[25] John Locke, *An Essay Concerning the True Original Extent and End of Civil Government,* esp. chap. V, "Of Property," and chap. IX, "Of the Ends of Political Society and Government." See also the summary in Frederick Copleston, *A History of Philosophy,* Vol. V (London: Burns and Oates, 1964), pp. 129-31.

[26] Jean Jacques Rousseau, *The Social Contract and Discourse on the Origin and Foundation of Inequality Among Mankind* (New York: Washington Square Press, 1967). See also the summary of Rousseau in Copleston, *op. cit.,* Vol. VI, esp. pp. 68-69 and 80-100.

tutions also included private property. According to him, when private property is introduced into a society, equality disappears. Private property marks a departure from primitive simplicity and leads to numerous injustices and evils such as selfishness, domination, and servitude. In the state he proposes, Rousseau supports a sharply increased tax on the property that is not necessary for a man to modestly support himself and his family. Beneath this level, there should be no tax at all. With regard to the illegitimacy of excessive wealth, Rousseau agrees with Locke.

Adam Smith's Capitalist Manifesto

The Scot Adam Smith (1723-1790) is the grandfather of capitalism and of free-enterprise economics. As a political economist and moral philosopher, he was among the first to emphasize free exchange and to present economics as an independent branch of knowledge. His classic work, *Wealth of Nations,* was published in 1776, and so provided independence for economics and business in the same year that the American colonies declared their political independence from England.

In explaining economics, Smith says, "Nobody ever saw a dog make a fair and deliberate exchange of one bone for another with another dog." A bit later he spells out the implications of this inability to exchange by showing that each animal is obliged "to support and defend itself, separately and independently, and derives no sort of advantage from that variety of talents with which nature has distinguished its fellows." Human beings, says Smith, are quite different in that they can take advantage of one another's unique genius. What a man is good at he does in abundance, sells to others, and thus ". . . may purchase whatever part of the produce of other men's talents he has occasion for."[27] Smith's first and most familiar example is of the division of labor of the pinmaker. One man, working alone and forming the entire pin, could perhaps "make one pin in a day, and certainly not make twenty." But when the operation is divided up into a number of separate operations so that "one man draws out the wire, another straights it, a third cuts it, a fourth points it, a fifth grinds it at the top for receiving the head," and so on, Smith says he has observed a man is able to make a batch which, divided by the number of workers in the group, comes to 4,800 pins.[28]

In addition to the value of exchange and the division of labor, Smith also examines the value of the free market, competition, and profit maximization. Smith was among the first to make a clear and convincing case that when individuals follow their own self-interest, it automatically works to

[27] Adam Smith, *Wealth of Nations,* ed. J. C. Bullock (New York: Collier, 1909), pp. 19-23.
[28] *Ibid.,* pp. 9-10.

the benefit of society as a whole. As individual competitors pursue their own maximum profit, they are all thus forced to be more efficient. This results in cheaper goods in the long run. Free competition in all markets and with all goods and services is thus to be encouraged; government intervention serves only to make operations less efficient and is thus to be avoided. The same principles apply to international trade. There should be a minimum of government interference in the way of duties, quotas, and tariffs. Smith's is the classical argument in support of free trade.

Smith takes some of his basic inspiration from the English philosopher Thomas Hobbes (1588-1679). Hobbes had maintained that individuals act simply to gain that which gives them pleasure, or to avoid that which causes displeasure. Since this may differ in each individual, there is no objective good or value in reality itself. Hobbes' view of human motivation is that of "egoistic hedonism." Since human nature is largely self-seeking, and further since there is no objective morality, it is not suprising that Hobbes held that might makes right. It is important to have power to protect one's person and goods. Whatever a person has the power to take belongs to that person. Hobbes acknowledges that this leads to conditions of insecurity and even war but maintains that they are an inescapable part of the human condition. On the theme of trade and economic activity, Smith quotes Hobbes that "wealth is power." It enables its possessor to purchase what he or she wants, and this in itself gives that person considerable control over others. So it is to the benefit of individuals to increase their wealth.

To explain profit maximization, Smith uses the example of rent. Even though the owner of the land contributes nothing to production beyond the fact of ownership, nevertheless the owner will strive for a contract that will give the highest rent the tenant can possibly afford to pay. The landlord will strive to leave the tenant as little as possible of what he or she earns. Smith contends that this is as it should be. On some occasions the landlord may leave the tenant a bit more for himself, but this is and should be exceptional; it is due to "the liberality, more frequently the ignorance, of the landlord."[29]

As the father of modern economics, Smith spells out clearly and graphically most of the current major principles operating in economic and business theory. He illustrates the great advantages of the division of labor, the free competitive market, and profit maximization, and how they all contribute to more efficient production. In pursuing these self-interested goals, Smith's famous "invisible hand" guides economic and business activities so that they are more productive and cheaper, and thus benefit society as a whole. Industry and commerce in the two centuries following Adam Smith have been extraordinarily successful. Moreover, these

[29] *Ibid.*, pp. 153-71.

activities have closely followed the model Smith described. The free market encouraged rapid economic growth. Economic motivation for most people up to Smith's time had been based more on obligations to a lord, proprietor, or one's family, and on threats, fears, and sanctions. The free market and potentially unlimited monetary rewards shifted the entire basis of economic activity.

The free market and the possibility of unlimited profits are at the heart of the system's greatest strength: it taps positive motivation and rewards. It draws a man or woman into greater activity and creativity, and quickly rewards those efforts. Furthermore, those rewards are tangible and measurable; by these standards there is little doubt as to who is a success. On the other hand, this new model for economic activity also includes the system's greatest weakness. It insulates a person from these older and clearly perceived obligations to friends, family, fellow citizens, and the larger community, and replaces them with an easily broken contract whose purpose is to obtain individual profit. Hence individuals can much more readily come to feel that they are alone, that they are isolated, and that they are easily replaceable. Current literature on the attitudes of managers and blue collar workers alike shows this feeling of isolation and alienation.[30]

Adam Smith, the grandfather of modern economics, provided a remarkably accurate and integrated picture of developing business activities. He clearly detailed the advantages of free exchange and the free market. As such, he was to people of the nineteenth century a father of "liberal economics." Smith is still widely quoted and, although challenged and criticized, remains to this day a principal spokesperson for capitalism and free enterprise.

THE PROTESTANT ETHIC
AND THE GROWTH OF A NATION

The year 1776, when a new nation was born on an unspoiled continent, is an appropriate time to shift our attention back to the United States. In Chapter 1 we surveyed the early values that developed in the American colonies with an examination of the Puritans and the work of Benjamin Franklin. After independence, those values and attitudes had an unprecedented opportunity to be realized. The nation provided an ideal testing ground for enterprising farmers, traders, prospectors, entrepreneurs, and theorists. Business and commerce grew at an extraordinary pace. It is im-

---

[30] See, for example, evidence of this dissatisfaction in Theodore V. Purcell and Gerald F. Cavanagh, *Blacks in the Industrial World: Issues for the Manager* (New York, Free Press, 1972), esp. pp. 72-75, 236-38.

portant briefly to examine that growth and, more to our purpose, the attitudes that undergirded it.

The early days of the new republic were dominated by the farmer. The colonial merchant provided the trading link between the early Americans, responding to needs and transporting food and goods. From 1800 to 1850, wholesalers took the place of merchants. They "were responsible for directing the flow of cotton, wheat and lumber from the West to the East and to Europe."[31] The rapid growth of the American industrial system that was to make the United States the most productive nation in the world had begun by the middle of the nineteenth century. "In 1849 the United States had only 6,000 miles of railroad and even fewer miles of canals, but by 1884 its railroad corporations operated 202,000 miles of track, or 43 percent of the total mileage in the world."[32] The number of those working in factories also grew very rapidly during this period. In terms of manufactured goods, "By 1894 the value of the output of American industry equalled that of the combined output of the United Kingdom, France and Germany."[33] Growth continued to accelerate, until within twenty years the United States was producing more than a third of the industrial goods of the world.

The mining city of the West was the site of new activities that called for strong, resourceful people. Tales of silver, gold, and other minerals in the mountains thrilled imaginations across the continent. Hundreds of thousands took the challenge: they risked their fortunes, their lives, and often their families to try to get at the newly found ore. Vast amounts of capital and superhuman energies were spent. The "get rich quick" spirit of these prospectors was a prelude to that of the entrepreneurs who came later. Virginia City, Nevada, was built over the famed Comstock Lode. What was bare desert and mountains in 1860 became within five years one of the most rapidly growing and thriving cities of the new West. The energies and genius of thousands sank dozens of shafts into the rock, supported them with timbers, built flumes—and an entire city. Between 1859 and 1880 more than $306 million worth of silver was taken from the mountains.[34] The magnitude of the effort and the accomplishment can be gathered from this description:

> In the winter or 1866 the towns and mills along the Comstock Lode were using two hundred thousand cords of wood for fuel, while the time soon came when eighty million feet of lumber a year went down

[31] Alfred D. Chandler, "The Role of Business in the United States: A Historical Survey," *Daedelus*, 98, 1 (Winter 1969), 26.
[32] *Ibid.*, p. 27.
[33] *Ibid.*
[34] Allan Nevins, *The Emergence of Modern America*, Vol. 8 (New York: Macmillan, 1927), p. 137

into the chambers and drifts. Since the mountains were naked rock, flumes had to be built from the forested slopes of the Sierras, and by 1880, there were ten of them with an aggregate length of eighty miles.[35]

Adolph Sutro owned a quartz mill on the other side of the mountains on the Carlson River, and he thought he saw an easier way to get the ore out of the mountains. He envisioned a three-mile-long tunnel through the mountains from the river valley that would intersect the Comstock mines 1,600 feet below the surface. The tunnel would drain the series of mines to that level, and would also enable the ore to be taken out through the tunnel for processing where fuel and water were plentiful. By 1866, Sutro had obtained contracts from twenty-three of the largest mining companies to use the tunnel when it was completed.

> . . . after incessant effort, in which any man of less marvelous pluck and energy would have failed, he raised sufficient capital to begin the project. In 1869 he broke ground for the tunnel and set a corps of drillers upon the task that was to occupy them for eight weary years. It was the labor of a giant.[36]

Sutro finished his tunnel and put it in use in 1877. But within three years, the boom collapsed. The value of the silver mining stock sank from a high of $393 million in 1875 to less than $7 million in 1880. People slowly began to leave Virginia City, and today it is literally a ghost town, with only remnants of roads, homes, and a few of the more substantial large buildings left to remind us of what it once was.

Virginia City illustrates how the great talents and wealth of a society can be quickly channeled to accomplish tremendous feats; it also shows how that accomplishment can and often is short-lived, and not designed to encourage stability. This sort of activity appeals to the energetic and fast-moving entrepreneur; it does not appeal to family people who look to their own and their children's future. Virginia City illustrates both the strengths and the weaknesses of the American entrepreneurial spirit. The same sort of Gold Rush a decade earlier in California left a more permanent mark, since the new inhabitants did not leave when the gold ran out. The prospectors, miners, and fortune seekers converged from all parts of the country, disrupting communities and families. Prior to their coming, California had had a unique style; "To these California imperatives of simple, gracious, and abundant living, Americans had come in disrespect and violence."[37] Exploitation of the land kept people moving, and California

---

[35] *Ibid.*, p. 136.

[36] *Ibid.*, p. 137.

[37] Kevin Starr, *Americans and the California Dream* (New York: Oxford University Press, 1973), p. 33.

chronicler Kevin Starr focuses on some of the problems they left in their wake:

> Leaving the mountains of the Mother Lode gashed and scarred like a deserted battlefield, Californians sought easy strikes elsewhere. Most noticeably in the areas of hydraulic mining, logging, the destruction of wildlife, and the depletion of the soil Americans continued to rifle California all through the nineteenth century.

> The state remained, after all, a land of adventuring strangers, a land characterized by an essential selfishness and an underlying instability, a fixation upon the quick acquisition of wealth, an impatience with the more subtle premises of human happiness. These were American traits, to be sure, but the Gold Rush intensified and consolidated them as part of a regional experience.[38]

Throughout these years of rapid economic change, the entrepreneurs' role has been central. Their brains, ingenuity, and willingness to risk have given us most of our economic success and growth. At the same time, their myopic desire for short-term gain has caused many failures and much personal anguish. With this as background, let us return to the leaders of thought who have had such a profound influence on American business values.

American Individualism, Ralph Waldo Emerson Style

To this day, the American business person is characterized as an individualist. One articulate, persuasive, and most influential champion of freedom and the importance of the individual is Ralph Waldo Emerson (1803-1882). Following on the French Enlightenment and Rousseau, Emerson is the best-known American proponent of individualism. He sees human nature as having natural resources within itself. Societal structures and supports tend only to limit the immense potential of the individual. Given freedom, individuals can act, grow, and benefit themselves and others. But they require an absence of restraints imposed by people, cultures, and governments. Emerson's friend Henry David Thoreau acted on this ideology and built himself a hut at Walden Pond, outside Boston, where he reflected and wrote alone in the unimpeded, open atmosphere of trees, grass, and water.

In his book of essays, *The Conduct of Life,* Emerson has one entitled "Wealth."[39] Here he applies his philosophy of individualism to economics and the marketplace. A person should contribute and not just receive. If an

[38] *Ibid.,* pp. 65-66.
[39] Ralph W. Emerson, *The Conduct of Life and Other Essays* (London: Dent, 1908), pp. 190-213.

individual follows his or her own nature, he or she will not only become a producer, but will also become wealthy in the process. Individuals contribute little if they only pay their debts and do not add to the wealth available. Meeting only one's own needs is expensive; it is better to be rich, and thus be able to meet one's needs and add to wealth as well. And doing both coincides with a person's own natural inclinations. Emerson insists that getting rich is something anyone with a little ingenuity can achieve. It depends on factors a person has totally under one's own control:

> Wealth is in applications of mind to nature, and the art of getting rich consists not in industry, much less in saving, but in a better order, in timeliness, in being at the right spot. One man has stronger arms, or longer legs; another sees by the course of streams, and growth of markets, where land will be wanted, makes a clearing to the river, goes to sleep, and wakes up rich.[40]

Emerson's heroes are the independent Anglo-Saxons. They are a strong race who, by means of their personal independence, have become the merchants of the world. They do not look to government "for bread and games." They do not look to clans, relatives, friends, or aristocracy to take care of them or to help them get ahead; they rely on their own initiative and abilities.

Struggle for Survival

The business person, and especially the entrepreneur, has always found the world to be nothing less than a struggle for survival. One may want to be humane and conscientious, but one cannot afford it. Herbert Spencer's theories of the survival of the fittest and what has come to be known as Social Darwinism were discussed in Chapter 1. Spencer's philosophy had an immense influence on the America of the late nineteenth century. In fact, it described the American experience.

William Graham Sumner (1840-1910) was a social science professor at Yale and a disciple of Spencerism. Sumner's father was an immigrant English workingman who gave his children the Puritan virtues of thrift, self-reliance, hard work, and discipline.[41] His son was convinced that egalitarianism, made fashionable by the French Revolution and the freeing of the slaves, would undermine the initiative and independent spirit that encourages the best people to develop their talents fully. According to Sumner, the less able and adept are jealous of the successes of the more

---

[40] *Ibid.*, p. 192.

[41] Donald Fleming, "Social Darwinism," in *Paths of American Thought,* ed. Arthur M. Schlesinger, Jr., and Morton White (Boston: Houghton Mifflin, 1963), p. 128.

talented, and through the political process they will require the latter to support them. This perversion undermines the creativity and motivation of the better and more talented people. Sumner applauded the era in which people would work and live not because of inherited position and status, but because they themselves chose to do so through the new democratic device of contract. He clashed with Yale President Noah Porter when the latter objected to Sumner's assigning Herbert Spencer's book to students but won the long-term battle with one of the first clear statements of academic freedom.

Sumner and Spencer urged a tight-fisted, unemotional aloofness. Both one's self and one's wealth must be saved and not spent without chance of a good return on investment. Free emotions and spontaneity were suspect; a person could lose all in a lighthearted or thoughtless moment. In the same vein, Sumner urged that government should not intervene in social and economic affairs. The environment should be kept clear of restrictions, taxes, restraints, and other needless and even harmful laws and regulations.

The opposition was led by Lester F. Ward (1841-1913). Ward's indictment in his *Dynamic Sociology* is that man should control his environment, not allow it to control him. Evolution and natural selection as outlined by Darwin led to change without direction and without goals. According to Ward, the great value of evolution and natural selection was that they had brought people to the position in which they found themselves now. Moreover, it was precisely in Ward's era that individuals became able to take over and control their own future, and not leave it to blind, natural chance. For him, it would have been the supreme paradox for men and women, now that they had discovered these natural laws and forces, to retreat and allow themselves to become victims of them. Ward labeled Spencerism a do-nothing philosophy.

Establishment Churches and Business

Churches have a double and often conflicting role to play in society: to help people to worship God, and to sensitize the consciences of their members. As a church becomes a large, recognized, and respectable institution in society, it can easily be deterred from its role as a prophet and prodder of consciences. A church ministers to its members, yet it can be so influenced by its "respectable" membership that it becomes part of the Establishment and preaches against change, "rabble rousers," and social justice. The church and its members risk losing too much by change. One lesson for today can be learned by examining the actions of the larger and more respected churches in the United States in the last century.

The dominant American churches in the nineteenth century, while preaching charity and concern for the poor, nevertheless vehemently defended the economic system that had grown up with the Protestant ethic. In this period, churches and schools had considerable influence over American life and morals. The prestigious private colleges of the eastern Establishment taught the values of private property, free trade, and individualism. These religiously oriented schools (both Harvard and Yale were founded as, and were still at the time, Congregationalist) generally taught conservative economic and business values along with their moral philosophy.

To many churchmen, since God had clearly established economic laws, it would be dangerous to tamper with them. Francis Wayland, president of Brown University and author of the most popular economics text then used, intertwines economics and theology in stating his basic position: "God has made labor necessary to our well being." We must work both because idleness brings punishment, and because work brings great riches; these are two essential, powerful, and immutable motives for work.[42] Wayland concluded from this simple principle that all property should be private and held by individuals. Charity should not be given except to those who absolutely cannot work, and the government should not impose tariffs or quotas, or otherwise interfere.

Approaching economic and social life from a different perspective, some religiously inspired groups did set up experimental communal and socialist communities. But the important churchmen and the major religious denominations vigorously defended the status quo against these new sectarian challenges. However, in the last twenty-five years of the century, these churches went through an agonizing reexamination. Up to this time, the major Protestant churches had bought Adam Smith's economics and canonized it as part of the Divine Plan. They defended private property, business, the need to work, and even wealth. Then three severe, bloody labor disturbances in these decades forced the churches to reconsider their traditional survival-of-the-fittest theories.

The first of these conflicts followed a severe economic depression in 1877. Wages of train workers were cut by 10 percent, and they protested. They picketed and halted trains. Army troops were called to defend railroad property, and they fought with desperate mobs of workers. In the confusion, scores of workers were shot. The churches generally sided with the Establishment and self-righteously preached to the workers on the Divine wisdom of the American economy. Hear the *Christian Union:*

> If the trainmen knew a little more of political economy they would not fall so easy a prey to men who never earn a dollar of wages by good solid work. . . . What a sorry set of ignoramuses they must be who

---

[42]Henry F. May, *Protestant Churches and Industrial America* (New York: Harper & Row, 1949), p. 15.

imagine that they are fighting for the rights of labor in combining together to prevent other men from working for low wages because, for-
sooth, they are discontented with them.[43]

The religious press, reflecting the attitudes of its patrons, took a hard line
against what it saw as anarchy, riots, and supporting weak and lazy men.

A decade later another serious confrontation occurred. On the occasion
of a labor meeting at the Haymarket in Chicago, the police shot several of a
group of strikers. A few days later, a bomb was thrown at the police. As is
often the case in such situations, facts and circumstances were forgotten as
near hysteria swept the religious press. The Protestant *Independent* was
typical: "A mob should be crushed by knocking down or shooting down the
men engaged in it; and the more promptly this is done the better."[44] Only
when these strikingly un-Christian outbursts had ended did the clergy have
the opportunity to reflect on what had happened and how they themselves
had reacted. It then became clear how biased, inflexible, and violent had
been their stance—hardly what one would expect of churches. During this
period the clergy were anxious to accommodate their churches' position to
the new industrial movements. They changed no creeds or confessions, but
"progressively identified [themselves] with competitive individualism at the
expense of community."[45] From the rubble of these mistakes and later recognized biases came the impetus toward a new social consciousness, specifically in the form of the Social Gospel.

Acres of Diamonds

Defense of free enterprise was not limited to the Establishment Congre-
gational and Presbyterian churches. The Baptist preacher Russell Conwell
traveled the country giving his famous speech, "Acres of Diamonds." He
delivered it more than five thousand times around the turn of the century to
enraptured audiences eager to hear that to gather wealth was God's will.

Conwell's speech tells of a man who goes out to seek wealth, and his suc-
cessor on the farm finds diamonds in the yard he had left behind. His message: any man has it within his grasp to make himself wealthy, if he is willing to work at it:

I say that you ought to get rich, and it is your duty to get rich. How
many of my pious brethren say to me, "Do you, a Christian minister,

[43] *Ibid.,* p. 93.
[44] *Ibid.,* p. 101.
[45] Martin Marty, *Righteous Empire: The Protestant Experience in America* (New York:
Dial, 1970), p. 110.

spend your time going up and down the country advising young people to get rich, to get money?" "Yes of course I do." They say, "Isn't that awful. Why don't you preach the gospel instead of preaching about man's making money?" "Because to make money honestly is to preach the gospel." That is the reason. The men who get rich may be the most honest men you will find in the community.[46]

Conwell demonstrates what to him was the happy confluence of deeply felt religious convictions and the life of the marketplace. Because of the more traditional religious values of poverty and humility, riches often brought qualms of conscience to contemporary believers. Conwell represents the tradition that tries to wed faith and fortune: there can be no better demonstration of faith in God than to use one's abilities to their fullest, to be a success and to accumulate the goods of the earth (to be used responsibly, of course). Conwell himself made a fortune from his lectures, and following his own advice on investment, used the money to found Temple University.

Carnegie's Gospel of Wealth

A handful of industrialists called the robber barons had an immense, enduring influence on America and American industry around the turn of the century. The immigrant Scot Andrew Carnegie was one who enjoyed his role as industrial and moral leader. With the help of the financier J. P. Morgan, Carnegie had put together United States Steel in 1901; he accumulated immense wealth in the process and loved to tell all who would listen why he deserved it. Furthermore, with millions at his disposal, Carnegie set out to establish libraries in every city and town in the United States, each proudly bearing the Carnegie name.

Carnegie had amassed a huge personal fortune, even though he was well aware that many of his own steelworkers were not well paid. But he made no apology for the inequality, and in fact defended it as the survival of the fittest. The millionaire's money would do no good if it were paid to his workers:

> Much of this sum, if distributed in small quantities among the people, would have been wasted in the indulgence of appetite, some of it in excess, and it may be doubted whether even the part put to the best use, that of adding to the comforts of the home, would have yielded results for the race at all comparable.[47]

---

[46] Russell Conwell, *Acres of Diamonds* (New York: Harper, 1915), p. 18.

[47] Andrew Carnegie, "Wealth," in *Democracy and the Gospel of Wealth,* ed. Gail Kennedy (Boston: D. C. Heath, 1949), p. 6.

According to Carnegie, it is only the wealthy man who can endow libraries and universities, and who can best look to the long-run good of society as a whole. The money is much better spent when he accumulates it in large amounts so that with it he can accomplish great things.

For this reason, Carnegie felt that the wealthy man should "set an example of modest, unostentatious living, shunning display or extravagance." He should hold his money in trust for society and be ". . . strictly bound as a matter of duty to administer in the manner which, in his judgement, is best calculated to produce the most beneficial results for the community."[48] Inequality and the accumulation of great fortunes is good for society, along with "the concentration of business, industrial and commercial, in the hands of a few." This concentration of wealth enables the most able to use the funds for the best interest of society.

Carnegie defended his fortune, his right to have it and dispose of it as he saw fit. He was not totally objective in his examination of the socioeconomic system; he was profiting too much from it. Thus, not surprisingly, he was able to overlook the injustices he and his company supported.

Manufacturing and Scientific Management

The growth of manufacturing did, in fact, provide a new and much faster means of attaining wealth and economic growth. With increases in productivity, higher wages could be paid and greater profits obtained for the owner at the same time. This was a considerable departure from past eras, when fortunes had been made by trade, transport, or lending (and, of course, wars and plunder). As a result, wealth had been considered more of a fixed quantity: what one person gained, another lost. The advent of manufacturing demonstrated clearly that the economy was not a zero-sum game—it was *possible* for each party in the exchange to benefit financially. It depended largely on productivity.

Frederick W. Taylor, founder of scientific management, focused on better methods in manufacturing as a way to increase productivity. Productivity is, of course, the amount of a product that is produced, given an hour of labor. Clearly mechanization and careful planning would enable workers to produce more than they might without planning. This was Taylor's insight: worker and management experience plus intuitive judgment is not enough. For the sake of greater production, which would benefit all concerned, the work setting and even the motions of the job itself ought to be carefully studied to discover the most efficient tools and techniques.

---

[48] *Ibid.,* p. 7. David M. Potter in his *People of Plenty: Economic Abundance and the American Character* (Chicago: University of Chicago Press, 1954) maintains that in an even more fundamental sense, a democratic system depends on economic surplus (pp. 111f).

As factory work became more complex, Taylor had greater support for his argument. No single person, worker or supervisor, could be aware of all the mechanical, psychological, and technological factors involved in planning even one job. Efficiency required careful planning by a team with varying competences. Intuition, experience, and seat-of-the-pants judgments would no longer do. Scientific management unwittingly undermined Spencer's notions of "survival of the fittest." Taylor pointed out that allowing the "best person" to surface naturally was inefficient. In the contemporary complex world, few single persons had the ability to achieve maximum productivity. Greater efficiency and productivity demanded the intervention of planners.[49]

Taylor was in favor of higher wages and shorter hours for workers, but he saw no need for the union. If scientific management is implemented, and the best and most efficient means of production achieved, there will be no grounds for petty quarrels and grievances. Policies and procedures will be set by scientific inquiry into what objectively is most efficient. And that which is most efficient will benefit worker and management alike, since both will share in the results of this greater productivity: greater profits. In Taylor's scheme, the personal exercise of authority would be eliminated. Managers would be subject to the same policies, rules, and methodology as the workers themselves.

Although he agreed with the traditional managerial ideology that workers pursue their own self-interest and try to maximize their own return, Taylor challenged the notion that each person worked out this struggle in isolation, apart from and even in competition with other human beings. In an industrial organization greater productivity can be achieved only when each worker, along with management, cooperates to achieve the best means of production. Taylor pointed out how the returns to all were diminished if a single worker is not working at his or her most efficient job and pace. Prior to this, a person caught not working was fired. Now Taylor set out to help both worker and management achieve maximum efficiency, which could only be done in cooperation.[50] Up to this time a lazy man or woman had been penalized; now Taylor proposed to reward workers by enabling them to work to their greatest capacity and receive greater financial return.

Scientific management was not greeted happily by either workers or management, because it tended to deprive each of a measure of freedom and judgment. Nevertheless, in the long run Taylor's methodology, and perhaps even more his ideology, have had an immense impact on industrial life. Even today we see company advertisements singing the praises of increased productivity.

[49] See Reinhard Bendix, *Work and Authority in Industry* (New York: Wiley, 1956), p. 275.
[50] *Ibid.,* pp. 278-79.

Schumpeter's Prediction of Decay

The dynamism and intensity of the single-minded effort directed toward economic growth in America throughout this period seemed boundless. The very best minds and talent were drawn into business and industry. Moreover, the effort was rewarded as the economy grew more and more rapidly. As long as a people's goals are to increase financial return and the amount of material goods available, seeking greater efficiency in production, and hence higher productivity, is paramount. Once these goals become less pressing, the talent, concern, and effort that go into industrial activity may decline. The possible result, decay of the economic system, was foreseen by the economist Joseph Schumpeter in the early 1940s.

In his *Capitalism, Socialism and Democracy,* Schumpeter provides a brilliant and detailed description of the undermining and decay of capitalism. He points out that the very success of the capitalist economic mechanism in providing goods and income paradoxically lessens dependence on and concern for the system. As free enterprise is successful, human needs are satisfied and investment opportunities tend to vanish. That same success undermines the need for, and so the position and prestige of, the entrepreneur, who is no longer a dominant or even a highly respected person in society.[51]

Contributing to the growing hostility to capitalism are the intellectuals. Academics and intellectuals are quick to see inequities and evils in any system. The problems are there for any perceptive eye to see, and it is the vocation of the intellectual to be a cultural critic. Moreover, Schumpeter would say that most intellectuals have had no experience in trying to manage an organization; at best they serve as staff persons or consultants. The ultimate responsibility for making an organization work has never been theirs, so they do not possess the wisdom and practicality of men who have gotten their hands dirty. In addition, they have a captive audience in the universities, and thus have a ready-made forum for their critical views. Schumpeter was convinced that the intellectuals had undermined capitalism.[52]

He was also convinced that these criticisms generated increasing government regulation to constrain the free movement of people and capital. Schumpeter is at pains to point out that he is not opposed to this change, but it is no longer capitalism. Moreover, the professional manager does not have the same long-term will and vision as the owner he replaces.[53] A manager need not stay and fight for the integrity of a firm or system; he

---

[51] Joseph A. Schumpeter, *Capitalism, Socialism and Democracy* (London: Allen & Unwin, 1943), pp. 131-39.

[52] *Ibid.,* pp. 143f.

[53] *Ibid.,* p. 156.

or she can move on to another job that offers greater financial return. Schumpeter's indictment is a broad-gauged one: he even goes into some detail as to how capitalism and its attendant attitudes tend to undermine family life and child rearing. In his view, capitalism faces imminent death.

Schumpeter picks out another increasingly obvious weakness of capitalism: it has no compelling, motivating, all-embracing ideology and set of values. It is a pragmatic system, designed and pursued for a rather narrowly conceived end—economic growth. He then contrasts capitalism with Marxism. Marxism has a vision of the world and a systematic ideology; it calls on its followers to sacrifice for the sake of the poor and the oppressed and for a more equal distribution of goods. Its vision is sufficient to inspire men and to initiate revolutions. According to Schumpeter, Marxism has all the marks of a religion: vision, doctrine, rules, and a call for self-sacrifice. In contrast, capitalism promises only a higher standard of living and in itself cares nothing for the poor and disadvantaged. It is effective in production, but crass and parochial in its view of man and his world.

Three decades later, the economist Paul Samuelson updated and paraphrased Schumpeter's penetrating assessment: "I told you so. The successes and rationalism of bourgeois capitalism will breed a swarm of discontented intellectuals—to fan the flames of hostility toward an efficient but unlovable system with no mystique to protect it."[54] Schumpeter's critique was widely quoted in his own day, but it is clearly even more relevant now. His insights remain valid and painfully obvious.

Measures of Success

Americans implicitly and often without much reflection look on rising gross national product and the level of median family income as yardsticks of a successful civilization. Since it is true that we have been eminently successful in the production and consumption of material goods, it is probably not so surprising that we would like to make that the measure of success for all cultures. Frederick Winslow Taylor, the founder of scientific management, put it succinctly when he said, "In my judgment the best possible measure of the height in the scale of civilization to which any people has arisen is its productivity."[55]

Another point of view was presented a generation before Taylor when England was at its height as an industrial and trading power. Matthew Arnold raised the same question, alluding to those who said that England's greatness was based on her railroads and her coal:

[54] Paul A. Samuelson, in *Newsweek,* April 13, 1970, p. 75.

[55] Frederick W. Taylor, *Hearings Before the Special Committee of the House of Representatives to Investigate the Taylor and Other Systems of Shop Management,* Vol. III (Washington, D. C.: Government Printing Office, 1912), p. 1471.

If England were swallowed up by the sea tomorrow, which . . ., a hundred years hence, would most excite the love, interest, and admiration of mankind—and which would most, therefore, show the evidences of having possessed greatness?

Would it be the England of the preceding two decades, a period of industrial triumph, or would it be an earlier period when culture was more valued? Arnold answers for his contemporaries:

Never did people believe anything more firmly than nine Englishmen out of ten at the present day believe that our greatness and welfare are proved by our being so very rich.

And then he goes on to give his own response:

. . . the use of culture is that it helps us, by means of its spiritual standard of perfection, to regard wealth as but machinery, and not only to say as a matter of words that we regard wealth as but machinery, but really to perceive and feel that it is so.[56]

This same question faces Americans in the 1970s. How are we to judge the success of our civilization? What is our goal, and therefore what are our criteria for judging whether we are successful or not? Frederick Taylor says it is simply productivity; Matthew Arnold says productivity and wealth are merely tools to achieve something more. In this perennial discussion, on which side do we stand? Or must we fashion some middle ground? If so, what elements will go into it? The point of this book is to provide some basis for resolving the dilemma.

THE AMERICAN BUSINESS CREED

Until the mid-1950s, when four distinguished scholars embarked on a joint effort, no major empirical study of the principal values and tenets of the American business system had yet been attempted.[57] Their inquiry focused on public and official statements of business people and organizations such as the U. S. Chamber of Commerce, the Committee on Economic Development, and the National Association of Manufacturers. Using material from the decade prior to 1955, they produced a comprehen-

[56] Matthew Arnold, *Victorian Prose,* ed. Frederick William Roe (New York: Ronald Press, 1947), p. 399.

[57] Francis X. Sutton, Seymour E. Harris, Carl Kaysen, and James Tobin, *The American Business Creed* (Cambridge, Mass.: Harvard University Press, 1956). Quoted with permission.

sive, heavily documented, and carefully constructed analysis of the American business creed.

According to the authors, the American business creed is not monolithic. Members of the business community disagree on many issues, sometimes publicly. There is no official text of the creed. But there is enough consistency in what is said and done that it is not inaccurate to call the business ideology a creed. This ideology or creed is similar to those we discussed in Chapter 1. It is a coherent, moving statement of goals and principles that therefore oversimplifies reality and is selective. Like other ideologies, this is both its strength and its weakness: simplicity and coherence move people to action, but they also admit of none of the shadings or subleties that characterize the real world. It is the theory of Sutton and his colleagues that the content of the business ideology is best explained in terms of the strains under which business people operate in fulfilling their roles: "Businessmen adhere to their particular kind of ideology because of the emotional conflicts, the anxieties, and the doubts engendered by the actions which their roles as businessmen compel them to take." Business people play conflicting roles in the family, the community, and the firm, and ideology helps "to resolve these conflicts, alleviate these anxieties, overcome these doubts."[58]

"Praise for the achievements of Americans capitalism is one of the dominant themes in the literature of the Business Creed."[59] Production and higher standards of living are listed first. In a secondary and quite subordinate position are nonmaterial achievements such as freedom. Even more important is the firm link that is forged between the accomplishments and the system: Without American capitalism, we would not have this prosperity. The achievements are a result of the system and thus validate it. Most business people would add American democracy and the free political system to free enterprise to form a highly interdependent system. To their minds, tampering with any one element will destroy the whole. Americans should defend the free market as strongly as they defend their right to vote.

Even in 1956, the word "capitalism" as a description of the American economic system was going out of favor. It had unfortunate overtones of exploitation, subsistence wages, and exorbitant profits. Moreover, it is the term consistently used by those who attack the system. Hence denying that the American free enterprise system is capitalistic is an initial effort at sidestepping the attack. When the term capitalism is used it is always modified by "American"; according to the creed, American capitalism is unique and therefore not open to the criticisms of traditional capitalism.

The four scholars also found two separate, discernible positions on the creed: the classical strand of business ideology, and what was then the

[58] *Ibid.*, p. 11.
[59] *Ibid.*, p. 19.

newer managerial strand. The classical strand emphasizes the traditional notions and values; it has continued with little substantial change since the days of the Puritans and Benjamin Franklin. In the scholars' opinion, Jeremy Bentham's description of economics as "the dogmatics of egoism" could easily be applied to the classical position. The newer managerial strand held many of the same positions, but broke sharply with the traditionalists on such issues as social consciousness and concern for the public image of the corporation and its members. It is more characteristic of the larger corporations and their managers. The Committee for Economic Development, a nationally respected group of business executives which publishes policy papers, generally represents the managerial strand of business ideology.

The creed itself maintains that the American business system has several important attributes. It is *unique;* there is nothing like it anywhere else in the world. The system is also *natural;* it flows from the natural, free needs and desires of people and so could operate in other cultures. Since it is natural, it is easy to see that it is also *stable.* Unless attacked from the outside, it will remain and continue. As a result, challenges to the system result not from its own deficiencies, but solely from outside, foreign interests. But the system, though natural and stable, must still be *chosen* by each individual. It cannot work well if large numbers of people do not understand it, or refuse to cooperate and contribute. This is a moral choice, and those who refuse to cooperate are considered "enemies."[60] Although these attributes obviously reflect the post-World War II atmosphere, they remain strong elements of the creed today.

When Sutton and his colleagues investigated business-government relationships in terms of the creed, they found the business view generally negative. Government power should be restricted; government should stay out of economic life as much as possible. On this point, both the classical and the managerial strands of the business ideology agree. Some regulation may be necessary, but restraints in general are evil because they are limitations on individual liberty.[61] Individuals are responsible for their own material well-being, according to the ideology. Whether executives or laborers, they are responsible for their own future. "Virtue pays; hard work, thrift, initiative, imagination, and venturesomeness are rewarded not only in the next world but in this. Failure, like success, is deserved."[62] The values found to be inherent in the business ideology are these:

- Individualism—moral responsibility and freedom
- Materialism and productivity

[60] *Ibid.,* pp. 36-44.
[61] *Ibid.,* p. 184-86.
[62] *Ibid.,* p. 208.

- Practical realism
- Activism based on realism
- The continuing goal of progress
- The need for optimism and the spirit of adventure
- Competition
- Democracy and equal opportunity
- Service and social responsibility (in the managerial strand)[63]

To take only the first two as examples, business worries about the so-called immoral climate of the United States and the rapidly changing morality. It sees welfare and health care programs as catering to people's laziness, encouraging a lack of thrift and planning, and undermining the virtues of honesty, sobriety, hard work, and prudence.

The ideology's most glaring weakness is its uncritical adulation of material prosperity. More material goods and a higher standard of living seem to be worthwhile for their own sake:

> Much of [the business creed's] apparent materialism arises from a tendency to value material riches without special regard to their ultimate uses. It does this above all in stressing the active pursuit of *productivity*. Business ideologists are not ashamed to stand with John Bright against Matthew Arnold and measure the greatness of a society in terms of its size and industrial equipment.[64]

Although the ideology does not necessarily encourage hedonism in the use of material comforts, it has never realistically faced the question: Productivity for what?

In their preface to the formal analysis of business ideology, Sutton et al. note the close interrelationship between ideology and institutions. The diversity of values and ideologies we have in the United States is dependent on the viability of our institutions, which give us the means to debate, compromise, and act. On the other hand, ". . . popular government, as we know it, is dependent on the existence of flourishing ideologies. The free discussion on which popular government rests must necessarily be largely ideological in character."[65] So strong institutions in a democracy depend on the existence of values and ideology, and the ability to function with a variety of values demands strong, flexible institutions.

Every ideology grows out of a total cultural tradition, and the business ideology is no exception:

[63] *Ibid.,* pp. 251-63.
[64] *Ibid.,* p. 255.
[65] *Ibid.,* p. 272.

The stamp of Western tradition is clearly set upon the general character of the business ideology. It is overwhelmingly secular in character; its values are temporal—almost embarassingly so. Despite its use of religious symbols, the creed does not proclaim the workings of God's ways to men.[66]

The business creed, following Franklin more than the Puritans, is secular. Its few references to God are ritualized; when examined, they have little content. To have a "calling" means to have an occupation; it has moved from being a religious duty to being an expectation of the larger society. When individuals understand their "calling" and the "dignity of work," they need make no apologies for the often narrow, specialized concern with production and sales that takes up the major portion of their lives.

In summary, the American business creed, although oversimplified and selective, has been and remains the basis for giving business a legitimate position within the larger society. Furthermore, it has given vision, provided motivation, and lessened anxieties for generations of business people. The creed proudly extols the material and practical achievements of the system, and holds these to be justifications in themselves for American capitalism. There are few claims of cultural or esthetic gain from the system, and spiritual and moral achievements are limited largely to those connected with freedom.

Free Men and Friedman

The central importance of free enterprise and its supporting values remains perhaps still the tenet most widely held by business leaders. That set of values, first outlined by Adam Smith and developed through two centuries of hard experience, is still vital and compelling for the vast majority of business people.[67] The most respected and articulate contemporary spokesperson for this free market ideology is the economist Milton Friedman. As a representative of the Chicago school of economists and policymakers, Friedman considers freedom the most important value in any economic or political system, and he sees economic freedom as absolutely essential to political freedom.

Friedman's position in defense of the free market and in opposition to government intervention goes all the way back to Adam Smith. His is the now familiar conviction that allowing every person the opportunity to buy

[66]*Ibid.,* p. 274.

[67]For a more detailed presentation of this view, see another volume in this series, Lee E. Preston and James E. Post, *Private Management and Public Policy: The Principle of Public Responsibility* (Englewood Cliffs, N. J.: Prentice-Hall, 1975).

and sell openly and without restriction will ensure that society will obtain the goods and services it needs at the lowest possible price. Free competition in the marketplace will bring about the greatest efficiency in producing the goods society is willing to pay for. The corporation, as the currently predominant economic institution, is the focus of Friedman's concern. He sees that institution as solely an economic one, responsible primarily to its stockholders. The corporation, or more properly corporate management, has no right to dispose of stockholders' profits in any manner that does not directly benefit the corporation. Management has no right to contribute to universities, to train disadvantaged workers, or to prevent pollution, unless in some way these actions benefit the corporation itself, at least in the long run.

Friedman vehemently denies that corporations do have, or even *can* have, social responsibilities: ". . . the only entities who can have responsibilities are individuals; a business cannot have responsibilities."[68] To presume that a corporation can have social responsibilities

> . . . shows a fundamental misconception of the character and nature of a free economy. In such an economy, there is one and only one social responsibility of business—to use its resources and engage in activities designed to increase its profits so long as it stays within the rules of the game, which is to say, engages in open and free competition, without deception or fraud.[69]

He is convinced that the growing sense of corporate social responsibility undermines basic freedoms:

> Few trends could so thoroughly undermine the very foundations of our free society as the acceptance by corporate officials of a social responsibility other than to make as much money for their stockholders as possible. This is a fundamentally subversive doctrine. If businessmen do have a social responsibility other than making maximum profits for stockholders, how are they to know what it is?[70]

He then goes on to point out the difficulty in making such a decision, citing the fact that some German business people contributed to the Nazi party in the early 1930s. Managers thus wrongly presumed an authority and a wisdom they did not possess.

Friedman argues for the abolition of all corporate taxes, and for ensuring

[68] Milton Friedman, "Milton Friedman Responds," *Business and Society Review,* 1 (Spring 1972), 6.

[69] Milton Friedman, *Capitalism and Freedom* (Chicago: University of Chicago Press, 1962), p. 133.

[70] *Ibid.*

that corporate profits are returned to the stockholders, who can then as individuals decide how they will spend their money. It is *their* money, so it should be their decision whether or not to use it for community purposes. His position is simple, straightforward, and consistent: the interests of stockholders, consumers, and citizens as a whole are best served if the corporation sticks to its legitimate role of producing goods and services and does that as efficiently and inexpensively as possible. This is the best long-run service that business firm can provide for society. He does, however, recognize the problem of unemployment and disability, and he was one of the first to propose a guaranteed minimum income (or "negative income tax," as he calls it) for all those of wage-earning age in the economy. He would substitute a minimum income for the variety of welfare, disability, and unemployment programs that have proliferated, all of which now require separate, expensive, and inefficient administrative apparatuses.

The same principles apply to such diverse areas as schooling and medical care. Friedman does not think the government should be in the business of education, for public education then becomes a monopoly insulated from the challenges to excellence and efficiency that come from *free* competition. Rather, the government should provide redeemable tuition certificates for parents and children to use at the school of their choice. As in producing goods and services, he is convinced that better and more effective education will result when there is free competition. His position on the medical profession and the monopoly that certification gives to the American Medical Association is the same. Better and surely more efficient and cheaper medical service would result if there were no monopoly. If anyone with some medical knowledge could hang out a shingle, the public would eventually find out who was giving better service and who should not be patronized. Friedman criticizes the guru status we have bestowed on the medical profession and claims that this does not produce the most effective and efficient treatment.

The Ideology of Corporate Chief Executives

For a decade beginning in the late 1950s, the chief executives of some of the largest corporations in the United States (General Electric, Sears, Roebuck, du Pont, U. S. Steel, American Telephone and Telegraph, and International Business Machines) delivered an annual lecture at Columbia University's Graduate School of Business Administration. The aim of the series, known as the McKinsey lectures, was to explore larger issues of value and ideology. The executives attempted to present their views of the business system and their conceptions of how that system relates to the larger society. In "The View from the Top," Robert Heilbroner analyzed these lectures for their approach, content, and basic ideology.[71] His definition of ideology is "the various ways in which privileges and dis-privileges of any society are justified to those who enjoy or suffer them." It is a pragmatic and self-serving conception, but we must probably concede that it accurately describes how ideologies are usually formed.

During the period of these lectures, there were few serious challenges to the ill-defined American business creed and no real alternatives to it. The business system provided the constraints within which any alterations must be made; if a proposed change in values challenged the operation of the cor-poration, it was doomed to failure. But the executive of the 1960s does not display the self-confident arrogance of his nineteenth- and early twentieth-century counterparts. Andrew Carnegie's righteousness has mellowed; there is a more cautious and sometimes even an apologetic tone to these lectures.

In making his analysis, Heilbroner looked for common threads. He found that these executives tended to dwell on several main themes. They emphasized a clear break between "old-fashioned" exploitative capitalism and modern capitalism. Modern capitalism is more responsible and more socially aware. Indeed, one of the main elements in this new capitalism is its professional responsibility. Like the proponents of what earlier was identified as the managerial strand of the business creed,[72] these executives too found a sharp break with the old brand of capitalism. Although very much in favor of the free market and free competition, they nevertheless argued the need for large-scale organizations. Not surprisingly, since each headed a giant firm, they did not see the need to revive federal antitrust acti-vities.

These executives acknowledged the need to be sensitive to the basic human needs of the men and women who work for them, whether managers or blue collar workers. In spite of the fact that this was the era of the "other-directed" and the "organization" man, they did not feel that the business corporation demanded too much loyalty and inhibited personal communication and growth. They split as to whether high salaries are necessary for high-ranking executives in the firm. Crawford Greenwalt of du Pont felt that these salaries were essential to attract the best talent to re-sponsible positions; T. V. Hauser of Sears Roebuck denied that "extreme practices in executive compensation" were necessary to obtain the services of the talented.[73]

Heilbroner is somewhat severe, and probably rightly so, in his criticisms of these lectures. He found that much of what these executives said was not borne out by their everyday actions. It was not that they deliberately set out

---

[71]Robert Heilbroner, "The View from the Top," in *The Business Establishment,* ed. Earl F. Cheit (New York: Wiley, 1964), pp. 1-36.

[72]Sutton et al., *op. cit.,* pp. 33-36.

[73]Heilbroner, *op. cit.,* p. 15.

to deceive; they seemed to take seriously what they said but never to have examined the inconsistencies:

> . . . one searches the McKinsey lectures in vain for a recognition of truly great issues. A few token gestures, a respectful doffing of the cap before the "challenges of our time," only serve to give greater inanity to the declarations of economic patriotism that follow. It is not moral leadership that the McKinsey lectures finally offer us; it is a pep talk.[74]

He goes on to ask what it is in these lectures that deprives the business ideology of the quality of inspiration it seeks. He says that it is, in part,

> . . . the more or less transparent defense of privilege masquerading as philosophy, the search for sanction cloaked as a search for truth, the little evasions and whitewashings that cheapen what purports to be a fearless confrontation of great issues.[75]

But there is something even more basic lacking in the business creed: "What it lacks is a grandiose image of society, a projection of human possibilities cast in a larger mold than is offered by today's institutions."

The values, ideals, and ideology of the American business community as presented in these lectures leaves us with the conviction that the business ideology is sincere, pragmatic, and well intentioned. These executives are intelligent and competent, even if often somewhat shortsighted and humorless. Whether they are becoming more sensitive to the demands of the larger society in which they live and work, however, remains an open question.

At the core of his *The 20th Century Capitalist Revolution,* the perceptive Adolph Berle located the "conscience of the corporation" in the person of the manager. Berle wrote during the same period and at the same university at which the McKinsey lectures were held; indeed, the lectures may well have been prompted by a desire to investigate his theories, which compare the power of the manager with that of the kings of earlier centuries and argue the necessity for restraint and responsibility. From the time of King William the Conqueror, power has been accompanied by responsibility. This is especially true of absolute power; and in the corporation, "within a wide range, management power is absolute."[76] Berle sees the necessity for such corporate and managerial power, but he also sees clear dangers.

In medieval times, there was a higher law; "the Cross could frequently

---

[74] *Ibid.,* p. 35.
[75] *Ibid.*
[76] Adolph A. Berle, Jr., *The 20th Century Capitalist Revolution* (New York: Harcourt, Brace & World, 1954), p. 64.

stop the king."[77] Some higher law would provide a more balanced exercise of power in contemporary society, but there is none. Hence, corporations need an active conscience: "This conscience must be built into institutions so that it can be invoked as a right by the individual and interests subject to corporate power."[78] Berle argues so strongly for management conscience that he adds this to the qualifications necessary for the corporate executive:

> for the fact seems to be that the really great corporation managements have reached a position for the first time in their history in which they must consciously take account of philosophical questions. They must consider the kind of community in which they have faith, and which they will serve, and which they will help to construct and maintain.[79]

This sort of vision is essential for the executive, for it is easy to forget that "Capitalism is not a way of life, but a method of achieving economic and social results." Yet the decisions of the management of Standard Oil of New Jersey or Sears, Roebuck & Company in the aggregate "do form life and community."[80]

Berle's thesis is well argued and substantiated with considerable evidence; furthermore, though it was presented twenty years ago, the question of how accurate he is remains unanswered. In the case of whether the free market has within itself the ability to handle current difficulties, or whether the increasing power of corporations must be balanced by a corporate conscience, Berle clearly comes down on the side of the latter. Laws and regulations must be developed, but Berle argues for the necessity of greater vision and moral sensitivity on the part of corporate executives. For although it is clear that corporate decisions in the aggregate help to create the type of society we have, the free enterprise economic system in itself as yet has no categories for the more subtle considerations of human happiness, interpersonal relations, and the quality of life.

Masculine Management

The world and the ideals we have been discussing in this chapter are those of the business*man*. For centuries, business, commerce, and trade have all been largely "for men only." Women did not even obtain the right to vote until the twentieth century. The fact that fully half the potential technical and managerial talent has been and continues to be lost is only now occur-

[77] *Ibid.*, p. 69.
[78] *Ibid.*, p. 114.
[79] *Ibid.*, p. 166.
[80] *Ibid.*, pp. 181-83.

ring to business. And it has been within only the past generation or so that religious prejudice in the executive suites of the largest corporations has begun to break down; the WASP (white Anglo-Saxon Protestant) clique is beginning to crack. Furthermore, a glance at any firm's equal employment opportunity figures, especially at the "officials and managers" category, immediately spotlights the results of centuries of racial prejudice. Blacks, Jews, Catholics, and women are only now scurrying up the managerial ladder into the executive suites.

SUMMARY AND CONCLUSIONS

From ancient times to the Middle Ages, Western attitudes toward work lost their negative cast and became progressively more positive. Biblical injunctions and monastic practices helped to integrate work, labor-saving devices, and a planned day into the average person's life. Then in the sixteenth century the Protestant Reformation made the successful performance of an individual's "calling" or occupation one of the primary duties of life. Although a rather joyless vision, it encouraged a focusing of energies that made rapid economic growth possible. The central importance given to private property and the freedom of the individual further supported this growth.

The American business ideology as described in this chapter was ideal for a period of expansion, rapid growth, and exploitation of land and resources. It gave the poor immigrant an opportunity; and it gave a new nation its railroads, mines, industries, and cities.

It was an ideology that advocated such personal qualities as hard work, competition, self-reliance and self-discipline, individualism, and saving and planning ahead. The vision that called forth these qualities, preached in church, school, and town meeting alike, was one of growth, superiority, and making the world a better place for the next generation.

Several elements converged to fashion this new and unique vision called the American business ideology:

1. The *frontier* and new lands opened up to the Europeans who had come to the New World opportunities for an exciting new life in farming, mining, or manufacturing whose potential material rewards were immense.
2. The *Protestant ethic,* which underscored the value of hard work in a person's occupation, was carried to the New World by the Puritans and translated into a secular vision by people like Benjamin Franklin.
3. *Faith in free enterprise* gave the individual security, confidence, and vigor. The system obviously worked well in encouraging economic growth, and moreover was shown to be intellectually sound by the classical economists.

4. *Competition* became more explicit and central with the advent of the theory of evolution and the recognition of the principles of natural selection and the survival of the fittest. Natural forces, if allowed to operate without constraint, would provide the best specimen of human being and, in a parallel fashion, the most efficient firm.

5. *The role of government* was to apply as few contraints as possible to business activity; its central purpose was to protect the private property of its citizens. In this Thomas Jefferson is often quoted, "That government is best which governs least."

It is an irony of history that emphasis on the rugged individualist peaked during the latter half of the nineteenth century, just at the time the business scene was dominated by oligopoly and trusts. A few firms in an industry virtually controlled production, prices, and even wages. It was difficult for an individual, no matter how rugged, to raise the capital necessary to compete. At that time and since then, it has become apparent that this American business ideology, although it may provide a motivation and a vision for the enterprising individual, does not really give an accurate description of the marketplace. For the market is not totally free.

The goal of the American business ideology is expansion and growth; its focus is material reward for the individual. But the assumption that an individual always wants more in the way of material goods leads us to further questions. Is the goal of more material goods sufficient to motivate the individual to give most of his or her physical and psychic energy to the business enterprise? If an individual is satisfied with less, why should he or she work harder, work overtime, or take work home? Even more basic, to what extent will one's "calling" continue to be central in one's life? On a policy level, is a goal of some sort of material growth necessary for any future business creed? These and other like questions will be examined in the following chapters.

CHAPTER THREE

Personal Values
in the Organization

Man is by instinct a lover, a hunter, a fighter, and none of those instincts are given much play at the warehouse!

Tennessee Williams, The Glass Menagerie*

The organizations and groups of which we are a part—from family to corporation—have a profound influence on our personal values and goals, although we are seldom explicitly aware of it. Personal values, a basic component of personality, are often accepted uncritically from parents, peers, teachers, and the mass media. During the working years, a person often so identifies with an organization that success within it becomes a measure of personal worth. Moreover, realization of the inadequacy of that measure often comes in mid-life, and brings with it profound questions, anxieties, and loss of perspective.

Additional occasion for conflict stems from the fact that Americans in general, and especially business managers, show low social concerns. As we will see later in this chapter, these managers show less concern about social conditions and less willingness to set aside personal gain for the sake of less fortunate people. These attitudes are in sharp contrast to the self-image most Americans have of themselves as generous, both personally and as a nation. Although we see ourselves as open-minded, empirical tests show that concern about others is not a primary value for us.

A major hypothesis of this book, and especially of this chapter, is that when such values are held uncritically and are not explicit, they contain the seeds of potential personal conflict and anxiety. Moreover, those in responsible positions who make decisions based on these uncritically held values are in danger of causing severe social disruption. We need look no further than the Nixon Presidency and ITT for examples of what can happen to individuals and nations. There is here a paradox for organizational managers, since they conceive of themselves as being objective, rational,

---

*Tennessee Williams, *The Glass Menagerie,* ed. Gilbert L. Rathbun of Random House. Quoted with permission.

and not led by personal whim. They are generally unaware of how strongly their unexamined personal values bias their decisions. Even more than most organizations, the business firm has carefully designed processes and structures for making decisions. A good manager insists on careful analysis of all the facts of a case before coming to a judgment. Market surveys, outside consultants, product planning groups, and computer analyses are indications of the high priority rational decision making has within the firm.

At the same time that the decision-making process is a source of pride to a manager, that manager is often unaware that the process itself rests on rarely examined assumptions. For beneath this structure[1] lie certain assumptions about the purpose of the corporation: to maximize profits, to expand market share, to enable the firm to survive and grow. These very ideological assumptions upon which the rational decision making is based are often accepted unquestioningly, much as we accept traditional cultural mores. The inadequacy of traditional business values and ideology does not appear until the goals of the corporation come into conflict with the goals of the larger society.

This chapter will examine the various factors that influence the values and goals of both the individual within the organization and the organization itself. It will focus on the factors that influence the values of the individual within the business firm.

THE ORGANIZATION'S INFLUENCE: SOCIALIZATION

A large organization exerts a powerful influence on its members and their values by means of the socialization process. Superiors' expectations, unwritten norms, and the career ladder have a profound influence on participants. Exposure forty hours a week to these expectations, coupled with the perceived importance of success within the organization, will lead to unconscious changes in and/or solidification of values.

Behavioral scientists who have studied the organization find that a bureaucratic form of organization is characterized by high productive efficiency but low innovative capacity.[2] When tasks are predictable and can therefore be repeated and codified, they can be done quickly and efficiently. Nevertheless, that very stabilization of tasks and roles can bring rigidity. It is difficult for the organization designed for efficiency to remain open and innovative; its very success tends to solidify and reinforce past ways of doing things.

[1]This point is well made by Robert Chatov, "The Role of Ideology in the American Corporation," in Dow Votaw and S. Prakash Sethi, *The Corporate Dilemma* (Englewood Cliffs, N.J.: Prentice-Hall, 1973), p. 51.

[2]Victor A. Thompson, *Modern Organization* (New York: Knopf, 1961), pp. 163-64.

Organizations generally reappraise their goals and values only in the face of new demands from the outside. Without such challenges, they tend to continue to operate in those ways that have proved effective in the past, and become more rigid and less open as the years go by. At the same time, the organization is quite effective in selecting individuals and socializing them into persons who "fit well" into the system. The organization has a subtle but potent influence on its members' attitudes and values, as the sociologist Robert Merton puts it:

> The bureaucrat's official life is planned for him in terms of a graded career through the organizational devices of promotions by seniority, pensions, incremental salaries, etc., all of which are designed to provide incentives for disciplined action and conformity to artificial regulations. The official is tacitly expected to and largely does adapt his thoughts, feelings, and actions to the prospect of his career. But *these very devices* which increase the probability of conformance also lead to an over-concern with strict adherence to regulations which induce timidity, conservatism, and technicism. Displacement of sentiments from goals onto means is fostered by the tremendous symbolic significance of the means (rules).[3]

The organization develops a life of its own, aiming at its own growth, protecting its own special interests, being jealous of its own position, power, and prerogatives. The corporation's way of doing things, especially when it has been successful in the past, can become rigid and ossified. The individual is expected to "learn IBM's way of doing things." Empirical studies show that managers tend to select for promotion subordinates who have values like their own.[4] Although we would expect these managers to make decisions that are objective and rational, there is evidence that personal likes and values play an important role.

When thousands of employees are organized to perform a certain productive task, it requires coordination among people and units of the organization. As these various relations and responsibilities are spelled out, either in writing or implicitly, there is correspondingly less discretion left to the individual. Even in decentralized companies, standard practices and procedures constrain new ideas and initiatives. Moreover, accepted goals and values become internalized by the individual employees. Deviant values are eliminated, either initially in the selection process, or through socialization. It quickly becomes clear which values are accepted and which are not.

In the large organization, the competitive, achievement-oriented manager wants to be noticed quickly as a success. He or she therefore tends to focus

[3]Robert K. Merton, "Bureaucratic Structure and Personality," in W. Lloyd Warner and Norman H. Martin, *Industrial Man* (New York: Harper & Row, 1958), p. 70.

[4]John Senger, "Managers' Perceptions of Subordinates' Competence as a Function of Personal Value Orientations," *Academy of Management Journal,* 14, 4 (December 1971), 415-23.

on short-run efficiency and performance, since these can be more readily measured and will make good material for a report to top management.[5] Hence corporate economic values become all-embracing, and permeate personal and social values as well.

Money and Markets As Goals

The corporation and material values influence much of Americans' lives. To foreign observers, it sometimes appears as if all Americans do is directed toward providing and acquiring material goods. The centrality of corporate life, advertising, and individualized suburban homes are but a few manifestations of the phenomenon. It is as if Americans really believed that "happiness is a new car or new home." Economic goals and the corporation can have a profound influence on our political values as well. The loud and clear voice of industry, through trade associations and the individual firm, often has a decisive influence on both domestic and foreign policy. Economic values dominate when we threaten war if foreign oil supplies are not available at a "proper" price.

Karl Marx was the first to charge that an industrial society separates people from their work and alienates them. We will examine Marx's critique in the next chapter. Here, we will see that work is not, as it happens, an attractive and rewarding activity for many Americans. Inquiries among assembly-line workers show that they generally find their work monotonous, impersonal, uncreative, unchallenging. An extensive study of assembly-line workers as early as the 1950s showed that nine out of ten of these individuals intensely disliked their immediate jobs.[6] The current high turnover, absenteeism, and tardiness in industry is mainly attributed to the fact that the work is so unattractive. Not only is there no incentive in the work, there is a positive aversion to it. On the assembly line a person is used like a single-purpose tool. The individual's actions are repetitive and paced from outside and thus demand little intelligence or imagination; the person is used as an addition to the machine. All this creates a distance between the workers and their work. They have little control, and the workplace is impersonal. Work values are material and not human: productivity and efficiency, even at the expense of pride, responsibility, and joy in one's work. Recent practical proposals for job redesign or job enrichment have not been

[5]Neil W. Chamberlain, "The Life of the Mind in the Firm," in the special "Perspectives on Business" issue of *Daedelus,* 98 (Winter 1968), 136.

[6]Charles R. Walker, "Human Relations on the Assembly Line," *Proceedings of Ninth Annual Industrial Engineering Institute,* University of California (February 1957), 50. See also the more complete study by Walker and Robert H. Guest, *The Man on the Assembly Line* (Cambridge, Mass.: Harvard University Press, 1952). These same findings are supported and updated in Theodore V. Purcell and Gerald F. Cavanaugh, *Blacks in the Industrial World: Issues for the Manager* (New York: Free Press, 1972), pp. 72-85.

widespread, and some attempts have already been discarded as too inefficient.

The executive, too, is exposed to this same impersonal emphasis on productivity. Ironically, the goals communicated to the corporate executive by the corporation, and thence to others, are not unlike those given the assembly-line worker. The manager's goals are productivity, return on investment, and a larger share of the market. Managers have no choice in this, if they and their firm are to survive. The individuals who are attracted to and make it to the corporate executive suite have a high need for success. They must be able to make decisions unencumbered by emotional ties to persons or groups. They must always be ready to move to a new location and leave old friends and associations behind. They must have sufficient detachment from their friends and neighborhoods. In fact, for many, there is little point in making deep friendships or getting involved in local activities; it would only make the parting more difficult. In his study of the executive personality, William Henry concludes:

> The corporate executive is a special type, spawned on impersonality and hurried into the task of defending his individuality in the diffuse and open competition of nonfamily life. His energy to prove his competence again and again is extreme, and his need to re-create a safe and personalized nest is minimal. . . . Undeterred by other than the purely conventional in personal life, he is able without sense of loss to devote his entire life to the executive task.[7]

Those attracted to corporate executive work are people who do not depend on close personal relationships. They obtain their major satisfaction from completing a task. Their personal values set the tone of the organization; these values are communicated and transferred to others in the firm. It becomes clear that the successful ones are more task- than person-oriented.

Many young people today find the business firm an unattractive place to work. This is probably largely because of what they would call the excessive and inhuman demands the corporation makes on its employees, whether they be on the assembly line or in the executive suite. Although the campus protests have quieted, probes of campus attitudes show that corporations and corporate leaders do not have the confidence of young people.[8] This erosion of trust in American institutions and its significance will be examined in greater detail in Chapter 5. All this says much about the goals and values of the corporation. The central accepted goal is economic—profit

[7]William E. Henry, "Executive Personality and Large-scale Organizations," in *The Emergent American Society,* Vol. 1, by W. Lloyd Warner, Dareb Unwalla, and James Trim (New Haven, Conn.: Yale University Press, 1967), p. 275.

[8]See for example, "Evidence of Campus Unrest," *Harvard Business Review,* 51 (May-June 1972), 86.

maximization and growth of the firm. It is a material goal of producing goods and services, some of which are valuable to society and some of which are trivial or even harmful. Since this is the organization's goal, it has a powerful influence on individuals, and generally becomes their goal as well. The identification at least decreases dissonance and frustration.

The corporation requires few of the many and varied talents of its employees. Although executives have the widest scope for their abilities, they are still constrained by accepted procedures and values. Their own values must be subordinated to those of the organization, which may be narrow, short-sighted and even potentially self-defeating. Some have even closed their eyes to, or have actually themselves participated in, poor workmanship, bribery, incomplete and dishonest testing of products, lack of sensitivity to valid customer complaints, and more.[9] In this sort of environment, it takes a strong character to "blow the whistle." Few of us want to be heroes or martyrs; we are coopted by the values of the organization that provides our livelihood.

Personal Growth Within the Organization

Organizational psychologists have spent considerable time and effort in attempting to unravel the many threads of influence binding together the organizational participant and her or his organization. Among the basic questions they ask is this: Is the corporation able effectively to pursue its corporate objectives, and at the same time encourage the development of its members as persons? Social scientists are amassing evidence that an individual can grow toward full maturity and self-actualization only in an interpersonal atmosphere of complete trust and open communication.[10] These open, trusting interpersonal relationships are essential to that growth. They are called "authentic relationships" by Argyris,[11] "genuine" by Rogers,[12] and characterized as "being-love" by Maslow.[13] Work relationships can seldom reach such openness and trust. Nevertheless, if the working climate inhibits personal growth, it will result in frustration and, eventually, a poor working environment. Managers are therefore concerned about the quality of these relationships within the organization.

Although not explicitly focusing on values and goals, psychologists and

[9]See the half-dozen cases of flagrant corporate evil-doing in Robert Heilbroner et al., *In the Name of Profits* (Garden City, N.Y.: Doubleday, 1972).

[10]Herbert A. Shepard, "Changing Interpersonal and Intergroup Relationship in Organizations," *Handbook of Organizations,* ed. James G. March (Chicago: Rand McNally, 1965), p. 1125.

[11]Chris Argyris, *Personality and Organization* (Homewood, Ill.: Dorsey, 1962).

[12]Carl Rogers, *On Becoming a Person* (Boston: Houghton Mifflin, 1961).

[13]Abraham Maslow, *Toward a Psychology of Being* (Princeton, N.J.: Van Nostrand, 1962).

many corporation executives have become vitally interested in supporting the personal growth and maturity of their employees. Executives are especially concerned if it can be established that this will benefit the corporation in the long run, or at least not detract from their basic goal of producing a good product at a profit. Can the sort of supportive relationships that are necessary for personal growth be achieved in an organization that is primarily concerned with production and efficiency? Or is the corporation to be an organization set apart, where the necessary trust, openness, communication, cooperation, and strong interpersonal relationships must simply be set aside in the interests of the primary goals of the firm? Does the essential dedication to the task, production orientation, short time span, and hard-headedness of the industrial corporation necessarily rule out the conscious pursuit of more subtle human values?

The case for shared decisions and encouraging individual initiative and creativity has been building for a generation. The concern that many firms have for these issues is often indicated by the size of the staff and the budget devoted to them. Although encouraging shared decisions and individual growth goes under a variety of names, from personnel research to organizational development, it is significant that a firm as productivity-oriented as General Motors has more than two hundred professionals working on what they themselves call organizational development. Firms face the prospect of losing some of their best talent if there is not sufficient opportunity for self-determination. In the long term, this loss also affects productivity.

In some of his earlier work, Chris Argyris maintained that there was a conflict between the traditional view of the goals of an organization and a healthy human personality. Under the traditional formal principles of organization (chain of command, task specialization), introducing into it persons who are fairly mature and are thus predisposed to relative independence, initiative, and the use of their important abilities will cause a serious disturbance, according to Argyris. He says that the results of this disturbance are "frustration, failure, short time perspective, and conflict."[14] Argyris then outlines some of the adaptive behavior in which a person in such a restrictive organization will engage: (1) leaving the organization; (2) climbing the organizational ladder; (3) manifesting defense reactions, such as daydreaming, aggression, ambivalence, regression, or projection; (4) becoming apathetic and disinterested in the organization, its make-up and goals. This then leads to employees' reducing their expectations of what they will achieve at work, and to goldbricking, set rates, restricting quotas, making errors, cheating, and slowing down.[15]

In his seminal *Human Side of Enterprise,*[16] Douglas McGregor contrasts

---

[14]Argyris, *op. cit.,* p. 233.
[15]*Ibid.,* p. 235.
[16]Douglas McGregor, *Human Side of Enterprise* (New York: McGraw-Hill, 1960), p. 33.

two views of man and his desire to work. The first, which he called Theory X, outlines the traditional view of man that has heavily influenced management style and control:

1. Man doesn't like to work and will avoid it if he can.
2. So therefore he must be coerced, controlled, directed, and threatened with punishment to get him to work.
3. Man prefers to be directed, wishes to avoid responsibility, has little ambition, and wants security.

In contrast to the traditional view, McGregor presents and proceeds to argue in favor of his Theory Y:

1. Work is as natural to man as play or rest.
2. Man will exercise self-direction and self-control in the service of objectives to which he is committed.
3. Commitment to objectives is a function of the rewards associated with their achievement (especially satisfaction of ego and self-actualization).
4. Man learns, under proper conditions, to accept and even ask for responsibility.

These divergent views of the values and goals of the person have a significant influence on the organizational climate and management style of an organization. Theory X provides the foundation for a formal, highly structured, control-oriented organization. One of the characteristic disadvantages of this sort of organization is goal displacement. Goal displacement is a bureaucratic process in which members of an organization tend to turn their procedures into goals. The petty organization official tends to make adherence to the rules and preservation of his office the purpose of his work, and most often this is at the expense of the persons or process he is serving. Studies of the French civil service in 1931 and the U. S. Navy in 1952 showed this tendency.[17]

Laboratory Research on Values in Groups

The importance of the individual and that individual's independent judgment has always been a paramount, explicit value for Americans. But although we mouth the value of independent judgment, laboratory research indicates it does not hold the high priority we claim. In fact, the opinions and attitudes of the group have a definitive influence on the individual. Individuals are often willing to deny their own perceptions and better judg-

[17]Bernard Berelson and Gary A. Steiner, *Human Behavior: An Inventory of Scientific Findings* (New York: Harcourt, Brace & World, 1964), p. 366.

ments because of the attitudes of their group. On the other hand, self-oriented competitiveness can undermine the cooperation and teamwork required in an organization.

One of the classic experiments in studying the influence of the group on the judgment of the individual was done by Solomon E. Asch.[18] Asch gathered groups of seven to nine college men for "psychological experiments in visual judgment." The group was shown two cards simultaneously; one card bore a standard line, the other bore three lines, one of which was the same length as the one shown on the first card. Of the men in the group, all were "confederates" (instructed ahead of time to pick the same erroneous line), except one who was "naive" and was therefore the subject of the experiment. The question was, How often would a subject pick the right length of line even in the face of unanimous agreement by the rest of the group that it was another line? It was visually quite clear which line was the same length; ordinarily, mistakes would be made only 1 percent of the time. The subject was seated near the end of the group, so that most of the others would have responded by the time it was his turn to do so.

For our reputedly individualistic society, the findings are significant: When the subjects were exposed to the incorrect majority, 75 percent erred in the direction of the majority. Only 25 percent braved conflict with the group and held to their own perceptions. As Asch himself points out, when a majority of reasonably intelligent and educated young men will call black white when faced with the opinions of the group, it is obvious that we are losing much of the benefit of an individual's independent assessment of reality. The opinions, norms, and values of the majority can become a tyranny. We can see this readily in Nazi Germany or Soviet Russia, but are often less able to see it in our own society.

In spite of their positive contributions, persons with an independent judgment are not always popular in the organization. This was established in experiments with problem-solving groups. A "deviant," a person whose values and attitudes did not coincide with those of the group, was placed in half the groups. In every case, the groups with a deviant had a better solution to the problem they were given than did the homogeneous groups. Each group was then asked to eliminate one member of the group before they received their next problem. In every case, the "deviant" was thrown out, and this in spite of the fact that it was fairly clear the deviant had significantly contributed to the work they were doing.[19] The group values harmony and "togetherness" more than challenge, new information, and perhaps irascibility. On the other hand, additional experiments have shown

[18]Solomon E. Asch, "Opinions and Social Pressure," in *Science, Conflict and Society.* (San Francisco: Freeman, 1969), pp. 52-57.

[19]Elise Boulding, *Conflict: Management in Organizations* (Ann Arbor, Mich.: Foundation for Research on Human Behavior, 1964), p. 54.

that in groups, competitive behavior (the individual looking to his own success and satisfaction) often leads to disruption and inefficiency in the
group's effort. Competitive behavior leads to greater efficiency when the
job can be done on one's own and does not require the help of others.[20]
Competition within the group often results in disruption and even
obstruction.

In sum, the corporation tends to inculcate and thus perpetuate its own
values. With other organizations, it shares the goals of survival and growth.
These, plus the characteristic goals of long-term profit and return on investment, have a profound influence on the attitudes and values of its members.
Members learn to accept the rules of the game as they are understood in
their organization. Although creativity is a long-term benefit to the firm, it
is not easily tolerated. The material goals of the firm often force individuals
into judging the success of their work in numerical terms: number produced
and dollars profit. The bias toward the concrete and measurable is satisfying, because it is objective and unarguable. But this bias can readily undermine more long-range and human values, such as creativity, trust, and
openness.

WHY MEN WORK:
INTERDEPENDENCE OF IDEOLOGY AND MOTIVATION

During the past decade, various theories of motivation have been quite
popular with business people. Executives have invested their own time in
reading, and company funds in leadership training programs based on
various theories of what moves a person to act and work. To determine why
they and their employees work is a bread and butter issue to managers. If
they can find out, perhaps they can influence people to work more efficiently and effectively. Dozens of men and women have researched the
motives that influence a person's work. Earlier in this chapter we mentioned
the work of Argyris, Maslow, and McGregor. These psychological theories
of motivation and their implications are an important part of the knowledge
and skills available to the professional manager. Hence, they are a core part
of any business school curriculum.

When psychologists ask why men work, they inevitably touch on values.
What sort of values move the employee, according to these specialists?[21]

---

[20]Alexander Mintz, "Nonadaptive Group Behavior," in *Basic Studies in Social Psychology,*
ed. Harold Proshansky and Bernard Seidenberg (New York: Holt, Rinehart and Winston,
1965), pp. 620-27.

[21]For a comprehensive overview of the questions and some suggested answers, see Theodore
V. Purcell, "Work Psychology and Business Values: A Triad Theory of Work Motivation,"
Personnel Psychology, 20, 3 (Autumn 1967), 231-58.

Most theories of motivation popular with business persons describe moving forces within the individual, but rarely or never explicitly discuss values, goals, or ideology. These theories generally implicitly presuppose traditional, accepted goals. In thus ignoring values and goals, and in that way seeming to hold that they are unimportant, motivational psychologists do business a disservice. This is especially so since there is actually an intimate and complex, although seldom acknowledged, relationship between ideology and motivation.

Among the questions we might ask are these: To what extent do theories of motivation (McClelland's need for achievement, Maslow's self-actualizer, Likert's System 4, McGregor's Theory Y) imply values and goals? Do they presuppose goals, or predispose one toward certain goals? Do these theories aid in a search for values and goals, or mask their absence? The greatly increased interest in motivation in the past few decades has paradoxically coincided with, and perhaps partially caused, a decrease in interest in values and ideology. Ideology is, as we have seen, a product of deliberate reflection and articulation. But psychologists warn us to be suspicious of stated reasons for actions. It is too easy, they remind us, to be unaware of unconscious or subconscious motives that have a powerful influence on our activities. We may think we know why we do something, and respond with that answer when asked. But according to psychologists, that may not be the real reason at all. In sum, the search for acknowledged values and an explicit ideology is not aided by the many psychologists who imply that straightforward verbal statements are generally self-deceiving and invalid.

Need for Achievement and Values

David C. McClelland's work on the need for achievement is well known to students of organizations. He has pointed out that the success of a society and of the individual is most often positively correlated with a high need for achievement. A person's need for achievement, according to McClelland, can be measured; indeed, it can even be increased. He has designed programs for increasing the need for achievement of poor and disadvantaged people.[22] It is not to our purpose to go into the details of McClelland's work. In this instance, as with the others that follow, we must be content with a brief examination of the psychologist's explicit treatment of the relationship between motivation and values. Of the motivation theorists, McClelland treats the relationship most explicitly. He examines the long-range impact of a person's ideology on motivation. McClelland

[22]See David C. McClelland's "Achievement Motivation Can Be Developed," *Harvard Business Review,* 43, 4 (November-December 1965), 6-24; and "Black Capitalism: Making It Work," *Think* (July-August 1969), pp. 7-11.

cites Max Weber's work[23] in showing how the Protestant ethic has contributed to attitudes supportive of modern capitalism. Protestantism encouraged independence and self-reliance. The Church was no longer the central agency for communicating values; the individual was much more on his own.

Attitudes of independence, self-reliance, and the need for achievement are very much influenced by the way parents bring up their children. Indeed, it is understandable and appropriate that parents' ideals and values do have an effect on how they rear their children. McClelland is able to predict from the content of children's stories, fantasies, daydreams, and dreams a high or a low need for achievement. Since parents' own values and ideology influence the stories they tell or provide their children, they then in turn have a profound effect on their children's motivation. In experimental work, it was found that boys who showed a high need for achievement had mothers who expected their sons to master a number of activities early in life: know their way around the city; be active and energetic; try hard for things for themselves; do well in competition; make their own friends.[24] On the other hand, the mothers of boys with low need for achievement reported that they restricted their sons more. These mothers did not want their sons to make important decisions by themselves, or make friends with other children not approved of by their parents.

McClelland theorizes that the Protestant Reformation encouraged a new character type possessing a more vigorous and independent spirit. This self-reliance was then passed on in families and especially through child-rearing patterns. Furthermore, McClelland follows Weber in maintaining that it is precisely this self-reliance that forms the foundation for modern capitalism. He cites evidence that the need for achievement is increased as an effect of an ideological or religious conversion, whether that conversion be Protestant, Catholic, or Communist.[25] In the wake of the reflection and forced reassessment a conversion entails, a felt challenge and resulting need for achievement emerges. According to McClelland, religion, ideology, and values are inextricably intertwined with motivation, and especially the need for achievement; and this relationship is especially close when these values are reassessed and changed.

In modern society, the need for achievement is generally exercised in the marketplace. McClelland cites Florence of the late Middle Ages as an example of the need for achievement being expressed in art, and thus in something other than economic development. In modern societies,

---

[23]Max Weber, *The Protestant Ethic and the Spirit of Capitalism*, tr. Talcott Parsons (New York: Scribner's, 1958).

[24]David C. McClelland, *The Achieving Society*. (Princeton: Van Nostrand, 1961), pp. 46-50.

[25]*Ibid.*, pp. 406-17.

however, business seems to be the major outlet for this need. McClelland's practical criteria for the success of the achiever today, and hence his implicit goal, is generally economic growth. In this fashion McClelland seems to accept rather unquestioningly the traditional business ideology and the prevailing social norms: that economic growth is the best final goal of a people.

McClelland denies that the business person with a high need for achievement is motivated by money. Nevertheless, he does hold that achievement is measured in money terms.[26] He notes that money is a *symbol* of success. An increase in salary, which is often demonstrated to friends and neighbors by a more expensive car and a larger home, is the reward that comes to those who have achieved; it is the sure sign of success, at least in the eyes of corporate superiors. Some further observations by Erich Fromm on money as a measure of personal success will be examined later in this chapter.

The Self-actualizing Person

Abraham H. Maslow was the principle proponent of a school of humanistic psychology that sees motivation as arising from a hierarchy of needs. Maslow maintained that his theory of motivation was based on observations of healthy, mature persons. He found that as "lower needs" (food, water, safety, security) were gratified, they ceased to be motivators. The person then moved on to "higher needs" (belongingness, love, self-esteem, and self-actualization), so that ". . . a healthy man is primarily motivated by his needs to develop and actualize his fullest potentialities and capacities."[27]

Of the various human needs, Maslow is quick to point out that some of the higher needs are not always strong. In spite of the fact that in the long run they can be vital for the individual, their importance is not often seen by those who do not have enough to eat or a roof over their heads. In Maslow's words, "The human needs for love, for knowledge or for philosohy, are weak and feeble rather than unequivocal and unmistakable; they whisper rather than shout. And the whisper is easily drowned out." For individuals to arrive at their own internalized personal values, to say nothing of their own philosophy and religion, demands that their lower needs be somewhat satisfied.

Maslow consistently maintains that as individuals become more mature and accepting, they will move correctly toward establishing their own values. He concludes that a firm foundation for a value system is automatically furnished by open acceptance of one's own self, ". . . of

[26]*Ibid.*, pp. 232-37.
[27]Abraham H. Maslow, *Motivation and Personality* (New York: Harper & Row, 1954), pp. 35-58.

human nature, of much of social life, and of nature and physical reality.'' A society made up largely of self-actualizers is characterized by more free choice and nonintrusiveness. Under these conditions, "the deepest layers of human nature would show themselves with greater ease.''[28] Maslow goes on to describe the personal characteristics of the people he has examined—those whom he calls self-actualizers. They tend to be "strongly focused on problems outside themselves"; they are problem-centered rather than ego-centered. Most often these mature, self-actualized individuals have "some mission in life, some task to fulfill''—a task outside themselves that enlists most of their energies. Significantly, especially for our purposes, these tasks are generally nonpersonal or unselfish; they are directed primarily toward the good of others. Furthermore, self-actualizers "are ordinarily concerned with basic issues and eternal questions of the type that we have learned to call philosophical or ethical.''[29] Their major concerns are not ego-centered, trivial, or petty; they have a wider breadth of concerns, larger horizons. They seem to have a stability that enables and encourages them to address the larger ethical and social issues.

The possession of basic, root values is described a bit later in more detail. Self-actualizers "are strongly ethical, they have definite moral standards, they do right and do not do wrong.'' They are less confused about their basic values. It is easier for them to distinguish right from wrong, although these values do not always coincide with those of the accepted, conventional, surrounding culture. Maslow holds that as persons grow and mature, they will become less selfish and more concerned with other people and larger problems. Their values will become clearer, more explicit, and highly ethical. Indeed, although Maslow finds that these people are not always theists, and most have scant loyalty to an institutional church, they are nevertheless the sort of people who a few centuries ago "would all have been described as men who walk in the path of God or as godly men.''[30]

Maslow gives values and goals an important place. Further, he is convinced that ethical values will emerge as the individual matures, and that this process is rather automatic. In so describing the process, Maslow implies that the development of internalized ethical principles and unselfish goals can *only* be accomplished as a person matures. He therefore has little room for a value system, asceticism, or a "spirituality" that seeks explicitly to develop unselfish, highly ethical principles and goals. Given Maslow's view, we would have to wait for a significant number of people to become self-actualizers before unselfish goals and policy could be developed. It is doubtful whether the problems that face our contemporary world can wait for this maturity to come about, or whether such maturity will *ever* characterize a significant number of the major world leaders and policymakers.

[28] *Ibid.*, pp. 276-78.
[29] *Ibid.*, pp. 159-60.
[30] *Ibid.*, pp. 168-69.

Human Resources

A team of motivational psychologists at Michigan's Institute for Social Research has proposed a more participative management style, which they call System 4.[31] By the traditional industrial criteria (productivity, lower absenteeism and turnover, less scrap and fewer grievances), this new emphasis on human resources is said to be successful. Led by Rensis Likert, this group maintains that probably the most valuable asset a firm has is its people, from unskilled workers to executives. Yet this asset is never presented in annual reports. Legitimate assets are considered to be plant, equipment, and inventory, as well as a firm's good name and markets. Likert proposes a system of "human asset accounting" designed to measure human resources and present them to the firm's publics.[32]

In a more recent article,[33] Likert urges the corporation to be more sensitive to social issues and to be more responsible, especially if it wishes to ward off government regulation. It is to the long-run benefit of all those who are influenced by the firm, whether they be shareholders, customers, citizens, or government, that ". . . business itself take steps to prevent the occurrence of abuses and to launch remedial action whenever abuses inadvertently occur." Nevertheless, besides making an exact and public accounting of its human resources, Likert offers little in the way of goals for the firm. He implies that its actions ought to be focused on satisfying the expectations of its various publics. At best, however, the firm ought to anticipate expectations and act accordingly. The initiative he speaks of is precisely that—to anticipate the expectations of others.

It is not to our purpose to go into the details of Likert's work, but suffice it to say that when it comes to ultimate goals and values, he leaves many questions unanswered. And in this he is more typical of motivational psychologists than are McClelland and Maslow. Likert holds, for example, that a group will be more satisfied and therefore more productive if it is able to participate in the decision-making process. But we are left with the obvious question, productivity for what? By default Likert leaves the impression that the goals of an organization are none of his concern. He even seems to imply that whatever an organization does, regardless of its goals, is good.

Along with most other motivational psychologists, Likert would probably reply that the goals and values of the firm are beyond his concern and competence. This may be true enough, yet there can be little doubt that an organization's values and goals will have some influence on the various participants' motivations. If values and goals are in conflict, it will lead to

[31]Rensis Likert, *The Human Organization: Its Management and Value* (New York: McGraw-Hill, 1967); also, *New Patterns of Management* (New York: McGraw-Hill, 1961).
[32]Likert, *The Human Organization*, pp. 104, 146-55.
[33]Rensis Likert, "The Influence of Social Research on Corporate Responsibility," in *A New Rationale for Corporate Social Policy* (New York: Committee for Economic Development, 1970), pp. 20-38.

frustration for the person and various inefficiencies for the organization, as Argyris has pointed out.[34] Moreover, our traditional neglect of values and goals leaves the impression that they are unimportant. In reality, we have taken organizational goals for granted; and we now find ourselves in the awkward position of wanting to probe these goals, yet having few tools and little expertise for doing so.

Unexamined Assumptions

More than a decade ago, after having worked with Maslow, Douglas McGregor began to dig into the accepted ideology, the conventional assumptions that lay beneath management and motivation literature. He was incisive in penetrating the "let's be practical; theorizing has no place in management" mentality and in demonstrating that "it is not possible to reach a managerial decision or take a managerial action uninfluenced by assumptions, whether adequate or not."[35] The assumptions and implicit goals and values are there. The relevant question is whether these assumptions and implicit goals and values are examined for their adequacy or not. McGregor pinpoints one of the most glaring deficiencies of this self-imposed managerial blindness: "The common practice of proceeding without explicit examination of theoretical assumptions, leads, at times, to remarkable inconsistencies in managerial behavior."[36]

It therefore becomes clear that there is no such thing as "valueless" management. Proceeding to carry out the unexamined goals of the organization without explicit awareness of what values undergird those goals is to have chosen a way of acting; it is precisely to have made decisions on the basis of values. These values are to accept without question the values of the organization. Rather than being value-free, decisions are supported by value judgments made by default. For example, that the present goals of the organization are acceptable; that in a conflict with the larger society or with another organization, loyalty demands that I pursue the good of my organization. The Watergate break-in and other "dirty tricks" bear testimony to the shortsightedness and ultimate inefficiency of this sort of loyal and "value-free" management.

PERSONAL VALUES AND THE BUSINESS CREED

We have examined how the structure and environment of the organization affect the values and goals of the manager. In this section, we will focus on the business manager as a person and on her or his values.

[34]Argyris, *op. cit.,* p. 233.
[35]McGregor, *op cit.,* p. 7.
[36]*Ibid.*

In the classic empirical study of the backgrounds, education, and attitudes of business executives by W. Lloyd Warner and James Abegglen,[37] the authors found that the executive is best characterized as a mobile person, able to leave and take up a new job in a new community rather easily:

> The mobile man must be able to depart: that is, he must maintain a substantial emotional distance from people, and not become deeply involved with them or committed to them; and he must be an energetic person and one who can focus his energy on a single goal.[38]

These top managers are not particularly sensitive to the needs of other people. Even though their own success is often built on decisions that result in considerable loss to others, this does not seem to disturb them. They do not set out to hurt others, but the fact that others are hurt does not seem to bother them; they do not allow themselves to become "distracted into personal duels, for they do not allow themselves to become so involved with others." Successful executives ". . . are not men who know guilt. The distractions of consideration for others, of weighing the potential damage to others of a contemplated move, do not enter into their calculations."

Mobility and lack of consideration for others enables them to approach managerial decisions dispassionately. This objectivity, combined with their other more obvious talents, contributes to making them successful. But their success does not allow them the satisfaction one might expect. There is rarely time to relax, to look back on one's successes, ". . . for an essential part of the system is the need for constant demonstration of one's adequacy, for reiterated proof of one's independence."[39]

What sort of a background is it that would give a person these qualities of mobility, lack of involvement with others, and the need to constantly demonstrate personal adequacy? The researchers found that these executives tended to have strong, demanding mothers and weak or even absent fathers. Although mothers of these successful executives are seen as even-tempered and hard-working, they are also stern, rigid, moralistic, and controlling. They hold out high standards of achievement and parcel out their love as reward for success. At the same time, the fathers are distant from their children; they are not supporting and reinforcing. These executives see their fathers as rather unreliable figures. They also could not identify with their fathers; it was their mothers who held out goals of achievement. According to Warner and Abegglen, if they were to win their mothers' love and others' respect, they must prove themselves; they must be a success at what they are doing. They can never be fully sure that they have

---

[37]*Big Business Leaders in America* (New York: Atheneum, 1963).
[38]*Ibid.,* pp. 81-82.
[39]*Ibid.,* p. 83.

achieved. The overwhelming majority of the families of these executives are upper or middle class: 76 percent of the managers' fathers were owners, executives, professionals, or white collar workers. They are conservative in their politics. Moreover, when they have any involvement with community activities, it tends to be with conservative movements—Chamber of Commerce, boys' clubs, conservative charities.

Warner gathered his material in 1950, but a survey twenty years later showed many of the same attitudes, especially on political and social issues.[40] The more recent survey showed that just short of 80 percent of the chief executives call themselves Republicans, and 80 percent are predictably Protestant. Only 9 percent are Catholics, nowhere near their 23 percent of the total population. Blacks and women, of course, are hard to find in executive suites. Most of these top managers have grown up in middle class or upper middle class homes.

When chief executives were asked what they would look for in their successors, suprisingly they do not give high priority to such attributes as youth or the ability to get along well with people of different races and classes. They are generally looking for men who are very much like themselves in background and attitudes. Organizations and their attitudes tend to be self-perpetuating. The ordinary struggle for growth and survival urges people and organizations to seek "their own kind."

Selling of Self

Although these goals and values are influenced by background, education, and age, they are also heavily affected by an individual's estimate of what sort of personal values will "sell" in the marketplace. The market concept of value, what a person will be able to obtain when he puts his body into the employment market, has a considerable influence on notions of self-worth.[41]

The individual begins to be concerned about how well he or she "sells" him or herself, how he or she appears to a prospective employer, what sort of a package he or she seems to be. The individual then becomes less concerned with personal goals of achievement, satisfaction, and happiness; attention is focused on pleasing someone else, rather than on determining personal values and goals. The more the individual sees self-esteem as largely dependent on his or her value in the market, the less control he or she has over that self-esteem. Individual notions of personal adequacy can

    [40]Robert S. Diamond, "A Self-portrait of the Chief Executive: The Fortune 500-Yankelovich Survey," *Fortune* (February 1970), pp. 180-81, 320-23.
    [41]Erich Fromm, "Personality and the Market Place," in *Man, Work, and Society: A Reader in the Sociology of Occupations*, ed. Sigmund Nosow and William Form (New York: Basic Books, 1962), pp. 446-52.

be a victim of unpredictable and insensitive market forces. One is not valued for the person one is, but rather for what one finds one can fetch in the marketplace. When such an individual receives an increase in salary, it is less the money itself that delights him than the fact that someone has recognized that he is worth more and is willing to pay for it. Without that salary increase, the person might sink into depths of lowered self-esteem and even self-pity.

Furthermore, since the market can be the principle determiner of self-worth and since value in the market is subject to many changing, unpredictable forces and fads, the individual must remain flexible. Her present value may collapse, simply because there are too many with the same talents on the market. She must then be able to shift to a new career. This phenomenon encourages an individual to maintain flexibility and maximum exposure, No matter how much she may like her present work or locale, it is to her advantage not to sink deep roots. If she becomes known as a one-talent person, her value, and hence her self-esteem, will be severely limited. This situation does not encourage developing expertise, and settling into and becoming involved in the community.

This notion of self-worth makes the individual totally dependent on others for his or her own self-esteem. Self-worth stems not from accomplishments, interests, loves or being loved, but rather from the impersonal forces of the employment market—in this case, from company superiors. This is the "other-directed" person. The heavy influence of a changing external environment on personal values contributes to making Americans practical and pragmatic. They will rarely dispute principles for their own sake; they find martyrdom to be the ultimate folly. Thomas More's beheading under Henry VIII makes superb drama in "Man for All Seasons"; Americans find the episode quaint and moving, but difficult to understand and perhaps even smacking of fanaticism or some other aberration. Indeed, the business person finds disputes over principles time-consuming and unproductive, and will rarely allow him or herself to be caught up in ideological battles.

The shallow soil in which the principles and values of most Americans are rooted was graphically demonstrated in the ability of the Chinese to "brainwash" American prisoners of war after the Korean conflict.[42] Most of us were astonished at the lack of deep convictions and the ease with which expert Chinese propagandists could undermine them. Explicit, articulated principles and values are not often a part of an American's baggage. This enables us to be flexible and pragmatic, but it also allows us to float and to become more victims of events and the environment than masters.

[42]See Edgar H. Schein, "Reaction Patterns to Severe, Chronic Stress in American Prisoners of War of the Chinese," *Journal of Social Issues*, 13 (1957), 21-30.

Mid-Life Identity Crisis

It is this same lack of internalized personal values and goals that enables a person to undertake a career or a life without much personal clarification of goals, examination of alternatives, and reflection. This then often leads to the much-publicized "mid-life identity crisis." Not many months go by without still another article on men who have opted out of the corporation.

In late 1973, John Z. DeLorean quit his job as vice president and group executive in charge of all General Motors car and truck divisions in North America. DeLorean felt that the GM committee system was too unwieldly; it dispersed authority and responsibility, and as a result he felt that no one could move aggressively.

His case is by no means unique. *The Wall Street Journal* ran a series of articles on scores of men who left well-paid corporate jobs to do something quite different at a fraction of their former pay.[43] These men found their work in the corporation to be confining and deadening, and most turned to a simpler and less structured life. Typical of them is Ross Drever, 52, who quit as director of Amsted Industries' research division at a $50,000 salary. He now spends his time working a cranberry bog in Three Lakes, Wisconsin. He says, "I have a lot of suits and shoes I'll never use again."

Most of these men felt they were giving too many hours to an activity that gave them little satisfaction. They yearned for a simpler life. They made the radical, lonely change; they left comfortable jobs, homes, and friends to carve out a new life. The increasing number of these men and women that we hear about tells us some people are beginning to examine their own life values and goals, and are willing to act on the values they find. Nevertheless, these sharp mid-life shifts may also tell us that few of us have sufficiently probed our own goals in order to chart our own course. Too often we leave it to opportunity, to "significant others," or to accepted norms to determine our life goals for us.

Normalcy and Anxiety

As in any culture, self-esteem is highly dependent on the feedback a person receives from others. That feedback can be either positive or negative. In the American culture, those who gain the esteem of their peers are considered to be successful. Such people are typically competent, goal-oriented, conscientious, ambitious, and hard-working.[44] These are qualities we have previously identified with the Protestant ethic. The culture, through its

[43]See the front-page articles in *The Wall Street Journal,* "The Great Escape," February 19, February 22, May 12, 1971.

[44]See H. J. Wahler, "Winning and Losing in Life: A Survey of Opinions about Causes," *Mental Hygiene,* 55, 1 (January 1971), 94.

family life, schools, churches, government, and business, is able to communicate its values to the individual. A culture does this in order to give itself direction and integrity. Otherwise it cannot develop; legal systems and economic growth become difficult or impossible. Without this socialization process, it is not even possible to know what one may expect of another in everyday dealings.

Although these cultural expectations have given American society strong direction and the ability to grow economically, they have done so at a price. American culture professes to value pluralism, and indeed it is more possible to take up beliefs and life styles counter to the majority here than in most other countries of the world. Nevertheless, persons who are not judged successful according to the norms of the Protestant ethic are often criticized by others; this causes stress, and they thus become victims of their own anxieties. And even those who are judged successful according to the prevailing norms of being competent, ambitious, and hard-working may by that very fact suffer anxieties. Earlier we have seen how successful corporate managers are those who are mobile: they are able to leave their present homes and jobs in order to move on to better positions. Psychologists tell us that anxiety is caused by moving from the known to the unknown. Having mastered one environment, it is unsettling to be asked to move to a new one. It is true that the challenge of life and that which encourages us to grow as persons often involves moving into the unknown. Nevertheless, when life consists largely of being uprooted every few years, leaving behind not just the confidence built in mastering a job but relatives, friends, and knowledge of the community, it can undermine willingness to commit oneself to a new job or neighborhood. Such persons may be forced in upon themselves, depending more on their aggressiveness and individuality than on the help and cooperation of co-workers, friends, and neighbors. When they choose to grow in this fashion, they force their families to undergo the same cyclic trauma of arriving and departing, along with the pain and anxiety it involves.

The unknown, and even more so the uncontrollable, produce anxieties. Ulcers and stress usually result when there are two conflicting demands on the individual. Neuroses have been experimentally induced in animals exposed to ambiguous stimuli. After the same or very similar stimuli, the animals were sometimes rewarded and sometimes not, or sometimes rewarded and sometimes punished. Gastric ulcers were produced in laboratory rats who spent one month in a special cage. During 47 hours of every 48-hour period, they had to endure an electric shock every time they went to the food box or the water cup. They needed the food, but also feared the shock. Furthermore, they were never sure they would get a shock along with their food. They developed ulcers. The conflict of wanting the food yet risking considerable pain, plus a lack of control over the situation, produced the ulcers. Control rats, which were simply deprived of food and water for 47 of the 48 hours, did not develop ulcers.[45]

Cats, which were first fed and then shocked following the same buzzer, exhibited a wide variety of aberrant physical activities, such as restless roving, clawing at wire cages, butting the roof with their heads, and ceaseless vocalizing—all indicating a high degree of anxiety. These cats were then given the opportunity to drink milk that had been laced with alcohol. Half the animals quickly learned that the alcohol relieved the symptoms of their anxiety, and they invariably chose the 5-percent alcohol mixture served in a distinctive cocktail glass. The cats preferred the alcohol as long as their tensions persisted and they remained neurotic. When the animals experienced uncontrollable psychic pain, they sought relief in periodic withdrawal, and their neurotic symptoms disappeared under the influence of the alcohol.

Decision Making Versus Sensitivity

Another aspect of the tension that is brought to bear on business people is the conflict between the characteristics that are rewarded on the job and those that make for a good spouse and parent. Much has been said about this, and here we will discuss but one example. The typical male manager is aggressive, decisive, and fact-oriented. He makes his decisions not on the basis of intuition or feelings, but rather on the basis of facts and clear, defensible reasoning. The mobile manager is one who does not become too involved with people and is not unduly influenced by human feelings. This talent of looking only to the articulated and measurable facts of the case does not work nearly so well when he is at home with his wife and children. When his wife asks him to take her out to a movie, it is not necessarily because she is enraptured with the particular film; it may simply be that she wants to be alone with him for a few hours away from house and children.

It is sometimes equally difficult for the fact-oriented father to determine what his son is saying beneath the flurry of words and argument. He has trained himself to look for the facts, and so he takes the words at face value. Furthermore, he can often be impatient with his son or daughter for not saying what they really mean. He finds it impossible to sift through the sentences to determine what his wife, son, or daughter is really saying—often enough nonverbally. Moreover, in his impatience he is often unable to be open enough to encourage them to communicate what they are really thinking and feeling. He is sometimes aware of this inability and conflict, and this causes additional tensions and anxieties.

[45]Berelson and Steiner, *op. cit.,* pp. 276-79.

EXAMINING PERSONAL VALUES

One solution to the problem of ambiguous, conflicting personal goals and values is to make an explicit attempt to clarify them. A scale that has been used for measuring personal values for more than a generation is the Allport-Vernon-Lindzey value scale. It attempts to discriminate personal values according to six potentially dominant personality characteristics: theoretical, economic, esthetic, social, political, and religious.[46]

The authors administered the value test to business students in college, who came out significantly higher on economic and political values and significantly lower on esthetic, religious, and social values, as compared with college students as a whole. The same scale was administered to those who had returned for the Advanced Management Program at the Harvard Business School. The predominant values these individuals espoused were economic, theoretical, and political (see Table 3-1). For the population as a whole, these same values tended to average out at around 40.

Economic man is primarily oriented toward what is useful and practical. Theoretical man is primarily interested in discovery of truth. Political man is characterized by an orientation to power—influence over people. Religious man is one "whose mental structure is permanently directed to the creation of the highest and absolutely satisfying value experience." Esthetic man is primarily interested in the artistic aspects of life—form and harmony. The highest value for social man is love of people.

TABLE 3-1
Personal Values in Business

	Score	
Value	*Business Students*	*Business Persons*
Economic	46	45
Theoretical	43	44
Political	46	44
Religious	34	39
Aesthetic	39	35
Social	33	33

Sources: For students, Gordon Allport, Philip Vernon, and Gardner Lindzey, *Study of Values* (Boston: Houghton Mifflin, 1931), p. 14; for business persons, William D. Guth and Renato Tagiuri, "Personal Values and Corporate Strategy," *Harvard Business Review,* 43 (September-October, 1965), 126.

[46]Gordon Allport, Philip Vernon, and Gardner Lindzey, *Study of Values* (Boston: Houghton Mifflin, 1931).

When we compare the relative strengths of the six values for the business people and the business students, the dominance of economic, theoretical, and political orientations is characteristic of both groups, and there is a significant gap between them and the lower three value orientations. Social values are the lowest by a wide margin for both business persons and business students. Religious values are stronger for the older business person, whereas esthetic values are stronger for students.

The scale of values was originally designed as a research tool to learn more about personalities and their values. It is now also widely used by interviewers and guidance counselors to determine the attitudes and potential vocational interests of students and employees. This use of the scale as an indicator of a person's compatibility with a future career underscores two of its principal limitations. The first of these is that the test measures only *relative* values. One person could possess exactly the same value *profile* as another, yet possess each value much more strongly. The test is forced choice and designed to measure only the relative value profile—for example, how strong social values are compared with the same person's political values. It gives no indication of how strong one person's social values are compared to another person's.

A second problem in using the test as a vocation indicator is that, based on profiles of successful business people, counselors often advise students who have relatively high social values to stay out of business. It is true that, according to the scales of those business people who have previously taken the test, social values are lowest. But to give career advice merely on the basis of how past persons in that career have scored is at best heuristic, and at worst prevents new values and creativity from entering a career or profession. It discourages young people with higher social values from entering business, and hence perpetuates and rigidifies an old pattern. The fact that in the past business people scored very low on social values may have been an unfortunate accident of a particular period of history. There are many who think it was only a temporary aberration. There is some recent evidence that persons choosing business and business education have higher social values than their counterparts of a decade or so ago.

Who school counselors advise to go into business and who they advise to stay away can have an immense influence on the values and goals of business itself. High school counselors have generally had little if any contact with business life beyond casual work to help pay for their college educations. Most have no direct experience of working in a corporation, and surely not of entrepreneurial activities. As a result, their attitudes toward business are often stereotyped and negative. Nevertheless, these counselors have considerable influence on young people's career choices.

Personal Experience Gives Values and Direction

In previous generations, children growing up in a family would witness their father and mothers doing work in or near the home. They would see not only the skill, effort, and challenge required in work, but also the joy of accomplishment. Since commercial work is generally done away from home today, the young person growing up in a family rarely has direct contact with it, and so hears only secondhand, and generally negative, comments on work and business. All Americans, and perhaps especially young people, are influenced by the media in their attitudes. Here again, most TV and film writers have no direct experience with business. The result is often caricature. There is rarely, if ever, a TV program or film that presents work and business in even an objective light, let alone a favorable one. Consider business as pictured in literature, on TV, and in films. The business person is generally portrayed as shallow, grasping, narrow, and petty, concerned only with status and position. Such a stereotype tends to perpetuate itself.

Current Scales for Measuring Personal Values

A newer scale for measuring personal values has been developed which asks an individual to rank 18 terminal and 18 instrumental values (see Tables 3-2 and 3-3) in order of importance for her or him.[47] Among the terminal values, Americans tend to rank at the top a world at peace, family security, and freedom. At the top of the instrumental values are honest, ambitious and responsible. The scale was administered to university business school teachers, and they tended to rank "a sense of accomplishment" significantly higher than do Americans in general. On the instrumental scale, the business educators ranked "capable" higher than did American men and women in the general population.

A third psychological investigation of the relationship between personality and career values tends to support these findings. Professional students in the fields of business, engineering, law, medicine, and theology show distinctive personality patterns when asked in a forced-choice test to rank their own personal values.[48] MBA (Masters of Business Administration) students are significantly differentiated from other professional students in describing themselves as being more able to inspire confidence and enthusiasm and as willing to accept leadership responsibility. They are self-confident and feel adequate to cope with life's problems; at work they are businesslike in dealings with others and avoid personal emotional involvement, being keenly ambitious and strongly competitive.

On the other hand, MBA students rank significantly lower than other professional students in such values as a concern about others and willingness to set aside personal gain and advantage in order to help others; strong involvement in working toward improvement of social conditions such as

[47]Milton Rokeach, *The Nature of Values* (New York: Free Press, 1973), esp. pp. 57-59, 144-46. Copyrighted and quoted with permission of the Free Press. Copies of the Rokeach value survey can be purchased from Halgren Tests, 873 Persimmon Ave., Sunnyvale, Calif. 94087.

[48]K. N. Kunert, *The Psychological Concomitants and Determinants of Vocational Choice.* Unpublished doctoral dissertation, University of California, Berkeley, 1965.

poverty, prejudice, social injustice; considering esthetic and cultural values as crucial to development of character and personal maturity. The graduate business student also shows that she or he is at home in new and challenging environments. Compared to other professionals, MBA students see themselves as dynamic, competitive, mobile, pragmatic. They have strong loyalties to family and also to the job. They see their own self-worth as being measured by what they accomplish in the competitive marketplace, not by what they can contribute to the welfare and happiness of those with fewer advantages. This picture of the values of business-oriented students corroborates the value profile presented previously. For a variety of reasons, the values and goals of business students differ significantly from the values of other professional students—and, indeed, from those of the population as a whole.

Examining One's Own Values

Planning for a career and for life itself can be much more solidly based if an individual is able to clarify and articulate her or his own goals and values. Rokeach's two value scales can aid in this examination. Each person is asked to arrange the values "in order of their importance to YOU, as guiding principles in YOUR life." The values are then ranked from 1 to 18, the most highly valued to the least important. The two scales are given in Tables 3-2 and 3-3.[49]

A more pointed aid for individuals attempting to formulate their own personal goals has been developed in an experiential organizational psychology context.[50] The authors suggest that each individual write out his or her major goals according to six categories: Career satisfaction, status and respect, personal relationships, leisure satisfactions, learning and education, and spiritual growth. Then, with regard to each individual goal, the individual determines: (1) the relative importance of the goal, compared to other goals; (2) how easy it would be to achieve the goal, compared to other goals; and (3) whether pursuing this goal involves a conflict with other goals. When finished, the individual has a much clearer picture of what her or his own major goals are, how important they are, their ease of attainment, and whether conflicts will likely arise in their pursuit.

Readers might rank their goals on the two 18-item scales and also state their major goals according to the six categories, and then compare the two

[49]Rokeach, *op. cit.*

[50]David A. Kolb, Irwin M. Rubin, and James M. McIntyre, *Organizational Psychology: An Experiential Approach* (Englewood Cliffs, N.J.: Prentice-Hall, 1971), pp. 273-93. See also Sidney B. Simon et al., *Values Clarification* (New York: Hart, 1972).

TABLE 3-2

Final Values

_____	A COMFORTABLE LIFE (a prosperous life)
_____	AN EXCITING LIFE (a stimulating, active life)
_____	A SENSE OF ACCOMPLISHMENT (lasting contribution)
_____	A WORLD AT PEACE (free of war and conflict)
_____	A WORLD OF BEAUTY (beauty of nature and the arts)
_____	EQUALITY (brotherhood, equal opportunity for all)
_____	FAMILY SECURITY (taking care of loved ones)
_____	**FREEDOM (independence, free choice)**
_____	HAPPINESS (contentedness)
_____	INNER HARMONY (freedom from inner conflict)
_____	**MATURE LOVE (sexual and spiritual intimacy)**
_____	NATIONAL SECURITY (protection from attack)
_____	PLEASURE (an enjoyable, leisurely life)
_____	SALVATION (saved, eternal life)
_____	SELF-RESPECT (self-esteem)
_____	SOCIAL RECOGNITION (respect, admiration)
_____	TRUE FRIENDSHIP (close companionship)
_____	WISDOM (a mature understanding of life)

Source: Milton Rokeach, *The Nature of Values* (New York: Free Press, 1973), p. 145.

TABLE 3-3

Instrumental Values

_____	AMBITIOUS (hard-working, aspiring)
_____	BROADMINDED (open-minded)
_____	CAPABLE (competent, effective)
_____	CHEERFUL (lighthearted, joyful)
_____	CLEAN (neat, tidy)
_____	COURAGEOUS (standing up for your beliefs)
_____	FORGIVING (willing to pardon others)
_____	HELPFUL (working for the welfare of others)
_____	HONEST (sincere, truthful)
_____	IMAGINATIVE (daring, creative)
_____	INDEPENDENT (self-reliant, self-sufficient)
_____	**INTELLECTUAL (intelligent, reflective)**
_____	LOGICAL (consistent, rational)
_____	LOVING (affectionate, tender)
_____	OBEDIENT (dutiful, respectful)
_____	POLITE (courteous, well-mannered)
_____	RESPONSIBLE (dependable, reliable)
_____	SELF-CONTROLLED (restrained, self-disciplined)

Source: Milton Rokeach, *The Nature of Values* (New York: Free Press, 1973), p. 146.

lists. Do the values support the major goals, or do they conflict? Are some personal values in conflict with career goals? How does my present work compare with my values and goals? Does this explain any satisfaction or dissatisfaction with my present job? What implications does this examination have for my future career and life plans? These questions have been raised and answered by graduate business students in brief papers in the author's classes. A vast majority indicated that the exercise was a great aid to them in clarifying their own values and goals.

Helping Experiments

It is not merely business people and business students who hold social values in relatively low esteem; their attitudes reflect the values of much of American culture. As laboratory experiments have shown, individuals in American culture are heavily influenced by the values and activities of others. Norms of right and wrong are inculcated by family, neighborhood, and environment in every culture, but the attitudes of bystanders in the immediate vicinity also have an unduly large influence on Americans. Some of the laboratory experiments were prompted by the murder of a young woman in New York City. She was stabbed to death in full view of many apartment dwellers. Later investigation showed that at least thirty-eight people saw or heard the attack, but not one tried to help; no one even phoned the police. This story shocked the country, and some university researchers decided to try to determine what elements influence helping behavior.

In one experiment, several individuals were placed in adjoining rooms connected by an intercom phone.[51] The subjects were led to believe that there were one, two, or five other persons present in successive experiments. In reality, the subject was the only person involved. During a discussion on a topic of current interest over the intercom, one "participant" suffered what seemed to be an epileptic seizure; that person choked, stuttered, and called out for help. The greater the number of persons the subject thought were present, the less likely he would be to help, and he would be slower to help. Apparently, the subject would think he could leave it to others. If he thought he was the only person present, the more likely he was to feel the responsibility and respond to the need.

Similar results were obtained when individuals were placed in a room and asked to fill out a questionnaire. Subjects were alone in the room, with two other subjects, or with two confederates who were instructed to remain im-

[51]Robert A. Baron and Robert A. Liebart, *Human Social Behavior* (Homewood, Ill.: Dorsey, 1971), esp. p. 492.

passive. After a few minutes, smoke began to pour into the room through a small wall vent. Results of this experiment again showed that the greater the number of individuals present, the lower the frequency of prosocial behavior. When the subject was with two passive confederates, he reported the apparent fire only 10 percent of the time.

These experimental studies show that individuals will act in a more socially responsible way when they feel the responsibility directly. When another unknown person is present, they are not as apt to stick their necks out. Nevertheless, these and other studies show that people *will* help others, even if they don't expect anything in return. Furthermore, subjects will tend to respond more quickly and in a more responsible fashion if they have been successful in similar earlier efforts, and also if they have been the recipients of help themselves in the past.

Authority

Evidence of a person's willingness actually to do harm to another individual when instructed by authority to do so was provided by another series of controversial laboratory experiments.[52] Subjects were told that they were to engage in experiments in memory and learning. They drew lots, and the subjects were placed at a shock generator with thirty intervals marked from 15 volts (slight shock) to 450 volts (danger—severe shock). The other person (a confederate), who was strapped in a chair with electrodes on his wrists, could be seen in an adjoining room through a glass partition. The subject was then instructed to shock the learner, increasing the intensity for every wrong answer the learner gave. As the shock level rose, the learner cried out in increasing pain, yet almost two-thirds of the subjects administered the highest level of shock.

The subjects would become nervous, agonize, and rationalize, but nevertheless administer the highest level of shock under the auspices of authority. The experiment has been criticized as being unethical. Indeed, it did play with people's consciences. However, it also gives us frightening evidence of what one human being is willing to inflict on another when it seems to be legitimized by some authority. Obedience in this experiment drops if the subject is in the same room as the learner, or if he must actually touch the learner to administer the shock. The more impersonal the situation, the more willing is the subject to do harm to another.

The modern organization is designed to produce results in an impersonal fashion. Layoffs, pollution, and exploitative advertising are more readily condoned when, even though they are the direct result of executives'

[52]Stanley Milgram, *Obedience to Authority* (New York: Harper & Row, 1974).

decisions and policy, they are able to convince themselves that they did not directly bring about the undesirable results. To executives, the system demands that they act in this fashion if they expect the firm to survive and grow.

THE BUSINESS PERSON'S ETHICS

The most widely quoted empirical study of the ethics of the business person was done in the early 1960s at the Harvard Business School by Raymond Baumhart.[53] Baumhart mailed a questionnaire to a sample of 5,000 subscribers to the *Harvard Business Review*. About one-third of that group returned usable responses. The same questionnaire was later answered by a cross-section of college students to compare their attitudes to those of the business people.

The popular evaluation of business ethics is negative, and students have an even lower respect for the ethics of the business person. This negative image is illustrated by a case. For a salesperson who earns $10,000 a year (1960s salary!) to pad his expense account by $500 a year is considered unacceptable regardless of circumstances by 85 percent of business people themselves. In contrast, only 17 percent of the students thought that business people would consider this act wrong. Indicating another cleavage is the fact that the 85 percent who themselves thought it was wrong nevertheless felt that only 62 percent of their peers would consider padding an expense account wrong. What emerges throughout the study is the fact that business people attribute significantly higher ethical standards to themselves than they do to their business peers. In addition, students have a widely divergent and much lower opinion of how ethical the average business person is in his or her daily decisions. Baumhart also shows that business people become more ethical as they grow older, and he hypothesizes that this may be due to their greater financial security.

Conscience is seen by executives as having a decisive influence on their ethical actions. But their level of moral thinking, and even more their conception of the influence of conscience, is often rather undeveloped. The ethical problems of greatest concern to these executives are personal problems; what we now call social responsibility was at least in the 1960s not a very important consideration. The morality that was and often still is generally held is often a personal morality, such as that opposed to stealing, sexual abuses, and lying. This leaves larger corporate decisions constrained largely by laws, competition, and what the traffic will bear, with less con-

---

[53]Raymond Baumhart, S. J., *Ethics in Business* (New York: Holt, Rinehart and Winston, 1968). See also Baumhart's "How Ethical Are Businessmen?" *Harvard Business Review,* 39 (July-August 1961), 6-8, 10-19, 156-76.

sideration for ethics. Business people themselves indicate that the most significant influence on unethical actions is competition. Unethical practices result from both too much and too little competition. If there is too much competition, the firm is drawn into unethical practices just to survive. If there is too little competition, the firm can grow fat, lazy, undisciplined, and free with its funds and in its actions. The most powerful positive influence toward ethical behavior is an ethical boss. An ethical chief executive can have a profound positive influence on the entire firm; an unethical executive can have a corroding influence. Most especially, Baumhart found that an ethical immediate superior had a vital influence on subordinates. The superior sets a tone and provides the constraints and criteria within which business decisions are made.

In spite of their unique role as prophets and custodians of morality, the churches are viewed by these business executives as having little influence on business ethics.[54] Executives affiliated with a particular church responded to the cases in much the same fashion as those who were unaffiliated. Although the American business ideology ritualistically supports the larger, established religions, it does not expect, and in fact most often resents, attempts at ethical moralizing from church people. Executives defend their lack of patience with church interference in business matters when they point out that clergy have no experience with and little sympathy for business. Their lack of concrete knowledge of what goes on in business makes them poor critics. J. Irwin Miller, chairman of Cummins Engine Company, was a highly ethical and sympathetic observer, but said that if the churches are to discharge their responsibility to aid in forming the business conscience, "they must be a great deal more competent, better informed, and far-sighted than they have shown themselves to be up to now."[55]

The Current Moral Crisis

A host of recent events signal a weak moral fabric in American business society. Large, illegal corporate gifts to the Committee to Re-elect President Nixon, ITT's $400,000 convention pledge plus its manipulation of American foreign policy to suit its private purposes, and a host of other misadventures have left most Americans highly suspicious of business ethics. Indeed, *Business Week* approvingly quotes historian Arnold Toynbee that Watergate is merely business ethics applied to politics. Says Toynbee, "One cause of the decline of political morality in America is that it has now sunk to the lowest level of American business morality."[56]

[54]Baumhart, *Ethics in Business,* pp. 186-205.
[55]*Ibid.,* p. 199.
[56]*Business Week,* September 15, 1973, pp. 178-182.

Each of these misdemeanors, and many others now familiar to us all, were perpetrated to further the interests of a group or firm. Firms that made illegal campaign contributions did so because the federal government has considerable power over their business actions, and it pays to have powerful friends on your side. Loyalty to the organization and its private interests took precedence over morality, law, and the larger public interest. On another level, the failure of the large oil and auto firms, plus the government, to come to grips with the long-predicted energy crisis is another example of both private industry and especially government itself pursuing short-term benefits and not looking to the long-term good of society as a whole. Narrow emphasis on sales and encouraging even more consumption has caused us to despoil many of our cities, forests, and seas with pollution. Clearly the attitudes that have led us into these difficulties need rethinking and amending, as we will see in Chapter 5.

Many executives feel that the pressures to continue in this narrow way, to produce only for the short term, have increased in recent years. A recent study by the American Management Association of 3,000 executives showed that most felt they were under pressure to compromise their personal standards to meet company goals.[57] Pressure for results, as narrowly measured in money terms, has increased. As firms become larger, more decentralized, and under absentee ownership, performance is measured in numbers and not by broader or more humane criteria.

As we live closer together and become more dependent on one another, planning becomes necessary. Most Americans agree that if problems can be solved by individual initiative this is a more efficient solution, and one less open to politics, favoritism, and bribery. On the other hand, the free market and private initiatives have not been particularly effective in dealing with the urban poor, pollution, and the developing nations of the world. Those with money obtain more than their share of goods. As shortages of oil became a reality, many firms began to scramble for fewer supplies. Many began to buy all available oil to hoard it for the time of critical need. This sort of "everyone for himself" mentality was encouraged by Richard Nixon's declaration in 1974 that he wanted to make the United States self-sufficient in energy. The United States, with its immense natural resources, including natural gas, oil, and especially coal, could afford to be a leader among nations in sharing needed materials. Most of the other countries of the world are not so fortunate, and they thus have no recourse but to look to their own individual national interests when other nations threaten and indeed do cut off needed supplies. The Arab oil boycott was no worse than the United States putting an embargo on the export of soybeans; American soybeans had become a staple of the Japanese diet, while we fed them to

[57] *Ibid.*, p. 178.

animals. Any sort of international trust and cooperation risks being eroded in the wake of such rationalized self-interest.

SUMMARY AND CONCLUSIONS

Empirical studies of business people have found them to be ambitious, achievement-oriented, disciplined, and adaptable. These values were inculcated largely by mothers, who were the more influential parent. Their personal goals are often to prove themselves, which commonly shows itself by achievement within the firm. Executives' goals are determined for them: success within the firm and, when they are in policy-making positions, success for the firm. Just as the rules of the game were set by someone else early in life, so too the economic rules of the game come from outside and are accepted. Perhaps largely because of this uncritical early acceptance of the system's criteria of success, we find many mid-career identity crises. Individual executives, for a variety of reasons, find themselves no longer able to make someone else's or the system's, goals their own. They begin to probe their own personal values and goals. Perhaps this will lead them back again to work within the private sector, and perhaps it will not. In either case, their goals are more their own, and they have a new perspective on their work.

The executive is energetic, capable, and urbane. Generally he or she tries to be carefully correct in working within the law, since the law is part of the rules of the game. On the other hand, he or she is impatient with discussions of business ethics and finds them difficult and fruitless. "Nice guys finish last"; idealism and preaching have no place in business. He or she also has little patience with social activists who criticize products or policies; such people are contemptuously labeled "do gooders."

Potential conflicts between the good of the firm and the person or the larger society are resolved by means of the free market ideology. That ideology says that the more successful the firm is (and this is traditionally measured in dollar terms), the better off individuals and the larger society will be. Even if its product is trivial or harmful, the public wants it and will pay for it. Pollution and decaying cities is a small price to pay for increasing personal income and gross national product. And these are the basic, unarguable criteria of a healthy, successful society.

In sum, until quite recently, ethics in business was narrowly construed to mean avoiding stealing, padding expense accounts, and procuring call girls for customers. Business executives have only recently accepted as part of their personal code the responsible use of power and their role in the effects the firm and its policies have on the larger society. In one sense, the American business ideology has just been accepted, much as one would accept rites and rituals in a traditional society. Until recently, to challenge or question it was to be labeled radical and un-American.

This chapter has brought us up to date on American business values and ideology. It remains to examine Marxism, the most incisive, persistent, and damaging critique of free enterprise both in its origins and in its current forms.

CHAPTER FOUR

Marx's Challenge
to Free Enterprise

The communist ideological and social system alone is full of youth and vitality, sweeping the world with the momentum of an avalanche and the force of a thunderbolt. . . . (communism) is the most complete, progressive, revolutionary and rational system in human history.

Mao Tse-tung*

No critique of free enterprise has proved as perceptive, trenchant, or appealing historically as that of Karl Marx. Marxism raises serious questions about the social and moral consequences of the economic system we have adopted. It also presents an alternative economic system and a supporting ideology. For Marxism has given us not only critics of the free enterprise system, but also a block of Communist nations whose people now outnumber those of the capitalist nations of the world. This chapter, then, takes a two-pronged look at Marxism: First, we examine the Marxist critique of capitalism, and then the Marxist realizations of communism, especially in the USSR and the People's Republic of China.

Free enterprise, or capitalism as it is called by its critics, is the socioeconomic system of most of the developed, industrialized countries. North America, Western Europe, and Japan form the powerful core of these wealthy "first world" countries. Russia, China, Cuba, and Eastern Europe operate with a Marxist socioeconomic system; they are called the "second world." The nations of Asia, Africa, and South America, which are very poor and do not clearly belong to either ideological camp, are thus called "third world" countries.

Although Marxism has been a remarkably successful system for organizing an economy, it is by no means the first social system to be built on cooperative ideals. Monastic living, discussed in Chapter 2, is an enduring model of living and working together and sharing goods in common. But such a community, which depends on closely shared values and a lifelong commitment at least on the part of some, was never intended for all people.

The principal author of this chapter is Arthur F. McGovern, S. J., professor of Marxist philosophy, University of Detroit.

*Mao Tse-tung, *Quotations from Chairman Mao Tse-Tung.* (New York: Bantam Books, 1967). Quoted with permission.

Medieval European communities were more cooperative than their contemporary counterparts. Guilds, stable populations, and extended families all living within walking distance gave these early communities cohesion. On the other hand, they also had a rigid hierarchical social system. If the father was a butcher, so was the son.

Criticisms of capitalism and advocacy of socialism did not originate with Marx. As the Industrial Revolution took hold of Europe in the nineteenth century, a plethora of critics and socialist theories emerged. Saint-Simon, Fourier, Cabet, Moses Hess, Blanqui, Robert Owen, and countless others attacked the capitalist system and proposed various ways of achieving socialism: state ownership, national workshops, voluntary communes, revolutionary overthrow by elitist conspiracy groups, revolutionary overthrow by the masses. The communes advocated by Cabet, who first coined the term "communism" in the 1830s, and by Fourier inspired some of the ventures in communal ownership attempted in the United States. One such was Brook Farm, which was located in West Roxbury, within the city limits of present-day Boston.

ALTERNATIVES TO CAPITALISM: THE EARLY AMERICAN EXPERIENCE

The New World was attractive not only to the individualist and those who were enraptured with the frontier mentality, but also to those with cooperative ideals. In the nineteenth century, as Europe was swept with the Industrial Revolution, many came to the New World to begin living and working again in a more cooperative fashion. Hundreds of cooperative, "communist" communities were formed in the United States during the nineteenth and early twentieth centuries.[1] These were not merely a few people or a single house like most of our contemporary communes; they were rather communities that counted their members in the hundreds and sometimes thousands. These communities shared work and income equally. They were opposed to the competition encouraged by capitalism, and felt that it was only in cooperation that a human society could develop. The clearly alternate life style they constructed was available to Americans through the early part of this century.

The Shakers were a religious group that at one time had nineteen separate communities scattered throughout New England the the Midwest; their land holdings reached nearly 100,000 acres.[2] The suburb of Cleveland called

[1]Rosabeth Moss Kanter, *Commitment and Community* (Cambridge, Mass.: Harvard University Press, 1972); see also Norman J. Whitney, *Experiments in Community* (Wallingford, Pa.: Pendle Hill, 1966), and the earlier account by William A. Hinds, *American Communities* (Chicago: Charles Kerr, 1902).

[2]Hinds, *op. cit.,* p. 27. See also Marguerite F. Melcher, *The Shaker Adventure* (Princeton, N.J.: Princeton University Press, 1941), p. 302.

Shaker Heights takes its name from the Shaker community there. Its beautiful Shaker Lakes were built as millponds by the Shakers. The men lived communally, as did the women; there was little contact between men and women at work or socially. There was no marriage; new members had to be converted. In the early days there were converts, and the number of Shakers eventually reached 6,000. They called themselves the Millennial Church; it was outsiders who observed the long, loud, and active shaking movements in their prayer services and dubbed them Shakers.

Most of the members of these communities farmed, like everyone else, but some later moved into manufacturing. Notable among the latter is Oneida Community in New York State, which was founded by the minister John Humphrey Noyes in 1848. Although it is no longer a commune, it has paradoxically developed into a multimillion-dollar international business. It is now the nation's largest maker of stainless steel tableware.[3] Probably the best known of the communal experiments was that of Robert Owen at New Harmony, Indiana. Owen was a wealthy Scots factory owner who was the first in England to limit the work day to ten hours. He both advocated and initiated other work and social reforms among his employees. But Owen's dream was a community in which all work, life, and leisure would be shared. Unlike most other early commune organizers, Owen's vision was not religious in origin.

In 1825, Owen purchased an established community built by a religious group called the Rappites and renamed it New Harmony. He advertised for members and accepted almost all comers; more than 900 came, among them some well-known professional people. But because of his other obligations, Owen himself found little time to be at New Harmony in the early days. Farming and other basic skills were scarce among the community members, and lack of common vision and subsequent discord brought the community to an end in 1827. It was a highly publicized, expensive, and noble experiment, but was shorter lived than most cooperative communities.

All these early cooperative communities began with strong leadership, and most were religious in origin. For a commune to survive, it must continue to attract the vigorous and talented, and not merely the weak and those who are looking for a refuge from the problems of the outside world. Self-discipline and external order are necessary to solve the multitude of differences that arise in a community, yet these values are impossible to sustain without a shared vision. Most of the communes failed after the original leader was gone and the early goals and inspiration for the community began to fade. It is thus clear that the counterculture communes we find in the United States today are not a new social phenomenon.[4] Moreover, in the light of history, it can hardly be said that communes and cooperative living are "un-American."

---

[3]Hinds, *op. cit.,* pp. 173-214. On recent successes, see "It Started Out As a Commune in 1848, and Today Oneida Is a Thriving Business," *The Wall Street Journal,* April 4, 1973, p. 8.

THE MARXIST CRITIQUE

Although French and English Utopian Socialists anticipated the idea of public or communal ownership as an alternative to capitalism, it was Karl Marx (1818-1883) who first forged a theory of communism as we know it today. Marx's criticisms of the capitalist system were incisive and based on careful empirical studies. His language is intentionally polemic. Marx and Marxists speak of "exploitation," "imperialism," and "alienation." Such language generally jars Americans and often provokes defensiveness and anger. The criticisms come from a viewpoint that is designedly quite foreign to that of the American business community. Marxist critics make little effort to be balanced or conciliatory. In addition, their criticisms recall the radical rhetoric of the late 1960s, and some may feel that we have already heard too much of it. But despite differences in language, values, and attitudes, the Marxist critique can provoke us to examine our own national priorities and the values that govern our economic, political, and social policies. If we are here attempting an objective examination of the goals and values of free enterprise, we must not neglect its harshest critics.

A man of real genius, Marx combined analytic and critical power with an ability to weld his ideas into an overall theory of history. According to his theory, economic forces are the primary determinant of history. Economic structures give rise to class differences; class conflicts provoke social and political struggles. The capitalist class conflict between workers and owners would inevitably erupt in revolution and would usher in a new socialist system of production. Our concern here, however, is not with the Marxist theory of history, but with its criticisms of our economic system. Not every author cited in this section is a strict Marxist (many would certainly not advocate social revolution), but all are severe critics of our current system. One critic acknowledged as a Marxist economist is Paul Sweezy. Sweezy contends that the essence of Marx's criticism can be found in the very method he used to analyze the economy.[5] Until Marx's time, according to Sweezy, economic theory viewed economic factors (commodities, wages, prices) as things. But Marx insisted that economics does not deal simply with things; it deals with *social relations.* Every commodity produced and sold, every wage paid, involves very definite relationships between human beings. In failing to recognize these social relations, capitalism and capitalist theory consequently ignore the real effects of the system on human society.

[4]For a well-written, carefully researched firsthand account of scores of contemporary communes in the United States, see Robert Houriet, *Getting Back Together* (New York: Coward, McCann & Geoghegan, 1971).

[5]Paul Sweezy, *The Theory of Capitalist Development* (New York: Oxford University Press, 1942), pp. 1-5, chap. II *passim.*

This basic critique can be divided into several accusations made by Marxists and other critics of the capitalist system. For some readers, these accusations may seem exaggerated, one-sided, and wearisome. But they are presented with the conviction that criticism can also lead to constructive change and a healthy reappraisal of views.

Exploitation of the Worker

The free enterprise system operates on the theory that when people work for their own self-interest, they will simultaneously contribute to the welfare of all. Everyone profits from economic growth, and presumably each person receives in proportion to effort and skill. Marxists challenge these assumptions. That economic growth has occurred since the beginning of the modern industrial age is evident. That all have profited from this growth in any degree proportionate to their work is quite dubious. For Marx, who knew the Industrial Revolution in its grimmest stage, it was difficult to see how the working class benefited at all from their labors. The masses of factory workers lived in hovels, worked exhausting ten- and fourteen-hour days, and died prematurely. Marx's classic, *Capital*, chronicles in page after page the price paid in human suffering for industrial growth: workers suffering from pulmonary diseases caused by the dust and heat of factories, small children working fifteen-hour days, a young girl dying of exhaustion after twenty-six consecutive hours of work.[6]

Today these extremes no longer exist, in the United States at least, and no contemporary Marxist would try to defend, as Marx did, the "iron law of wages" that keeps workers' pay at a level of bare subsistence. But Marxists do sharply question the assumption that economic growth tends toward an egalitarian redistribution of wealth and the decline of poverty. In the 1960s Gabriel Kolko demonstrated with extensive statistical data how unfounded is this liberal redistribution thesis. More recently, Weisskopf has argued that great inequalities in the distribution of income and wealth not only accompany economic growth but are actually essential to the capitalist mode of production.[7]

Graduated income taxes are supposedly designed to redistribute wealth. In fact they do not, according to the contention of a group of writers in *The Capitalist System*. A study of incomes in 1962 showed that the poorest

[6]Karl Marx, "The Working Day," *Capital*, Vol. I (New York: International Publishers, 1967), pp. 244-54.

[7]Gabriel Kolko, *Wealth and Power in America* (New York: Praeger, 1962); Thomas E. Weisskopf, "Capitalism and Inequality," in *The Capitalist System*, ed. Richard C. Edwards, Michael Reich, and Thomas E. Weisskopf (Englewood Cliffs, N.J.: Prentice-Hall, 1972), pp. 125-33. The essays in this volume are an excellent collection of almost every aspect of contemporary Marxist economic criticism.

one-fifth of the population receives less than 5 percent of gross income while the wealthiest one-fifth receives 45.5 percent. Income distribution after taxes remains under 5 percent for the poorest group; the richest one-fifth still receives 43.7 percent.[8] For a Marxist, the reason for this disparity is clear. There are only two possible sources of income in the capitalist system: selling one's own labor and ownership. Real wealth accrues only to owners. It does so, according to Marx, because ownership of the means of production enables owners to exploit workers who have only their own labor power as a source of income. Workers are not paid the worth of their work but only what they need to sustain themselves and their families. The difference (surplus value) between what they should receive and the actual wages they do receive is the real explanation of the owner's profit.

A Belgian Marxist explains this notion of surplus value and the exploitation it involves quite graphically.[9] As long as the productivity of labor remains at a level where one person produces only enough for his own subsistence, no social division of owner and worker occurs. But once a surplus is available, the possibility of exploitation develops. Exploitation was blatantly clear in the slave plantations of the Roman Empire. On six days of the week the slave worked on the plantation and received nothing. Most often he had to produce his own food by working a tiny plot of land on Sundays. The great domains of the Middle Ages furnish another illustration. The serf worked three days on land whose yield belonged to him; the other three days he worked on the lord's land without remuneration. The revenue of the capitalist class, according to Mandel, is simply a more subtle form of the same exploitation. It is the uncompensated labor the wage worker gives to the capitalist without receiving any value in exchange. Or in Marx's own words: "Suppose the working day consists of 6 hours of necessary labor and 6 hours of surplus labor. Then the free laborer gives the capitalist every week 6 times 6 or 36 hours of surplus value. It is the same as if he worked 3 days in the week for himself and 3 days gratis for the capitalist."[10]

It is not sufficient to respond that the executive also works and merits his salary, or that costs of raw materials and maintenance must also be computed. Marx argues that profit is precisely the surplus over and above all costs and salaries. The Marxist recognizes the need for capital investment for expansion and new industry; his quarrel is with its private possession and control. If workers are the prime source of production, then they, and not private owners, should be the prime beneficiaries and should also have a

[8]Frank Ackerman et al., "The Extent of Income Inequality in the United States," in *The Capitalist System,* p. 210.

[9]Ernest Mandel, *An Introduction to Marxist Economist Theory* (New York: Pathfinder Press, 1970), pp. 7-9.

[10]*Capital,* Vol. I, p. 236.

significant voice in the whole process of production. The fact that labor unions have reduced the inequities between wages and profits does not alter the basic fact of exploitation for a Marxist. The capitalist still seeks to pay as little as possible for workers' services. The resulting profits or "surplus" are not the rewards of the capitalist's hard work or enterprising spirit, but due simply to ownership of property and control over the work of others.

The contemporary Marxist challenges the contention that wealth in the United States has really been the product of "free" enterprise. Can American business be said to have "earned" its total income in the past without reference to the takeover of Indian territories, to slavery, or to the minimal wages paid immigrant workers? Or in the present, do even the relatively well-paid blue collar workers receive a share proportionate to their work when executives of the same company earn ten times or more their salary? Today one can hardly speak of "private ownership" of companies. Ownership is corporate. But for critics of the capitalist system, this change has not basically altered the situation. Corporate profits go to the stockholders, and America's stockholders are the rich. According to one study, "About 1.6 percent of America's adult population owns 82.4 percent of the publicly held shares in the nation's corporations."[11] In addition, Marxist critic Felix Greene maintains that the same 1.6 percent of the population in the United States owns 32 percent of all the personally owned wealth, and that at the lower end of the scale 50 percent of the adult population owns only 8.3 percent of the nation's wealth and has assets averaging only $1,800.[12]

Salary differences between executives and workers are not the bone of contention. Such differences exist in Communist countries. The main issue is income through investment. "Let your money work for you," the advertisement reads. That is precisely the problem for a Marxist critic. It is not hard work that is rewarded most, but investment. C. Wright Mills illustrated this quite graphically. If you had bought $9,900 worth of General Motors stock in 1913 and then gone into a coma for forty years, you would have awakened in 1953 worth $7 million.[13] Lundberg, in his *The Rich and the Super-Rich*, comments on the 398 persons who reported million-dollar incomes in 1961. Of their total income, less than $30 million came from salaries or partnership profits; nearly $700 million was derived from dividends and capital gains.[14] Even our tax system favors investment over

---

[11] Jack Newfield and Jeff Greenfield, *A Populist Manifesto* (New York: Praeger, 1972), p. 41. See also Ferdinand Lundberg, *The Rich and the Super-Rich* (New York: Bantam Books, 1968), p. 154.

[12] Felix Greene, *The Enemy: What Every American Should Know About Imperialism* (New York: Vintage, 1971), p. 254. See also Lundberg, *op. cit.,* pp. 8-9.

[13] C. Wright Mills, *The Power Elite* (Oxford University Press, 1956), p. 111.

[14] Lundberg, *op. cit.,* pp. 43, 935-36.

worked-for income. A person who works for $10,000 pays full income taxes; if the $10,000 comes through investment or capital gains, only half of it is subject to taxes.[15] So the contemporary Marxist not unreasonably concludes that private ownership, in the form of investment, still remains the real source of disproportionate wealth in capitalist countries.

Alienation of the Worker

In his earliest writings, Marx used the term "alienation" to describe the effects the capitalist method of ownership and production had upon the working class. Capitalism alienates the workers first of all because it takes from them the product and profit they produced. Their life energy is poured into their work, yet they have little to show for it. "The more the worker exerts himself, the more powerful the alien objective world he fashions against himself; the poorer he and his inner world become, the less there is that belongs to him."[16]

But Marx's concern was not just distribution of wealth and fair return for work done. He felt an almost greater concern for the way people work. Under capitalism, he charged, work is forced and dehumanizing. The work is forced because the average worker, though theoretically free to accept a job or not, has little choice but to take a job or go unemployed. Nor does he have much freedom in the way he carries out the work. He does the work assigned, at the pace designated. The work is thus dehumanizing because it does nothing to develop the human potential of the worker (for example, his power to be inventive, to make decisions, to develop different skills). The worker is simply an appendage to a machine. He "does not affirm himself in his work but denies himself, feels miserable and unhappy, develops no free physical and mental energy but mortifies his flesh and ruins his mind."[17] The capitalist works him as he would "a horse that he has hired for a day."[18]

Though not a Marxist, Kenneth Keniston describes the impact of alienated work in terms that echo Marx's analysis a century before. In most traditional societies, he observes, a man's work was his life; work, play, and social life flowed into each other. Work meant simply tasks to be done, without any division of life into work and nonwork. For most Americans, in contrast, work has unpleasant connotations. The reason why lies in the

---

[15]Newfield and Greenfield, *op. cit.,* p. 92.

[16]*Writings of the Young Marx,* tr. and ed. Loyd D. Easton and Kurt H. Guddat (Garden City, N.Y.: Anchor, 1967), p. 289.

[17]*Ibid.,* p. 292.

[18]*Capital,* Vol. I, p. 185.

characteristics of most jobs. With increasing specialization, each worker finds herself or himself assigned to a smaller and smaller portion of a task. The product is finished far down the line: out of sight and out of mind. There is little sense of satisfaction from work. Moreover, too few jobs challenge one's abilities, imagination, or spirit; most call simply for a capacity to follow exact routines in an orderly way. As a result, most Americans speak of "working for a living" and rarely "living for their work." We have long since stopped even expecting work to be meaningful, Keniston concludes.[19] Among workers in America, the problem of dehumanizing labor has received much less attention than the issues of higher wages, shorter hours, and pensions. But the strikes in the early 1970s at the automated General Motors plant at Lordstown, Ohio, and recent auto worker demands suggest that the issue of how the production process is determined and carried out will become an increasingly important one in the years ahead.[20]

In part, different attitudes toward work explains the divergence between American and Communist views on this point. The American view has been pragmatic. Work was not chosen because of its intrinsic value or interest but because it achieved other goals—new products and the money needed to obtain a car, a home, an education for the children. Marx stressed the importance of work itself. Work is a person's main activity; it should then be truly human work. It should be satisfying. It should be freely chosen. It should develop as many of a person's capacities and talents as possible. Marx therefore attacked "division of labor" (fitting a person into a job "slot" someone else has designated) as vigorously as he did private ownership of property.

One certain objection that will be raised against the demands of labor unions, whether in regard to wages or working conditions, is that unions already have too much power. Every grievance, every demand, can occasion a strike. Often these strikes affect not only big industry, but the ordinary citizen. They create grave inconveniences, particularly when public services are involved—for example, when truckers, city garbage collectors, or even grade school teachers strike. But for a Marxist, these strikes only confirm what is wrong with the capitalist system—not just the problem of inequity, but the pervasive "dog-eat-dog" spirit it engenders. Capitalism builds on and

[19]Kenneth Keniston, "The Alienating Consequences of Capitalist Technology," in *The Capitalist System,* pp. 269-73. See also Herbert Gintis' essay on alienation in the article that follows Keniston's.

[20]See H. Sheppard and N. Herrick, *Where Have All the Robots Gone: Worker Dissatisfaction in the 1970's* (New York: Free Press, 1973); also, *Work in America,* Report of the Special Task Force to the Secretary of Health, Education and Welfare, Foreword by Elliot L. Richardson (Cambridge, Mass.: MIT Press, 1973); *The New York Times,* Sec. 3, September 9, 1973, "Lordstown—Searching for a Better Way of Work."

encourages self-interest, competition, and individualism. Strike demands simply reflect this free enterprise spirit of getting what you can. No group in the system really looks to the common good. Or in Marx's language, capitalism leads to the "alienation of man from man."[21]

But isn't competition essential for economic growth? The Marxist does not deny this; what he criticizes is its basis in self-interest alone, and the degree to which individualistic competition is stressed to the detriment of other values. Marx sought to restore a social aspect to work, a sense of mutual collaboration. We ought to be able to work not just out of self-interest, but with satisfaction in the thought that our work contributes to the welfare of others: "In your satisfaction and your use of my product I would have the direct and conscious satisfaction that my work satisfied a human need . . . that it created an object appropriate to the need of another human being."[22]

Perhaps more than any other aspect of Marx's doctrine, Communist nations have attempted to build this social dimension into their economies. Competition exists between brigades, communes, and even individuals. But the competition stresses a common goal of "building a socialist nation." Competition on the broadest scale becomes the striving of the whole nation to outstrip its capitalist rivals.

Imperialism: Exploitation of Other Countries

The wrath of contemporary Marxists is particularly directed against American business overseas, against "imperialism." If the free enterprise system has exploited and alienated workers in the United States, the harm it has inflicted on the poorer nations of the world is far greater. In the name of democracy and free enterprise, American business has gouged out the natural resources of underdeveloped countries, established corporations to control profits from their major industries, and influenced American foreign policy in favor of right-wing dictatorships willing to protect American business. Nor, say the Marxist critics, is it simply a matter of increasing already enormous profits. The capitalist system needs foreign markets for its own survival. Without these markets in which to sell goods and reinvest profits, the free enterprise system would face economic crisis. Franklin D. Roosevelt once acknowledged: "Foreign markets must be regained if America's producers are to rebuild a full and enduring domestic economy for our people. There is no other way if we would avoid painful economic dislocations, social readjustments, and unemployment."[23]

Profit always has exploitation as its source, according to Marxist critics.

[21]*Writings of the Young Marx*, p. 295.
[22]*Ibid.*, p. 281.
[23]Quoted in Carl Oglesby, *Containment and Change* (New York: Collier-Macmillan, 1967), p. 67.

If workers in the United States are less exploited, the profit must derive from exploitation of cheap labor in foreign countries. Between 1950 and 1969, the asset value of American foreign private investments grew from $19 billion to $110 billion.[24] Americans generally believe that these investments contribute to the welfare of underdeveloped countries. But do they? Between 1947 and 1960, the flow of investment funds on private capital account from the United States to Brazil was $1,814 million, while the capital flow of profits, royalties, and other transfers from Brazil to the United States totaled $3,481 million. For the seven largest Latin American countries (Argentina, Brazil, Chile, Peru, Venezuela, Colombia, Mexico) United States Department of Commerce figures for the years 1950 to 1961 indicate $2,962 million of investment flows on private account out of the United States, and remittances of profits and interest of $6,875 million.[25] In Venezuela during the decade of the 1950s, barely 10 percent of oil profits ($600 million of $5 billion) remained within the country.[26] In Cuba, prior to the revolution against Batista, the United States controlled 80 percent of Cuba's utilities, 90 percent of its mines, and almost 100 percent of its oil refineries. "United States firms received 40 percent of the profits on sugar, a crop that represented 89 percent of all Cuban exports."[27]

But even more detrimental than ownership is the power the United States, together with other developed nations, exerts on prices so that the poorer nations must sell cheap and buy dear. Nearly all the economies of the underdeveloped countries depend on the export of just a few commodities; and this dependency is most often created by the foreign countries that once colonized them. Sixty-three percent of Bolivia's exports are of one commodity, tin; 69 percent of Colombia's exports are in coffee and oil; 84 percent of Equador's exports are coffee, bananas, and cocoa.[28] The slightest drop in prices greatly affects these countries' economies. A drop of only 1 cent per pound in coffee results in an estimated loss to Latin American producers of $50 million.[29] The problems Salvador Allende's Marxist government faced in Chile were quite similar. After his overthrow by a military junta, American analysts tended to blame "mismanagement" and lack of majority backing. But Oxford scholar Alan Angell sees other factors as far more decisive. Allende inherited an enormous foreign debt;

[24]Thomas Weisskopf, "United States Foreign Private Investment: An Empirical Survey," in *The Capitalist System,* p. 427.

[25]Andrew G. Frank, "On the Mechanisms of Imperialism: The Case of Brazil," in Charles Perrow, *The Radical Attack on Business* (New York: Harcourt Brace Jovanovich, 1972), p. 98.

[26]John Gerassi, *The Great Fear in Latin America* (New York: Collier-Macmillan, 1968), p. 370.

[27]Greene, *op. cit.,* p. 139.

[28]Harry Magdoff, *The Age of Imperialism* (New York: Modern Reader, 1969), pp. 99-100.

[29]Greene, *op. cit.,* p. 175.

copper prices fell by 25 percent after 1970, while food prices rose sharply. Moreover, the United States refused any renegotiation of loans from the Inter-American Development Bank.[30] All this was in addition to the now-acknowledged active intervention by ITT and the CIA in order to overthrow Allende. The United States proves hostile to any government not friendly to American business.

The United States has become less committed in recent years to foreign economic aid. But even in the early years of the Alliance for Progress, most aid was in the form of loans, and most of the loans in the form of credits, with stipulations that money be spent on American goods.[31] Certainly the United States has rendered significant aid to other countries. The Marshall Plan after World War II contributed greatly to rebuilding Europe's economy. But for the Marxist critic, even this aid was motivated primarily by self-interest. One critic cites a leading magazine of that period, *United States News,* which described the Marhall Plan as a "way to check depression":

> If world buying power is exhausted, world markets for U.S. goods would disappear. The real idea behind the program, thus, is that the United States, to prevent a depression at home, must put up the dollars that it will take to prevent a collapse abroad. The real argument for the support of the Marshall Plan is the bolstering of the American system for future years.[32]

American leaders justified the war in Vietnam as an effort to "help" another country in need, to preserve democracy in the world. Marxist critics, not surprisingly, viewed the war as an effort to protect American business interests in Southeast Asia. They find support for their thesis rather easily. As early as April 4, 1954, *U.S. News & World Report* ran an article entitled "Why U.S. Risks War for Indochina: It's the Key to Control of All Asia":

> One of the world's richest areas is open to the winner of Indo-China. That's behind the growing U.S. concern . . . tin, rubber, rice, key strategic raw materials are what the war is really about. The U.S. sees it as a place to hold—at any cost.[33]

Years later, Presidential advisor Walt W. Rostow reaffirmed this same point: "The location, natural resources, and populations of the under-

[30]Alan Angell, "Counterrevolution in Chile," *Current History 66,* 389 (January 1974), pp. 6-7.

[31]Gerassi, *op. cit.,* pp. 262ff.

[32]Greene, *op. cit.,* p. 125. Greene cites *United States News,* February 20, 1948.

[33]Quoted in Greene, *op. cit.,* p. 108. See also Oglesby, *op. cit.,* chap. 3.

developed areas are such that, should they become effectively attached to the Communist bloc, the United States would become the second power in the world.''[34]

If wars protect overseas markets, the massive defense industry also serves a vital need in the capitalist system. Imperialism alone is insufficient to create new markets. The defense industry, according to Marxists, is essential to the survival of free enterprise. Defense contracts ensure new markets, new jobs, and new uses for capital.[35] Without the artificial stimulus of defense spending, the United States would face crises of unemployment and recession. Exploitation of other countries, war, and a giant defense industry—these alone, say the Marxists, provide the outlets without which the free enterprise system would collapse.

Capitalist Domination of the State

Americans take pride in their democratic system: "Whatever its faults, it's the best in the world." Every citizen has a voice in the government. All can vote; all can aspire to political office. The two-party system offers alternatives in the choice of policies and candidates. The division of executive, legislative, and judiciary creates a balance of power.

The Marxist believes otherwise. According to Marx's analysis, society simply reflects its economic base. The state really serves as a protective shell for private economic interests. When land ownership dominated the economy of the Middle Ages, the state protected land interests. The hierarchical structure of political rule (princes, barons, vassals, serfs) and of Church rule (pope, cardinals, bishops, laity) reflected the hierarchical structure of economic classes. When free enterprise came to dominate the economy, a corresponding political structure and political philosophy emerged; and often the new system triumphed through the force of revolution. As free enterprise and free trade characterized the economic system, so freedom of speech, freedom of religion, and universal suffrage characterized the new political governments. Political democracy was simply the counterpart of an open, competitive market economy. Private property was essential to the new economy, so we find the seventeenth-century English philosopher John Locke claiming that "the great and chief end, therefore, of men's uniting into commonwealths, and putting themselves under government, is the preservation of their property."[36] In Marx's eyes, the new political freedoms gained by democracy simply confirmed the

---

[34]Cited in Magdoff, *op. cit.,* p. 54.

[35]See *Fundamentals of Marxism-Leninism,* ed. Clemens Dutt (Moscow: Foreign Language Publishing House, 1961), p. 330.

[36]John Locke, "An Essay Concerning the True Original Extent and End of Civil Government," in *Treatise of Civil Government and A Letter Concerning Toleration* (New York: Appleton-Century, 1937), chap. IX, no. 124, pp. 82-83.

narrow self-interest and individualism generated by free enterprise. The new freedoms were simply rights "of egoistic man, man separated from other men, and from the community."[37]

The Marxist explains the supporting ideology by the same economic forces. The Puritan ethic of work, the individualism, and the frugality that characterized early capitalism simply reflected the values needed in a production-oriented society. The contemporary, more hedonistic "playboy" morality mirrors the transition to a more consumer-oriented society. But in addition to motivating production and consumption, ideology also serves to defend and justify the prevailing economic system.[38] In short, the Marxist argues, the establishment of modern democratic society was not the result of noble, human ideals. It simply best fitted the interests of the new economic system. Although it claims to represent the common good of all its citizens, its real purpose is to protect the self-interest of the ruling capitalist class: "The executive of the modern state is but a committee for managing the common affairs of the whole bourgeoisie."[39] Although its laws now protect workers and minority groups, these have simply been necessary concessions to maintain power.

This whole thesis may appear quite one-sided and exaggerated, but the contemporary Marxist need not strain for evidence to support his position. Wealth does carry with it political power. In theory, public office is open to all, and all segments of the population are proportionally represented. In fact, power is not so proportionally distributed. Almost every recent Presidential election has presented us with a multimillionaire candidate (Franklin Roosevelt, Adlai Stevenson, John F. Kennedy, Lyndon Johnson), though they represent a mere fraction of 1 percent of the population of the country. Over a thirty-year period (1932-1964), Domhoff notes that five of eight secretaries of state and eight of thirteen secretaries of defense were listed in the elite Social Register.[40] Ambassadors have consistently been men of great wealth. Indeed, many important ambassadorial posts are awarded to wealthy men because they have contributed substantially to the successful candidate's treasury. Congress has a broader composition, but even today one would look in vain for a worker or farmer. The law profession and big

[37] *Writings of the Young Marx,* p. 235.

[38] For comments on the transition from a production-oriented society to a consumer-oriented one, see Amitai Etzioni, "The Search for Political Meaning," *The Center Magazine,* 5, 2 (March-April 1972), 2-8. For a discussion of how capitalist economists justify their system, see Robin Blackburn, "A Brief Guide to Bourgeois Ideology," in *The Capitalist System,* pp. 36-45.

[39] "The Communist Manifesto," in *The Marx-Engels Reader,* ed. Robert C. Tucker (New York: Norton, 1972), p. 337. For a fuller discussion of Marx's theory of the state, see Sweezy, *op. cit.,* chap. XIII.

[40] G. William Domhoff, *Who Rules America?* (Englewood Cliffs, N.J.: Prentice-Hall, 1967), pp. 97-99, 105-7.

business are disproportionately represented. In addition, ITT, Vesco, and the many illegal corporate campaign contributions have made all too apparent the influence of wealth on our political system.

Critics find our laws susceptible to the same inequities. The wealthy are protected and favored in tax credits and tax loopholes. In theory we have a graduated income tax, with the wealthiest surrendering more than 90 per cent of their incomes to the government. But in fact some multimillionaires have managed to pay no taxes at all. In 1970, no fewer than 394 families making more than $100,000 avoided paying even a nickel to the treasury.[41] In Philip Stern's phrase, our greatest "welfare program" are the tax "loopholes" granted to the wealthy of the country.[42] It is the wage and salary earners who bear the brunt of the tax burden. Every dollar they make is subject to taxes. Those wealthy enough to invest in stocks, in municipal bonds, and in real estate do not pay the same rates. Those who have managed to pay little or no taxes are precisely those with little or no *earned* income. In 1968, people with total earned incomes of less than $2,000 were paying half their incomes in taxes (including sales taxes), as opposed to only 45 percent for families with incomes over $50,000.[43] In addition, the executive can write off a luncheon or a trip as business expense, but it is actually thus taken at the taxpayers' expense; the ordinary worker has no such fringe benefits.

How the tax system works to favor the wealthy was exemplified rather dramatically with the disclosures about former President Richard M. Nixon, whose net worth tripled between 1969 and 1973. Documents released by his tax accountants and lawyers revealed that he had paid only about 7 percent of his total income in federal taxes, and had paid no state income taxes in California or the District of Columbia during his presidency.[44] For the Marxist critic, the fact that reputable tax experts and lawyers came close to enabling a man with a gross annual income of more than $250,000 to effectively avoid paying taxes simply confirms the privileges built into the whole legal system. It protects the wealthy, and thus puts a greater burden on poor and middle income families.

Most government spending benefits the prosperous much more than the poor. Defense contracts and public housing quite obviously increase the profits of big business. But government payments to farmers exemplify more strikingly how the rich get richer. In 1967 farm owners in the top 20 percent bracket of farm incomes received 70 percent of government

[41]Philip M. Stern, *The Rape of the Taxpayer* (New York: Random House, 1973), p. 68. See also Stern's earlier *The Great Treasury Raid* (New York: Random House, 1964), p. 4.

[42]Stern, *Rape of the Taxpayer, op. cit.,* pp. 5ff.

[43]*Ibid.,* pp. 25-26.

[44]*The Detroit News,* Sunday, December 8, 1973, p. 1.

payments; farmers in the lowest 20 percent received 1.2 percent.[45] Even in government expenditures on welfare, much of the money goes to white collar administrative staffs.

Social Consequences of Capitalism

To these major themes might be added a host of other issues, problems the Marxist considers directly related to the capitalist economic system. The inequality of women and their subservient role in society are for Marx consequences of private property and the division of labor. He viewed the family itself, with the husband dominating his wife and children, as the first form of property and as a "latent slavery."[46] Engels argued:

> . . . to emancipate woman and make her the equal of man is and remains an impossibility so long as woman is shut out from social productive labor and restricted to private domestic labor. The emancipation of woman will only be possible when woman can take part in production on a large, social scale, and domestic work no longer claims anything but an insignificant amount of her time.[47]

Lenin writes in a similar vein that "women are still in an actual position of inferiority because all housework is thrust upon them."[48] Needless to say, what the founders of Marxism had to say about the "woman question" has now become an open, sensitive, and pressing issue in the United States.

In a chapter entitled "The Face of Capitalism," from his book *The Enemy,* Felix Greene details the social problems in America he considers direct consequences of an economic system that subordinates social concerns to profit-making.[49] The problems are all too familiar. Capitalism has ravished the continent. The United States has killed off 85 percent of its wildlife and 80 percent of its forests; millions of acres of farmland have been misused and lost. Pollution is rampant. New York City dumps 200 million gallons of raw sewage in the Hudson River each day. Medical care for all citizens has been neglected. Three million children have untreated speech disorders. Crime and violence have come to be an almost accepted part of urban life. Armed robbery in Washington, D. C., runs 1,760 percent higher than in London; the number of homicides per year in Detroit is several times higher than for all of England. Drugs, inadequate housing, racial prejudice—the list goes on and on.

[45]James Bonnen, "The Effect of Taxes and Government Spending on Inequality," in *The Capitalist System,* p. 243.

[46]"The German Ideology," in *The Marx-Engels Reader,* p. 123.

[47]*The Woman Question: Selections from Marx, Engels, Lenin, Stalin* (New York: International Publishers, 1970), pp. 10-11.

[48]*Ibid.,* p. 52.

[49]Greene, *op. cit.,* pp. 3-43.

The charge that these problems are consequences of the free enterprise system is perhaps too facile an explanation. But the "face" of America is marred by serious social problems that make the charge difficult to dismiss. The United States prides itself as enjoying the highest standard of living in the world. The average American enjoys far more material benefits than any people in history. But the Marxist critic questions even this achievement. How much of what we consume corresponds to *real* needs? Marcuse charges our consumer-propelled economy with the creation of mostly false "needs."[50] Advertisements keep us in a state of perpetual dissatisfaction with what we do have. Automobiles could be made to last for years, but that would reduce production and profit. So new "styles" become the selling point. Advertising seeks to convince us of our "need" for ever-drier deodorants, electric toothbrushes and combs, and automatic garbage compactors. We can no longer even be sure of what kind of vacation we would naturally like because advertisements have programed us into what we *should* like.

The charges made by Marxists against our economic and political system are many. The wealth produced by industry profits owners and executives far more than workers. Financial investment multiplies the disproportionate distribution of wealth. Factory work stunts the capacities of workers engaged in it. Initiative, self-determination, a voice in decision making, are more possible in sales and management, but not for the labor force. Competitive self-interest characterizes work at every level. Poverty and unemployment become stigmatized as one's own fault. A wealthy power elite controls the highest public offices. Laws favor the wealthy and protect their incomes by tax loopholes. Women are made subservient. Pollution, crime, drugs, racial discrimination, and false needs are by-products of an economic drive that considers only more and more goods and profits. The system stands condemned.

But has any system done a better job? Would communism provide a better way of life? The instinctive response of most Americans is probably "no." The Communist nations of the world have hardly achieved any utopia. Their economies still lag far behind our own. Their political regimes appear intolerably regimented and coercive. Any reader of Solzhenitsyn's *The Gulag Archipelago* or observer of the persecution of Jews in Russia will hardly desire to live under a Soviet political system. The inefficiency and bureaucracy of the Russian economy and the still-undeveloped state of the Chinese economy make them inadequate models for an alternate economic system for the United States. Even severe struggles with inflation and recession are not likely to make most Americans eager to risk overthrowing our present political and economic system for socialism. But not being willing to

---

[50]Herbert Marcuse, *One Dimensional Man: Studies in the Ideology of Advanced Industrial Society* (Boston: Beacon Press, 1964), chap. 9, pp. 225-46.

trade places with Russians or Chinese should not be equated with not being willing to learn from them. For they have constructed economic systems that give special priority to eliminating some of the social problems which beset our own. Their failures as well as their achievements can contribute to a reappraisal of American business ideology and practice.

MARXIST IDEOLOGY: THE USSR AND CHINA

Marx was a social critic, not a social planner. He never developed a model of how a Communist economic system should operate. But implicit in his criticisms of capitalism were norms and principles that have served as a basis for the ideology Communist nations have sought to embody. Marx used the term "ideology" pejoratively to refer to the efforts made to legitimate or rationalize capitalist economic and political systems. In relation to communism, he spoke rather of "theory." But if ideology can be defined as a "simplified view intended to motivate," then modern communism certainly employs a very explicit ideology. In fact, one of the most obvious features of communism is its very conscious, clearly formulated, and oft-repeated ideology. The language and ideas of communism are uniform and easily recognizable whether the source is a Russian Party program, a Chinese government declaration, or Marxist newspapers in the United States. For in contrast with American business and political ideology, which developed almost unreflectively through many differing sources and theorists, Communist ideology has quite intentionally grounded itself in the writings of Marx, Engels, Lenin, and now Mao Tse-tung. Consequently, its economic ideology cannot be isolated from the overall view of history Marx formulated. To an outsider, the Communist world view would seem to have all the elements of a fundamentalist crusade: victory through arduous struggle, the example of its heroes and heroines, combat against its enemies, conformity to true doctrine, the promise of a glorious future, the call for tasks still to be fulfilled.

A 1961 draft of the Program of the Communist Party of the Soviet Union gives this ideology typical expression:

> The great October Socialist Revolution ushered in a new era in the history of mankind, the era of the downfall of capitalism and the establishment of communism. . . . The brilliant genius of Lenin, whose name will live forever, illumines mankind's road to communism. . . . Socialism will inevitably succeed capitalism everywhere. Such is the objective law of social development. Imperialism is powerless to check the irresistible process of emancipation.[51]

[51] *Program of the Communist Party of the Soviet Union* (New York: Crosscurrents Press, 1961), pp. 7-9.

The program goes on to describe the mission of communism to deliver all men from social inequality, from oppression and exploitation, and from war. It claims that all the productivity achieved under capitalism will be maintained and improved upon by communism while the social problems caused by capitalism will be eliminated. Under communism, the program continues,

> . . . the all-round development of people will be accompanied by the growth of the productive forces through continuous progress in science and technology, all sources of public wealth will gush forth abundantly. . . . Communism puts an end to the division of society into classes and social strata. . . . Under communism all people will have equal status in society. . . . Labor and discipline will not be a burden to people, labor will no longer be a mere source of livelihood—it will be a generally creative process and a source of happiness.[52]

The task of "building a Communist society" thus becomes the cornerstone of the Communist ideology of work. Individual fulfillment is realized through identification with this common goal. The state does the economic planning and sets priorities; most of the program, for example, is devoted to setting forth these plans and priorities—increased industry, a higher standard of living, and so on. The task of the individual is to join fully in this noble enterprise, and the Party sets down a moral code for him to follow:

> Devotion to the Communist cause, love of the Socialist motherland and of the other Socialist countries
> Conscientious labor for the good of society—he who does not work, neither shall he eat
> Collectivism and comradely mutual assistance: one for all and all for one
> An uncompromising attitude to the enemies of communism
> Fraternal solidarity with the working people of all countries, and with all peoples[53]

This is the expressed ideology. But how have Communist nations attempted to achieve these goals, and to what extent have they made good on their claims? Quite obviously only a very limited answer can be given in a few pages. The People's Republic of China is still too closed to outsiders to permit fully accurate evaluation. The Soviet Union has been the subject of more studies, but many Western Marxists reject it as an aberration from Marx's true idea of a Communist society. Given these limitations, some general observations can certainly be attempted about the two best-known Communist countries and how they have dealt with three primary goals of communism.

---

[52]*Ibid.*, pp. 60-62.
[53]*Ibid.*, p. 109.

One observation might be made at the outset. The two countries under consideration, the USSR and the People's Republic of China, differ considerably. To the Chinese and many other non-Russian Marxists, the Soviet Union is little more than "state capitalism." Comparisons with the American economy are therefore more easily made, but the challenge of a true alternative is much less evident when one studies Russia. Ideology there has yielded too easily to efficiency. Bureaucracy, managerial control over workers, individualistic incentives, preferential treatment, and marked differences in income characterize the Soviet system almost as much as they do the American. China, on the other hand, while impoverished if we compare GNPs, offers a more challenging example of alternate attitudes toward the economy. China has taken its ideology much more seriously and has often placed noneconomic, social objectives above productivity and efficiency. The Maoist claim that the very nature of man can be changed, that cooperation can replace self-interest as a basic economic motivation, stands in real contrast to Western capitalist values.

Social Equality and Social Consciousness

The most obvious goal of communism is to put an end to class antagonisms and economic inequities, to create a society in which people mutually support and aid one another rather than compete against each other. Although a truly classless society is still a distant dream, the great gap between the very wealthy and the poor has been narrowed in Russia, and all but eradicated in China. By law no one may exploit another. In the USSR it is illegal for an individual to have even a single employee or to sell what another person has produced.[54] Private ownership of productive facilities is minimal and is generally restricted to crafts and small landholdings. The state or collectives own or control the rest.

Wage differences do exist in Russia. Skilled workers may make three to four times the earnings of unskilled workers. Managers, Party bureaucrats, and university professors may make even twenty times the salary of an unskilled worker. But developing wealth through investment, which is the greatest source of wealth in the United States, is impossible. There are no stocks or bonds; and "The individual can acquire only consumer goods and strictly limited categories of property for personal use."[55] There are a "negligible number of individual savings accounts."[56] Banks are not run for the purpose of profit and are hence unconcerned with attracting investors. As in the United States, personal income taxes serve as a leveler, but the average worker in Russia pays no income taxes at all. Differences in

---

[54] Alec Nove, *The Soviet Economy*, 2nd ed. (New York: Praeger, 1969), pp. 27-28.

[55] George Garvey, "Finance and Banking in the USSR," in *The Soviet Economy*, 3rd ed., ed. Morris Bornstein and Daniel Fusfeld (Homewood, Ill.: Irwin, 1970), p. 142.

[56] *Ibid.*, p. 155.

status, prestige, and income remain, but there is no longer any real wealthy class.

Since the People's Republic of China remains somewhat closed to investigation, evaluation of success can only be tentative. But Western observers who have visited China and studied its economy are impressed with the degree of social equality they have found. Commenting on income distribution, one China expert concludes:

> . . . the overwhelming body of visual, qualitative and admittedly impressionistic evidence, coupled with whatever quantitative evidence is available, strongly supports the conclusion that the Chinese have been remarkably successful in narrowing income inequities and thereby assuring a certain minimum standard to most, if not all, elements of the population.[57]

An executive or party leader averages only twice, or at most four times, the salary of the ordinary worker.

Foreign correspondents in China have been strongly impressed by the sense of equality evident among the people. Hotel maids, peasant farmers, streetcleaners—all are treated with respect. Gone are all signs of the subservience that characterized China in the past. Waiters who were called "boys" in pre-Communist China are addressed as "comrades" today.[58] Students destined for professions or higher posts must put in two years of manual labor with peasants or factory workers to learn respect for them and for their skills.[59] Chinese professors are often required to do the same thing. The great Cultural Revolution (1966-1969) was geared to shake up Party officials, managers, and anyone else who might have begun to develop a sense of privileged position.

This sense of social equality and the sacrificing of individual gains to social progress results from a very definite economic ideology. Gurley makes this point in contrasting capitalism's stress on efficiency with the Maoist concern for involving the "masses" in the whole process of economic development.[60] Capitalism, he notes, uses the best, the most skilled workers available, the most ideal locations, the best managerial expertise. Efficiency results, but so does an ever-widening gap between the gifted and the disadvantaged. Maoism, on the other hand, quite deliberately builds on the worst. It gives top priority to raising the level of the populace as a

[57] Alexander Eckstein, "Economic Growth and Change in China: A Twenty-year Perspective," *The China Quarterly,* 54 (April-June 1973), 238.

[58] Seymour Topping, "Canton: A Society Transformed," in *Report from Red China,* ed. Frank Ching (New York: Avon Books, 1972), p. 141.

[59] Seymour Topping, "Rural China: Change and Continuity," in *Report from Red China,* ed. Frank Ching, p. 157.

[60] John W. Gurley, "The New Man in the New China," *Center Magazine,* III, 3 (May-June 1970). See also Jack Gray, "The Economics of Maoism," in *China After the Cultural Revolution* (New York: Random House, 1970).

whole. By developing the skills of the poorest, all advance together. Efficiency is secondary; human development is primary. Of course, when a worker moves from being unemployed to being employed and efforts are made to increase his skills, overall production generally increases. In the long run, even productivity also often rises.

There is very little sense of private property in China. The English correspondent Felix Greene comments on his hours spent watching Chinese children play without ever seeing fighting or arguments over what is "mine."[61] The same correspondent tells of a village commune where the people freely chose to restrict their own eating of fish to three times a year—though fishing was a major project of the commune—until they had saved enough money to improve their hospital, schools, and old people's homes.[62] Equality for women is an essential Communist goal. The economic dependence of a woman on her husband, which Marx and Engels criticized in "bourgeois" marriages, has been eliminated. The family structure remains intact, but child-care centers enable women to be as fully a part of the work process as men. Katkoff, speaking of the progress already made twenty years ago, indicates the extent of the integration of women into the work force of the USSR:

> Women are taking an active part in all phases of the Soviet economy. According to the latest information, they constitute 65 percent of all graduates from the institutions of higher learning. Women comprise 76 percent of all physicians and 70 percent of all teachers, and about one-third of all Soviet engineers and technicians are women.[63]

In China, women's liberation has become, in the words of one American correspondent, a "fact of everyday life."[64] One may still, however, question the level of equality. Women remain very disproportionately represented in the highest posts of the government and the Party in both countries. Nevertheless, the degree of equality seems certainly more advanced than in the United States.

Social consciousness, in theory, serves as the primary incentive for work in Communist countries. "Building a socialist society" should be the first task and highest goal of each citizen. But how successfully does it work? Can incentive be high if it does not base itself on personal advantage?

Mao's Social Motivation

In China, social motivation appears remarkably operative. The Chinese take great pride in the progress of the nation as a whole and are reluctant to

[61]Felix Greene, *Awakened China* (Garden City, N. Y.: Doubleday, 1961), pp. 60-61.
[62]*Ibid.,* pp. 166-67.
[63]Vladimir Katkoff, *Soviet Economy, 1940-1965* (Baltimore: Dangary, 1961), p. 62.
[64]Robert P. Martin, "China Revisited," *U. S. News & World Report,* March 13, 1972, p. 26.

speak about what they have achieved or attained personally. They attribute that progress to the inspiration of Mao Tse-tung. American businessman Harold Willens observes that "nowhere in the world have I seen men and women work with more zeal," and that "the source of this is the 'thought' of Mao Tse-tung."[65] A German journalist confirms this impression: "Mao is everywhere." He considers the omnipresence of portraits and Mao's Little Red Book the most significant change to have occurred in China between his visits in 1957 and 1971.[66] How do the Chinese explain their progress? "We studied the words of Chairman Mao and found our inspiration in Chapter III of the Little Red Book, where it says that China is poor but that poverty gives rise to the desire for change, the desire for action, and the desire for revolution."[67] Whatever the endeavor, Mao is credited with inspiring its success—the developing of a precision tool for grinding, a new way to preserve tomatoes, a world record in the high jump, successful surgery. Everyone in China spends a half-hour each morning studying Mao's thought, and three evenings a week in group study sessions. By the middle 1970s, the focus on Mao had diminished, but reliance on his thought appears deeply embedded still.

But have the Chinese renounced all individual, monetary incentives? In his important work *Industrial Society in Communist China,* Barry Richman raises doubts about the ultimate efficacy of incentives that neglect personal gain. But he notes that at present, even among directors, technical experts, and Party leaders, income and material gain do not play a key role. Extensive use is made of socialist emulation; workers are rewarded with titles, praise, and publicity. Richman thus concludes: "In general, non-material incentives have undoubtedly been highly effective in motivating enterprise personnel in Chinese Communist industry."[68] Individuals are paid on a scale determined by a point system based on skill, seniority, and political consciousness. Everyone is presumed to be doing his or her best; to work for higher wages is considered "unworthy." Galbraith compares the Chinese economic system to "a great battalion in which some lead, in which many march, and in which there is much emphasis on the soldiers' sense of purpose."[69] Incentive is built on exhortation—exhortation to build the nation, to advance the revolution, to please Chairman Mao. The Chinese people appear to have responded with enthusiasm.

[65]Harold Willens, "Make Deals, Not War—An American Businessman's Eye-Witness View of China," *Center Report,* 3 (August 1973), 9.

[66]Klaus Mehnert, *China Returns* (New York: Signet, 1972), p. 161.

[67]*Ibid.,* p. 123. On the use of Mao's thought, see also E. L. Wheelwright and Bruce McFarlane, *The Chinese Road to Socialism* (New York: Modern Reader, 1971), p. 188.

[68]Barry Richman, *Indistrial Society in Communist China* (New York: Random House, 1969), p. 817. For more on nonmaterial incentives in China, see also Wheelwright and McFarlane, *op. cit.,* chap. 8.

[69]John K. Galbraith, *A China Passage* (New York: Signet, 1973), p. 106.

One can object that social consciousness has been achieved at the expense of submission to a manipulative thought control and depersonalizing conformity. One can also question whether this motivation will change as China moves out of the heroic, pioneer stage of socialism and the people become more conscious of consumer goods. But social incentive has been impressively effective thus far. Richman draws attention to the dramatic change in the "image" of the Chinese people as viewed by outsiders. Prior to 1949, their image was characterized by favoritism, corruption, venality, and a lust for money. Today the Chinese are described by visitors and Sinologists as hard-working, energetic, honest, and cooperative.[70] Galbraith concurs: "The Chinese do work hard, effectively and intelligently for six days a week and without vacations. The impression of diligent effort. . . is overwhelming."[71]

In the Soviet Union, pure social incentive appears to be more compromised and individual reward plays a greater role. This is one reason why radical Marxists criticize Russia. The Soviet compromise dates back to the very beginning of socialism in Russia, when Lenin was compelled to introduce "capitalist" incentives because of the upheavals caused by the Russian civil war in 1918. Factory workers in Russia are paid according to their skill classification, which is more pronounced than in the United States.[72] The classification serves as an incentive to workers to learn new skills and improve their education. The workers are further rewarded if their production team overfulfills its production targets. The USSR also uses the piecework system to a much greater extent than the United States, with bonuses based on the number of "pieces" produced. Finally, in earlier decades at least, negative sanctions were used. Each worker had a labor book in which his performance and his times late or absent were recorded. Sanctions could be strict and harsh. In respect to its workers, then, Russia uses more individual, competitive incentives than does the United States.

What of managerial incentives? In many respects, according to the excellent study made by Joseph Berliner, motives in Russia closely parallel those of the American executive.[73] In neither case is "profit" a direct motive. The American executive works primarily for a salary, bonuses, and promotion, and so does his Russian counterpart. Incentive for the aspiring young Russian works on two levels: first, in the choice of career, and then in working within that career. In the choice of career, higher education is a much greater prerequisite for success than has been the case in the United

[70]Richman, *op. cit.,* pp. 224-25.

[71]Galbraith, *op. cit.,* . 107.

[72]Robert W. Campbell, *Soviet Economic Power* (Cambridge, Mass.: Riverside Press, 1960), p. 135.

[73]Joseph S. Berliner, "Managerial Incentives and Decision Making: A Comparison of the U.S. and the Soviet Union," in Bornstein and Fusfeld, *op. cit.,* pp. 163-94.

States. Though socialism has tried to make manual work respectable, the prestige of "working with one's mind" is still much greater and the incomes higher.

In the United States, bright and ambitious students are most likely to choose one of the professions or business. In Russia, the most lucrative and prestigious careers are in science, education, and industry. An engineering rather than a business education best prepares one for a role in industry. In addition to prestige and salary, executive positions may bring with them expense accounts, use of automobiles, and even a home. Careers such as law and medicine, because they cannot be profit making and because they enjoy relatively little prestige, are much less desirable in Russia than in the United States. Within industry, personal gain is perhaps as much a factor in the USSR as in the United States, and the gain comes chiefly through bonuses. "The principal incentive in Soviet industry is the bonus paid for overfulfillment of plan targets."[74] Once the career choice is made and a basic salary established, bonuses become the principal incentive for achievement. Social consciousness certainly plays an important incentive role in Russia as well, but its influence is less dramatic and obvious than in China. What the Russian economy does show is that, though appeals to self-interest remain, incentives for work do not depend on private ownership, profits, or investments.

Economic Planning

Marx believed that capitalism had outlived its usefulness. It had veered out of control and would inevitably collapse. Capitalism had no direction because individual owners worked blindly for personal profit without any sense of social or overall economic consequences. Production was regulated only by the unpredictable method of supply and demand. This led to overproduction, which created a regular cycle of ever-worsening economic crises. These crises of overproduction and massive unemployment would eventually compel workers to revolt. Only a planned socialist economy could restore economic balance and order.

These criticisms are now being voiced anew not only by Marxists, but also by mainline economists as well. In early 1975, seven Nobel Prize winners, including the economists Gunnar Myrdal and Kenneth Arrow, signed a statement saying that the current economic crisis "in the advanced industrial democracies raises serious questions about the very nature of the economic systems in these societies."[75] They addressed their statement to a socialist convention and they urged that "the exploration of alternatives to

---

[74]*Ibid.,* pp. 165-66.
[75]*The New York Times,* January 26, 1975, p. 30. See also *The Wall Street Journal,* February 5, 1975, pp. 1, 30.

the prevailing Western economic systems must be placed on the agenda at once." The new edition of Paul Samuelson's widely used economics textbook has a full chapter on Marxist economics, and Marxist economists are teaching at most of the better universities in the Western countries. Inflation, coupled with unemployment, cannot help but raise serious questions about the efficacy of the free enterprise economic system. Nevertheless, Marx's prediction of the collapse of capitalism has not come true, even though the planned socialist economy he envisioned has developed in many parts of the world. Critics who not long ago pronounced communism unworkable have been proved as wrong as Marx. But how well has communism succeeded economically?

If judged by its "starting points," the results are quite impressive. Socialist revolutions did not occur in already highly developed industrial countries, as Marx anticipated; they occurred instead in less developed countries. Communism's task, therefore, has been to transform poor, peasant economies into more prosperous, industrial societies. Khrushchev's boast that Russia would surpass American industrial output by the 1970s has not been realized. After impressive gains during the Khrushchev era, the Soviet economy has struggled with a drop in industrial growth rate in recent years.[76] Russia's total output of goods and services increased 213 percent from 1950 to 1971, compared with only 108 percent in the United States during the same period.[77] But the Soviet economy remains only half as big in absolute figures and the gap is widening rather than narrowing.

The Chinese economy can hardly be compared in absolute terms with that of the United States. But its success relative to its own past poverty, or to other large and poor nations, has greatly impressed those who have seen the changes. "That part of the country I have just seen is healthier, more prosperous, and far more orderly than the China I left in 1949," writes one correspondent.[78] The people are better fed, better dressed, bigger, and huskier. Cities that were once slums are now faultlessly clean, writes another observer.[79] There are no beggars on the streets; no one starves. Crime and prostitution are almost nonexistent. By 1972 the People's Republic of China had an industrial output 10 to 11 times higher than in 1949 and had reached a GNP of $140 billion.[80] In short, in Galbraith's words,

---

[76]Marshall I. Goldman, "The Soviet Economy: New Era or the Old Error?" *Current History,* 65, 386 (October 1973), 168.

[77]"Can Russia Surpass America?" *U.S. News & World Report,* May 15, 1972, 29-33.

[78]Robert P. Martin, "China Revisited," *U.S. News & World Report,* March 13, 1972, p. 22.

[79]Audrey Topping, "Dirt Is Now a Dirty Word," in *Report From Red China,* ed. Frank Ching, p. 126.

[80]Kuan-I Chen, "China's Industry: Strengths and Weaknesses," *Current History,* 65, 385 (September 1973), 115.

"There can now be no serious doubt that China is devising a highly effective economic system."[81]

If judged by the availability and quality of consumer goods, socialist economies suffer by comparison to the United States. But this norm can be very misleading. Besides starting at a poorer level, the Communist nations have given greater priority to industrial growth and to social goals (elimination of social inequities, improvement of health and education), than to consumer goods. Especially misleading are statistics that purport to show how much longer the average Russian must work than his American counterpart to pay for consumer goods (46 months for a car vs. 6 months for an American worker; or 17 minutes for a loaf of bread vs. 5 minutes for the American).[82] Consumer goods are more expensive in Russia because they include a "turnover tax" (a kind of sales tax) that may account for nearly 50 percent of the price.[83] Weeks and even months of an American worker's yearly wages may go to pay income taxes, insurance premiums, medical bills, and some educational costs, while the Communist worker receives all these free. One commentator estimates that the Russian worker has twice as much of his income available for consumer goods as does the American worker.[84] China is still too poor even to attempt comparisons about consumer goods. The average wage is only $30 per month, and though food and clothing prices are low and housing costs as little as $1 or $2 per month, this still leaves little more than pocket money for other consumer goods.

Grass Roots Participation in Planning

In one sense, any strict comparison between communism and free enterprise is impossible because neither system exists in its theoretical state. Communism proclaims the need for more economic planning than does capitalism. Americans tend to identify socialist planning with heavily centralized, bureaucratic state control. But even in the USSR, which has relied greatly on state planning, more subsidiary levels of planning have been

---

[81]Galbraith, *op cit.,* p. 104. Richman, *op. cit.,* p. 913, concurs with these judgments: "Very few poor countries in the world have done so well in economic growth or industrialization as China has since 1950. There is no doubt in my mind that in 1966 when I was in China the average Chinese citizen was living substantially better—and could expect to live about twelve to sixteen years longer—than the average Chinese citizen did at any time before the Communists came to power."

[82]" 'Good things' of Life for Russians—Can Kremlin Deliver?" *U.S. News & World Report,* July 24, 1972, p. 52.

[83]Janet G. Chapman, "Consumption in the Soviet Union," in Bornstein and Fusfeld, *op. cit.,* pp. 329-31.

[84]Victor Perlo, *USA and USSR* (New York: International Publishers, 1960), p. 72.

developed. More important, many Marxists would strongly dispute the identification of social planning with state planning. Marx himself did not envision state control. Marxist Oskar Lange argued the advantages of a "market socialism" in place of government plans; Yugoslavia in practice has developed a form of market socialism.[85]

China also has moved quite dramatically away from any bureaucratically planned, top-down economy. "Those who imagine the Chinese economy to be a pure 'totalitarian command economy' in which enterprise managers merely carry out orders have no conception of the reality."[86] The state still determines production quotas, sets prices and policies, and collects taxes. But since the Cultural Revolution, most of the planning occurs at lower levels. The stress is on a "cellular" economy built upon small, self-reliant units.[87] China is now divided into some 75,000 communes varying in size from 5,000 to 40,000 persons, but averaging about 10,000 persons. These are subdivided into brigades, averaging 1,000 persons; and these into production teams, averaging 150 to 200 persons. In recent years even the communes have become less significant. They serve primarily to provide services such as hospitals, large-scale industry, and research centers that lower units are too small to provide. The brigade has become the heart of the system. It is a small enough unit for people to know each other and to feel they have a real voice in decisions about what products to develop, what methods to employ, what social needs to give priority. Finally, a great deal of responsibility is left with the production team—for example, the determination and distribution of wages.

Free enterprise, on the other hand, has moved in the direction of greater planning. The largest two or three hundred corporations in the United States effectively control most of the economy. Economic planning is corporate and long range, no longer totally dependent on a fluctuating market. Economic decisions are no longer in the hands of a few capitalist owners, but now involve many managers and technical experts. Profits still dominate as a corporate goal but are less operative as an incentive for the managerial class, which is rewarded by salary and bonuses.[88] Government intervention in the economy has introduced a significant degree of planning. Government subsidies, tax shelters, oil depletion allowances, the highway trust fund, and government housing programs hardly exemplify free enterprise, yet they now exist as a pivotal influence on the United States

[85] Gregory Grossman's *Economic Systems* deals in chap. 6 with the USSR's "command economy," and in chap. 7 Oskar Lange and Yugoslavia's "market economy" are discussed (Englewood Cliffs, N.J.: Prentice-Hall, 1967).

[86] Richman, *op. cit.*, p. 42; see also Mehnert, *op. cit.*, pp. 70, 239.

[87] See Audrey Donnithorne, "China's Cellular Economy," *The China Quarterly,* 52 (October-December, 1972), 605. See also Wheelwright and McFarland, *op. cit.*, pp. 201ff.

[88] These are points made in John K. Galbraith's *The New Industrial State*.

economy. The Pentagon alone, with assets larger than many European countries, has been characterized by one of its critics as "military socialism."[89] In short, various aspects of socialism have influenced free enterprise, just as capitalist influences have had their effect on socialism.

There remain, nevertheless, rather basic differences between the two economies. The United States economy remains primarily a consumer-directed, market economy. The Communist nations are production-directed, planned economies. In the socialist system administrative decision determines prices, and efficiency depends on capital allocations and cooperation. In the United States supply and demand still dictate prices to a significant extent, and the drive to maximize profits and cut costs encourages efficiency. The American economy succeeds rather well on total production and income, but suffers from a lack of social priorities. The Communist system, with its centralized economy, can control priorities but often suffers from lack of flexibility and loss of efficiency.[90]

Democracy and Worker Control

Through socialist revolution the workers, the masses, would take control of their own "conditions of existence," according to Marx.[91] They would eliminate private property and division of labor, and with these would be abolished all domination of owners over workers. The workers would govern that state until society no longer required a special government force to regulate it, and the state would then "wither away." The domination of capitalist rulers has come to an end in Communist countries. But has a "proletarian democracy" replaced their rule? Or has a Party bureaucracy taken their place "in the name of workers"?

In Russia, after the Bolshevik revolution of 1917, despite real efforts to include broad representation in the Party, Lenin found that strict Party rule was needed to ensure the results of the revolution. The masses were inexperienced in self-government and lacked the managerial skill to run factories. Civil war and the threat of counterrevolution made strict controls and policing a necessity. The underdeveloped state of the economy called for administrative controls not envisaged by Marx. This created a state bureaucracy, which under Stalin became a totalitarian, dictatorial rule.

Though not reaching the extremes of Stalinism, socialist revolutions in China, Cuba, and elsewhere have faced similar problems in attempting to realize worker control (or in China peasant and worker control) of the economy and government. But factory workers and peasants do get elected

[89]Richard J. Barnet, *The Economy of Death* (New York: Antheneum, 1969), p. 117.
[90]Campbell, *op. cit.*, p. 113.
[91]*The Marx-Engels Reader*, p. 162.

to legislative offices at local and national levels in far more proportionate numbers than happens in the United States. Economic and political planning, however, remains primarily from the top down and under strict control of professional Party officials. Trade unions exist in the USSR, but their primary purpose is to stimulate output of production through "socialist competition" between production teams and individuals. The unions also serve to protect workers from abuses by management and to present grievances. Western critics see government policy as superseding workers' complaints and suggestions.[92] The Russians themselves see worker input as integral to their whole planning process.

Mao Tse-tung has attempted to achieve in China what would seem to be contradictory goals—maintaining the revolution along "correct" lines, yet encouraging popular participation in policy formulation and implementation. A good deal of self-determination is permitted for production teams, and discussion at least of policy decisions at the commune level. Although top-level policies guide the overall direction of the economy, the motivational factor of self-reliance appears to play a very significant role in the Chinese economy.

Although the Marxist critic would challenge how much real political self-determination is possible for the average American, it is precisely on this issue of political freedoms that Americans find themselves most opposed to communism. One-party rule, censorship of the press, repression of religious freedom, not having even the liberty to leave the country—these run wholly counter to all we identify with freedom and democracy. To Russians, who previous to the revolution of 1917 knew only absolutist rule by a czar, and to Chinese who knew only the predatory rule of warlords, these political restrictions may seem less oppressive than they do to us. But it remains true that political democracy and even worker control of the economy are the least realized of all Marxist goals.

SUMMARY AND CONCLUSIONS

Karl Marx perceptively pinpointed the weaknesses of the capitalistic economic system. He and his followers have shown that capitalism possesses a series of undesirable characteristics. According to Marx, capitalism results in:

1. Exploitation of the worker
2. Alienation of the worker
3. Imperialism: exploitation of other countries
4. Capitalist domination of the state

[92]Nove, *op. cit.,* p. 142-44.

Although Marxists are at their best in criticizing capitalism, they also propose an alternate method for organizing a society. That system has been developed and tried in such countries as the USSR, the People's Republic of China, and Cuba. China is perhaps the best large-scale example of Marxist ideology in practice, and it is held out as a model by most contemporary Marxists.

An evaluation of communism for many Americans goes no further than concluding that "We have more and better consumer goods available, and more money with which to buy them. Moreover, we are free; they are not." True, but the Communist nations also possess much that we lack: greater cooperativeness, greater pride in work, less unemployment, less disparity of wealth, greater equality of all—including women and the disadvantaged—and less crime, drugs, and violence.

Each system has its strengths and weaknesses. A bureaucratic, totalitarian system is hardly desirable to most Marxists. Unemployment, poverty, and crime are certainly not advocated by the defenders of free enterprise. But the comparison does raise the question of priorities and how they are formulated. Who decides what specific values and goals of a society are to be given priority? In the Communist nations, the Party and the government set priorities, both economic and political. The system is devised precisely to encourage cooperation, to provide greater participation, and to eliminate unemployment. Through meeting these goals, the system also thus encourages production and economic growth. With free enterprise, conscious priorities are set only in the political sphere. Government can regulate and sometimes subsidize, but it generally does not set specific economic goals. Free enterprise advocates firmly defend this nonintervention as more efficient and effective. When it comes to priorities, free enterprise in theory recognizes only one: "Will it return a profit?" The system does not ask how important is the need the product fulfills; it has no method of rating products or services on any human scale of values.

Perhaps profits should be the sole concern of the corporation. But then who, if anyone, does set national economic priorities in the United States and sees that they are implemented? Do individual consumers have the vision to look to the long-term economic and social good of the majority of the people? Who decided that automobile travel was better than urban rapid transit systems? Who decided that the sale of cat food and cosmetics would have priority over programs to eliminate world hunger? As we will see in the last two chapters, it is not clear where this responsibility lies. The new movement advocating greater corporate responsibility has focused attention on the moral and social consequences of some business policies—for example, minority hiring, pollution, withdrawal from urban areas. But the issue of national priorities goes beyond these. Perhaps at least this much can be learned from the Marxist critique of free enterprise and the goals Communist nations set for themselves. They can stimulate us to examine our priorities. They can help us see the inadequacies and the limits of our own ideology, so that we may improve it.

CHAPTER FIVE

New Challenges to Free Enterprise and Its Values

Practical men, who believe themselves to be quite exempt from any intellectual influences, are usually the slaves of some defunct economist.

*John Maynard Keynes**

In the last decade profound questions have shaken the foundation of the American free enterprise economic system. Just a few years ago, it was inconceivable that anyone who was not "misguided" would question the adequacy of a system that had been so successful in providing so much in the way of goods, income, and wealth for so many people. Indeed, as recently as the early 1960s, it would have been thought by most to be "un-American" and disloyal to include a chapter on Marxism in a book on American business values. Now, confidence in the efficiency and the values of free enterprise has been seriously eroded. Moreover, public opinion has shifted so much that many business persons are anxious lest the questioning bring additional government regulation, more drastic constraints on the operation of business, or perhaps even something akin to nationalization.

Many of the more serious challenges to free enterprise have come from idealistic people; some are public-spirited citizens, others are religiously motivated or person-oriented socialists, still others are teachers and young people. Defenders of free enterprise generally point out that these people are not practical, not hard-headed enough; they have never gotten their fingernails dirty or met a payroll. Perhaps this is true. But in any case dialog and listening is essential to mutual understanding. This chronicle of challenges should aid that growing dialog. Although the last chapter presented the classical Marxist critique of capitalism, such challenges are not limited to Marxists or to those whose sympathies lie with China, Russia, or Cuba. Free enterprise has been questioned by a wide variety of people and organizations. Moreover, many of these questions are wide-ranging, quite profound, and have already had a significant impact on the operations, goals, and values of the business firm.

*John Maynard Keynes, *General Theory of Employment, Interest and Money,* (New York: Harcourt Brace Jovanovich, 1965). Quoted with permission.

BUSINESS AS A CRIPPLED GIANT

Americans in general and youth in particular have serious quarrels with assumptions that form the basic fabric of our free enterprise economic system. Business and the corporation are not now viewed in the positive light they had almost come to expect. For a variety of reasons, many of which we will discuss later in this chapter, confidence in the business system and its leaders has fallen dramatically in the last decade.

A series of opinion surveys was done by Daniel Yankelovich, Inc., for *Fortune* magazine and for the John D. Rockefeller, 3rd, Fund. Some of the questions pertinent to our inquiry are shown in Table 5-1. An examination of these attitudes indicates the roots of dissatisfaction with our business and economic system. More than nine out of ten young people are convinced that business is too concerned with profits and does not attend enough to its public responsibilities; indeed, more than a third of business executives feel the same way. Here, as with other items, it is clear that there is a large divergence in opinion between the business community and young people. Distribution of goods and services is another vital aspect of our business system, and more than three-fourths of young people and almost one-half of the executives polled feel it is unjust and unfair. These attitudes of youth are now more widely held in the population, according to more recent surveys by the same group: "What seemed to be a generation gap was actually the leading edge of a new morality and quest for new, self-fulfilling life styles that have now spilled over from the campus to influence all American youths—and many of their parents as well."[1]

Paralleling public distrust of the justice of the distribution system is disenchantment with the leadership of our major institutions. A recent Harris poll[2] shows that only 21 percent of the American people express confidence in the leadership of our major companies. This is down from a high of 55 percent in 1966. The leaderships of other major institutions—government, the military, labor, and the churches—fare little better. Even more unsettling is the conviction expressed by 76 percent of the people that "the rich get richer and the poor get poorer"; this is up from 45 percent who felt that way in 1966. With this sort of dissatisfaction, we must conclude that either people are uninformed or that there are indeed serious inequities in our business and economic system.

Frank T. Cary, president of IBM, points to these attitudes as the most important problem facing the country. He feels that "the nation's lack of belief in its own institutions and in the leadership of these institutions" is the major problem facing the United States.[3] Pointing to the Harris poll, he

[1]"Startling Shifts Found in Youths' Views of Work, Morals," *The Chronicle of Higher Education,* 8 (May 28, 1974), 3.

[2]*Detroit Free Press,* September 30, 1974, p. 6; *Newsweek,* December 10, 1973, pp. 40-48.

[3]*The New York Times,* January 7, 1973, Sec. F, p. 37.

TABLE 5-1

Attitudes on Issues Underlying the Business System

Issue	Percent of Group Agreeing					
	Man-agers	Youth			Graduate Business Students	
	1969	1969	1971	1973	1974	1975
Business is overly concerned with profits, and not concerned enough with public responsibilities.	36%	92%	93%	93%	75%	69%
Economic well-being in this country is unjustly and unfairly distributed.	46	76	82	—	80	68
Today's American society is characterized by injustice, insensitivity, lack of candor, and inhumanity.	18	59	69	—	55	56
Our foreign policy is based on narrow economic and power interests.	36	75	88	88	70	68

Sources: The 1969 figures are taken from "What Business Thinks," *Fortune,* 80 (October 1969), 139-40, 196; attitudes for 1970 and 1971 are added in Daniel Yankelovich, *The Changing Values on Campus.* (New York: Washington Square, 1972), pp. 62-63. The 1973 attitudes are from Daniel Yankelovich, *The New Morality* (New York: McGraw-Hill, 1974), p. 122. Graduate business students'attitudes are from the author's classes at Wayne State University.

says, ". . . not one of our professional, social or governmental institutions commands a majority vote of confidence from the people queried." He is especially concerned that public confidence in business, which was only a bare majority, ten years ago, has now fallen to half of that. Henry Ford II tries to probe the roots of this malaise. He says that our most important national problem is "our failure to achieve the level of human relations and basic human satisfactions that we, as a society, are capable of achieving."[4] He goes on to say: "Divisiveness and deep-seated antagonisms have weakened our will to listen to each other. The decay of inner cities is an alarming symptom of widespread denial of fundamental human values." Ford concludes, "If we do not pull ourselves together into a more humane, cohesive and tolerant society, we will have neither the will nor the strength to meet effectively the many other problems besetting us." Disenchantment of Americans and their business leaders is clear, and conditions have not improved since these men expressed their concern. In the wake of inflation, recession, the energy crisis, and the spectacle of a recent Attorney General of the United States being found guilty in a federal court, confidence in American institutions has fallen to a new low. Moreover, Americans seem

[4]*Ibid.*

to be exhibiting a sense of powerlessness: the problems seem to them to be too large, too complex, and not open to traditional solutions.

Institutions here, as everywhere, depend for their existence and successful operation on the trust of the people. There is serious question as to how long these institutions can last in their present form when that confidence and trust is so obviously lacking. But before speaking of new values and reform, it is essential to probe some of the underlying reasons for this disillusionment.

The Contemporary Corporation: Cornucopia or Citizen?

The reasons for the decline in confidence in the business system are many, but the way in which business persons view their own purpose is fundamental to that decline. Business has rather complacently assumed that, by pursuing its own rather narrowly construed ends, it was by that very fact contributing best to the welfare of the majority of American citizens. This attitude is probably best characterized by the oft-quoted statement of the General Motors president Charles Wilson some years ago, "What is good for General Motors is good for the United States." This rationalized self-interest stems from the conviction that the best thing that General Motors can do for society is to provide quality automobiles at the lowest possible price, and in so doing provide a good return for stockholders. Assuredly, if GM fails in this, it is a failure as a business firm. On the other hand, being successful within these narrowly conceived limits is no longer sufficient.

Earlier we examined the value system that held that when the firm and even the individual pursued her or his own self-interest, the play of market forces and Adam Smith's "invisible hand" brought about the most efficient use of resources and resulted in the satisfaction of everyone's needs. Clear challenges to this simplistic ideology have recently arisen on such issues as employing minorities, pollution, the energy crisis, and the automobile. Pursuing narrow self-interest was a cause of these problems in the first instance, so we can hardly expect that rationale to contribute to a stable solution.

Rationalized self-interest has for many decades worked rather well for both the firm and the individual. Furthermore, it was justified by economic theory and blessed by the Protestant ethic. The unrestrained right of individuals and businesses to pursue their own self-interest has taken us fast and far in economic growth. Enlightened self-interest builds upon the recognition that man tends to be selfish. Capitalism or free enterprise takes into account this human quality and tries to direct it to work for the benefit of the entire society. When it does work in this fashion, it is one of the system's strengths.

These attitudes can also breed an arrogance in pursuing narrowly construed goals, a self-righteousness that results in indifference to consequences. The attitudes thus engendered in those directing the corporation have been described flippantly as "creative greed": acquisitiveness coupled with creativity makes our economic system successful. Critics point out that the system thus lionizes those who are most innovative in their selfishness, provides them with material and psychological rewards, and thus reinforces and institutionalizes self-centeredness and narrowness of vision.

These personal values are judged effective and worthwhile, since it can be readily shown that they contribute to achieving our national economic goals. Moreover, these economic goals—continually increasing gross national product and average personal income, greater productivity, and the availability of more and better goods—are even said to be the most important goals of our society. These material and measurable ends of American society were graphically paraphrased by President Calvin Coolidge in an adage we all heard in grade school, "The business of America is business."

Rationalized Self-interest

Focusing narrowly on the ends of profits and productivity provides both theoretical and psychological support to those business people who "look out for number one first." Colonial Pipeline, jointly owned by nine of the largest American oil companies and itself the largest oil pipeline firm in the country, was finishing the construction of its line into New Jersey in 1962.[5] A site for a storage area was needed, and tank farms were not popular with the people of Woodbridge, New Jersey, the area selected. Although public hearings were required by law, both the mayor and the president of the town council said they would see to it that Colonial received its building permit if the firm would give a $50,000 "campaign contribution." To look for another site would delay the project, and laying additional pipeline to the spot could cost the firm millions, so they paid the $50,000 (and later an additional $100,000). It is illegal for a firm to contribute to political campaigns. In addition, the firm and the local leadership conspired to deprive citizens of their right to be heard on the issue. Nevertheless, it was a far less expensive alternative for management. Management had counted on not being caught, having decided it was better for the firm to break the law than to expose itself to additional costs. In spite of cleverly hidden accounts and transfers of funds, however, the scheme was accidentally exposed. Ensuing events showed that similar campaign contributions by large firms are

---

[5]Morton Mintz, "A Colonial Heritage," in Robert Heilbroner et al., *In the Name of Profits* (New York: Warner, 1973), pp. 59-96.

common practice. Rationalized self-interest thus leads firms to seek the lower cost alternative—not surprising in the context of an "every man for himself" ethic.

An empirical investigation of the values of corporate managers also showed that their personal and organizational goals can be characterized as centered on self and success. Personal goals of achievement, success, and creativity were valued significantly more than those of autonomy, dignity, and leisure. The most important goals of the organization for these managers were efficiency, high productivity, profit maximization, and organizational growth; these goals were far more important than employee welfare and social welfare.[6] Such self-centered and success-oriented goals inevitably create conflicts, diseconomies, and injuries to society. One example is that of pollution, which is generated when the source of the damage is not willing to pay the full cost of its operations. It is cheaper for the producers of pollution to push that part of the cost off onto someone else. For example, additional expense is required to clean effluents. It is cheaper for the firm to dump the waste into the air and water and let the costs be borne by others. Users of the product are thus not paying the full costs. Those who live in congested neighborhoods surrounding the plant, including those too poor to be customers, bear a large share of those costs by breathing foul air that may take months or years off their lives. They therefore subsidize those who, for example, drive automobiles. Environmentalists claim that justice demands manufacturers "internalize" these real costs of production and pass them on to those who actually use the products. The Environmental Protection Agency was set up just to accomplish this transfer. Whether we feel the agency is overregulating or not, it is clear that the free market has no mechanism for eliminating pollution; in fact, it encourages firms to pollute as long as they can get away with it.

There are other instances of how primary emphasis on dollar return often works to the detriment of the larger society, and even ultimately to the efficient operation of the firm. The rise of the conglomerate in the late 1960s (for example, Litton Industries and International Telephone and Telegraph) shows how large corporations acquired other firms largely because it would look good on the annual report. Little attention was paid to whether the parent firm's management would be able to improve product quality or even increase efficiency. Often the newly acquired firm would be closed, its assets liquidated and its employees thrown out of work, simply because the parent company judged it had better uses for the funds acquired. No consideration was given to the welfare of employees, customers, the general public or even the stockholders themselves when these mergers took place.

---

[6] George W. England, "Personal Value Systems of American Managers," *Journal of the Academy of Management,* 10 (March 1967), 53-68.

Aside from the immense political influence that firms such as Litton and ITT have exerted to get their own way on these mergers, aside from the influence peddling, pressure, illegal campaign contributions, and interference in foreign governments' operations,[7] these mergers show how the economic system can work to the disservice of the very people it is designed to serve. Generally, the major index of success for these conglomerate executives is the rising price of the firm's stock. Since this is largely based on expectations, and since expectations can be influenced and managed, success for these men and their firms is far removed from quality products and even further removed from sensitivity to citizens' needs.

Executive salaries are also judged by the public to be grossly beyond what a person is worth. Harold Geneen, chairman of ITT, earned $814,000 in 1973, and there was no personal risk in his job. He, like other corporate executives, has unique talents and works long hours, but he is no entrepreneur. He has personal security and there is absolutely no danger of his going into bankruptcy unless he is totally inept in managing his personal fortune. Geneen is the same executive who offered $1 million to the Central Intelligence Agency to interfere in the Chilean elections to ensure that the eventual winner, the late Salvadore Allende, would not be elected. Political contributions by corporations are illegal in the United States. What about clandestine interference in the internal political affairs of a foreign country? How would Americans react on hearing that a French corporation secretly offered $1,000,000 to influence a Presidential election? Moreoover, if Geneen admits to tampering with the internal affairs of Chile, what are we to say of the multitude of other domestic charges leveled against ITT, such as the $400,000 pledged to the Republican campaign just when ITT was seeking government approval of its proposed merger with Hartford Life?

Corporations are surely the wealthiest and the most powerful institutions in our society. The American public is not about to allow institutions so visible and so powerful to follow only their own narrowly construed interests. In thinking that they may, the corporate managers are adding to the lack of confidence in the business corporation and the American business system.

The Federal Government as Mediator

In a system characterized by enlightened self-interest, only the government is left as a protector of the public interest. Given the business ideology, it could be expected that individual firms would not of their own accord take into account most issues of public concern. In fact, it is

[7]See, for example, on ITT, "Harold Geneen's Tribulations," *Business Week,* August 11, 1973, pp. 102-7; see also the fuller account by Anthony Sampson, *Sovereign State of ITT* (Greenwich, Conn.: Fawcett, 1973).

sobering to recall that during the last hundred years business has fought almost every piece of social legislation that would have tended to constrain its activities. Child labor laws, the minimum wage, recognition of labor unions, and legislation eliminating discrimination on the basis of race, sex, or age were all passed over the loud and sometimes violent protests of business and groups representing business.[8] Today executives are surprised and indignant at the suggestion that at one time they were opposed to any of this legislation. Memories are short. Nevertheless, history does provide clues that are important in determining future policy, whether corporate or government. Many people are asking for more information on corporate activities. The public is not looking for more "public relations" (indeed, it has long been suspicious of public relations), but rather for honest and fuller disclosure on products, finances, forecasts, equal employment opportunity data, pollution expenditures, and other matters of public concern.

The citizen often feels powerless and cynical when confronted with these immense public problems. He feels he should be able to look to the government to protect his interest. But many recent government efforts are designed more to protect special interests; when they do attempt to promote the common good, they are too little or too late. The energy shortage, for example, has been building for decades. The major oil companies, for all their profit-taking and other faults, have been warning us for years of a coming shortage of petroleum. The federal government nonetheless continued to encourage the building of roads, disrupting and destroying portions of cities and farms, and at an immense cost. In 1968 the federal government repealed the excise tax on American-built cars, precisely when it could have been discouraging the use of large cars. At the same time, it placed a new import tax on the smaller, fuel-saving foreign-made autos. Rather than encouraging conservation of oil and other resources, it encouraged additional use. Also undermining the credibility of the federal government as a protector of the individual citizen is its tolerance and even encouragement of tax loopholes and tax shelters for the wealthy. In 1969, 301 families with an income of $100,000 or more paid *no* federal income tax. In addition, "An oil investor was able to shield his entire income of $1,313,811 from the tax collector."[9] So many other examples of the wealthy avoiding their share of taxes are available that even *The Wall Street Journal* entered the fray with an editorial entitled "Trimming Tax Shelters."[10]

Federal regulatory agencies have been less than successful in protecting the public interest. Charged with setting standards and rates, they hear testi-

---

[8]Albert Z. Carr, "Can an Executive Afford a Conscience?" *Harvard Business Review*, 48 (July-August 1970), 58-64.

[9]Philip M. Stern, *The Rape of the Taxpayer* (New York: Vintage, 1974), p. 14. This inequity is often also cited by Marxist critics of capitalism (see Chapter 4).

[10]*The Wall Street Journal*, November 6, 1973, p. 20.

mony almost exclusively from the regulated firms, and rarely from groups representing the public interest. They have also not always been staffed with the most talented people available. When public-minded regulators such as Mary Gardiner Jones of the Federal Trade Commission or Nicholas Johnson of the Federal Communications Commission are appointed, their outspoken defense of the public interest rarely earns them a reappointment. The hope of the federal government's defending the public interest has been further eroded in the last decade. The attempted politicizing of the Internal Revenue Service, the actions of the "plumbers," the use of the Federal Bureau of Investigation domestically and the Central Intelligence Agency internationally to suppress antiwar activities and leftist social justice activites all provided convincing evidence that the reins of power are in the hands of the wealthy and powerful.

The New Left critique, which sees *all* power in the hands of a few wealthy men, may seem somewhat paranoid. Nevertheless, recent evidence leads us to the conclusion that the average man in the street is not wrong when he concludes that his government cares little for him personally, that the wealthy are able to protect their own interests through the government, and that there is little that he can do about it. Moreoever, in the modern organization power is typically separated from its source.[11] Because an organization is larger than and outlasts its founders and participants, the institutions of our society have assumed greater power than that of natural persons. This gives rise to individual feelings of powerlessness. Much like in science fiction, the organization and technology, originally created by man, take on a life and a purpose of their own. The corporation's purpose becomes independent of that of those who created it. It acts in a single-minded pursuit of its own narrow interests.

Business Schools: Goals or Techniques?

Business schools have been criticized as being exclusively concerned with teaching competition, control, and the techniques of success. The Harvard Business School, the "West Point of capitalism," has been a special target of this criticism.[12] Like other schools, however, Harvard faced its own "crisis of legitimacy" in early 1971. A series of discussions were held at the school among faculty, administrators, and graduate students. Moreover, two position papers were written by Professors Theodore Levitt and George C. Lodge to prepare for this large-scale inquiry. Among the many important

[11]James S. Coleman, *Power and the Structure of Society* (New York: Norton, 1974), pp. 36-37, 57.

[12]Peter Cohen, *The Gospel According to the Harvard Business School* (Garden City, N.Y.: Doubleday, 1973).

questions raised was the very legitimacy of the school itself if it continued to ignore the issues basic to the survival of the corporation and the business school. In his colorful but precise style, Theodore Levitt stated the problem when he said, "The Harvard Business School, where such things aren't supposed to happen, is headed for a crisis of legitimacy. It may already be there." He indicted the school because it taught only skills and techniques, and nothing about values.

A new need for clarifying goals and values has arisen because the accepted rationale has dissolved. This disintegration has occurred on two levels: (1) the disappearance of delayed gratification for the individual, and (2) the questioning of traditional capitalism itself. The old postponement of gratification and delayed personal satisfaction is, especially among young people, "almost totally gone when it comes to sex, automobile ownership, sartorial possessions, travel, and social power." Everything must be had now. There is a narcissistic concern with self and "doing one's own thing." In fact, this new attitude is more consistent with traditional enlightened self-interest than is delayed gratification.

Moreover, "the moral legitimacy of traditional capitalism is under siege. Everything that goes with it is under jeopardy. . . . The spiritual cement has let go, the moral legitimacy of this beautiful machine is under question."[13] Students, in asking that business and business schools direct themselves more to basic value questions, are not attacking but rather are trying to save the system. They are looking for new values and goals that will provide a new legitimacy. Furthermore, in facing these problems, business students and others are asking for more than just responsiveness. They are looking for leadership, for lack of leadership and an inability to articulate new values and goals indicates a personal and corporate vacuum.

In merely responding to questions on a stopgap basis and continuing to teach competitiveness and techniques, the business school thus "confesses its own lack of self-esteem. It stands for nothing. . . . Opportunism and pragmatism are its style. Integrity is a word in the dictionary."[14] Yet even the best business schools can get caught up in running without a clear purpose and contribute to the "American way"—compete for the sake of competing, achieve for the sake of achieving. And he who does continually achieve is honored; he is the smartest, the cleverest, the richest, and that is the goal of any good American, is it not?

Graduate business schools in urban areas have generally gone further in recognizing these new social issues and values and integrating them into the curriculum. Most business schools now offer one or more courses on social

---

[13]*Crisis and Legitimacy on the Wrong Side of the River,* Committee on the School and Society in the 70s (Boston: Harvard Business School, 1971), pp. 22-24.
      [14]*Ibid.,* p. 26.

issues, and in many cases, the new course is part of the required core curriculum. In several schools—for example, Columbia, Harvard, Berkeley, and Pittsburgh—it is now possible to obtain a business doctorate with a major in social issues. Students at business schools located in small towns and rural areas, such as most of the land grant universities, are not faced with problems of pollution, the employment of blacks, or urban transportation as they walk out of their classrooms. Hence rural schools are further behind in acknowledging these new issues and attempting honestly to address them.

A traditional and appropriate role of the university is to transmit the best elements of a culture, and also to be a critic of that culture. One of the university's major concerns has therefore always been values and philosophy. A university can hardly claim to be a university if it does not encourage its students to probe their own values and goals and those of their society. If a business school restricts itself to passing on the tools and techniques of achieving material success and neglects this larger and more important role, it aids society little more than does a barber college.

THE MALAISE OF AMERICAN SOCIETY

A generalized feeling of confusion, powerlessness, and frustration has swept America in recent years. It is a malaise that stems both from the widening gap between the American promise and reality and from shifting values. According to a prestigious group of corporate executives and government, civic, and religious leaders of the National Urban Coalition, the national ideal is a country where every American "gets an equal chance to perform, where a job exists for everyone who wants one, where health care and personal safety are assured, where we live in harmony with each other, and where each of us has a decent place to live."[15] In sharp and embarrassing contrast stands the national reality, according to these same leaders. The cities are in trouble, poverty continues in the midst of wealth, unemployment is high, malnutrition is widespread, injustice exists, and tensions endure. "In sum, we know that our society is not functioning the way it is supposed to."

Shifting attitudes affect more than just the business firm, although here we are primarily concerned with the way changing attitudes and values of the larger society help us to understand the current challenges to the values of the corporation. Change has been so rapid in recent years that it has been

---

[15] *The National Urban Coalition Counterbudget*, ed. R. S. Benson and Harold Wolman (New York: Praeger, 1971), p. xiii.

extremely difficult or even impossible to cope with, whether as an individual or as an organization. Confidence in our institutions and our way of life has been shaken. Pinpointing the sources of confusion may help us to find our way. In the material that follows, we will attempt to spell out some of the changes that have affected all our institutions—including the business firm.

The Inadequacy of Institutions

As we pointed out early in this chapter, confidence in our institutions has dropped dramatically in the past few years. In the 1950s and the early 1960s, Americans felt a moral superiority over other nations and had confidence in their own leadership. We were successful, and we knew it. We exhorted other peoples to follow our example of democracy, free enterprise, and freedom, and our foreign aid program was designed to further these convictions. Now, in the wake of Watergate, the ITT manipulations, influence peddling, and more, these basic values and the institutions that embody them are seen by many Americans as being narrow, self-centered, competitive, interested largely in their own survival and growth, and thus not deserving of unswerving loyalty. Once institutions are seen as no longer working for the best interests of the majority of the people they lose support, their goals come into question, and their very legitimacy begins to erode. Some people will even advocate dismantling them.

In spite of loss of confidence in them, American institutions, especially government, business, and the schools, are still the major centers of power in our society. Herbert Marcuse, a long-time critic of these institutions, a decade ago articulated what increasing numbers of citizens are beginning to feel: that these institutions use their power to pursue their own narrow self-interest, and that that power at times is considerable and could even be called "totalitarian." Marcuse explains that "totalitarian" is "not only a terroristic political coordination of society, but also a non-terroristic economic-technical coordination which operates through the manipulation of needs by vested interests."[16] This sort of unresponsive, self-seeking use of power has been evident not only in the marketplace, but in political elections and teacher-school board conflicts. The self-interest of institutions without a counterbalancing sense of the needs of the larger society has been seen often enough by Americans to call into question these very institutions.

Let us look first briefly at the effectiveness of economic institutions in the international arena. From the perspective of developing peoples, the self-seeking and injustices are seen in a sharper light. International Telephone and Telegraph ran an advertisement recently to defend itself

---

[16]Herbert Marcuse, *One Dimensional Man: Studies in the Ideology of Advanced Industrial Society* (Boston: Beacon Press, 1964), p. 3.

against the charge that it was exporting jobs, which would hurt American labor and the American ecnomy. ITT boasted that it had a net return from foreign investments of $332 million in 1972; these are the returns that came back to the United States after deducting any outflow of funds for new investments. The company went on to say that of the $180 million newly invested in the same year, "half of these dollars were reinvested in the countries in which they were developed. The other half were fresh funds borrowed abroad."[17] ITT's ad confirms the accusations of the New Left that American multinational firms tend to exploit developing countries in the sense that these firms take far more dollars out of a developing country in profits than they bring in via investments. Moreover, what help they provide the host country in the way of paychecks and job skills is secondary to their main goal of bringing more dollars home to what is already the wealthiest country in the world.

Even though per capita income in the United States is many times that of developing countries, there is still a net flow of capital from the poorer countries to the richer countries. This is true even when the relatively small and declining dollars of American foreign aid are taken into account. John F. Kennedy pointed out how in one year, 1960, the capital inflow from underdeveloped countries to the United States was $1,300 million, while the capital outflow from the United States to these same countries was $200 million.[18] At the 1974 GM Conference on Areas of Public Concern, Chairman of the Board Thomas A. Murphy cited similar figures, showing that GM's foreign operations, rather than being a drain on the American economy, had since 1946 resulted in a net inflow of $15 billion.[19] In a discussion after his presentation, Mr. Murphy, a sensitive and knowledgeable executive, admitted to the author that this inflow from poorer nations was a "two-edged sword." Although it improves the United States economy and is a stimulus to business, Murphy recognized that it is a drain of much-needed capital from poorer peoples.

The private investors, the multinational corporations that seek to begin operations in another country look for political stability, local banks willing to lend, and a potential work force that is willing and trainable. They prefer

---

[17]*Newsweek,* November 26, 1973, pp. 12-13. Peter Gabriel, "MNCs in the Third World: Is Conflict Inevitable?" *Harvard Business Review,* 50 (July-August 1972), urges multinational management to be more aware of local needs. For a more recent and detailed treatment of these issues, see Richard J. Barnet and Ronald Muller, *Global Reach: The Power of the Multinational Corporations* (New York: Simon and Schuster, 1975).

[18]Andrew Gunder Frank, "On the Mechanisms of Imperialism: The Case of Brazil," in *The Radical Attack on Business,* ed. Charles Perrow (New York: Harcourt Brace Jovanovich, 1972), p. 99.

[19]Thomas A. Murphy, "The Worldwide Corporation: An Economic Catalyst," in *General Motors Corporation 1974 Report on Progress in Areas of Public Concern* (Warren, Mich.: GM Technical Center, 1974), p. 8.

a society in which the government can guarantee law and order and a sympathetic environment. Brazil, for example, has received billions in foreign investments in recent years, and its per capita income is going up rapidly. But that increased income is going largely to a small minority of the already wealthy, and the very poor benefit hardly at all. In the period during which the Brazilian GNP has increased by 25 percent, the wealthiest 20 percent of the people received 50 percent of that increase, while the poorest 20 percent received but 5 percent.[20] Even Brazilians who have jobs work at wages a fraction of what they would receive in the United States, and Brazilian law forbids them to strike. Brazil is ruled by a right-wing military dictatorship that has an expressed goal of bringing in more foreign investment and of keeping the country stable, even if that be at the expense of citizens' rights.

For years, Litton Industries had been unable to negotiate a contract with Greece to aid national development. Then came the military coup in 1967, and the rightist military dictators *invited* the company in.[21] Litton could help the new government gain legitimacy in Washington, and also worked well with a government much like its primary customer, the Pentagon. The military government of Greece had a clear chain of command; there were no conflicting and uncertain interests to be considered. In a military dictatorship, it is obvious where the power lies. It is not surprising that a corporation prefers to operate in a stable, law and order, rightist, dictatorial type of society—precisely the kind of society American citizens would find intolerable. Working cooperatively with private business interests, the American government itself has for decades been helping to "stabilize" most of the Latin American countries by means of the aid, loans, and support it has given rightist military regimes that deny individual freedoms. Chile, when it had a freely elected leftist government, was denied American aid and loans. After the military dictatorship took over, aid flowed freely. Chile, Brazil, Bolivia, Uruguay, and a number of other Latin American countries not long ago had free, elected governments. With encouragement from the American government and from American business interests, these countries now have rightist military dictatorships.

From the perspective of the developing nations, this support for right-wing military dictatorships, plus the flow of dollars out of their poorer economies, often appears to be an unjust and intolerable burden. Frantz Fanon, the French-educated psychiatrist, is one of the best-known advocates of developing peoples' taking control of their own economic systems, and force if necessary.[22] Severely critical of Western nations, he urges

---

[20]Lecture of World Bank Officer, Wayne State University, Detroit, November 1973.

[21]David Harowitz and Reese Erlich, "Litton Industries: Proving Poverty Pays," in Perrow, *op. cit.,* pp. 48-54.

[22]Frantz Fanon, *The Wretched of the Earth: The Handbook for the Black Revolution* (New York: Grove Press, 1968).

poorer nations to use violence and revolution to obtain self-determination. It is sobering to read this distinguished black psychiatrist's analysis of exploitation, and his advocacy of violence and revolution to right it. Fanon's opinion of the corporation as an exploiter of the poor is held in the United States today by a small but growing number of people. The Port Huron Statement of Students for a Democratic Society sounded shrill and revolutionary when it was first published in 1962. It pointed to men who "still tolerate meaningless work and idleness. When two-thirds of mankind suffers undernourishment, our own upper classes revel amidst superfluous abundance."[23] This attitude is corroborated by World Bank President Robert McNamara when he says that the wheat the United States sold to Russia was used to feed Russian livestock and that the sale left our reserves so depleted we could not aid the tens of thousands who were starving because of poor crops in sub-Saharan Africa. It is no longer merely radical youth who recognize the injustices in our social system and institutions; average citizens have a growing conviction that the enlightened self-interest of the corporation and its sister institutions does not always work to their best interests.

Lack of Satisfaction

People look to their roles and work within a society for satisfaction and fulfillment. Satisfaction generally comes from raising a family, from doing a job well, from contributing to the success, growth, and happiness of people. This fulfillment, this feeling that one's life is worthwhile, gives a person not only satisfaction but also renewed motivation to direct his or her energies to the unfinished work. Industrial society demands specialization of task and interchangeability of personnel. Because the industrial bureaucracy is designed to maximize efficiency, the hierarchical organization thus exacts "complete loyalty from men and reduces them to utterly dependent and depersonalized cogs in a machine."[24] As work becomes segmented and depersonalized, much of the joy of success is taken away from the individual. Workers rarely produce the finished good themselves; they perform but one small portion of the process because of the lower cost of specialization of labor. The large corporation and automation further this segmenting of the job and the resulting distance between the individual worker and the finished product.

As a result, in contemporary industrial society something that "is vital and essential for human life is left out, neglected, suppressed and repressed."[25] Sociologists and Marxists call this vacuum "alienation";

---

[23]See Perrow, *op. cit.,* pp. 10-18.

[24]Charles H. Anderson, *Toward a New Sociology* (Homewood, Ill.: Dorsey, 1971), pp. 178-84.

[25]Walter A. Weisskopf, *Alienation and Economics* (New York: Dutton, 1971), p. 16.

theologians call it "estrangement." The purposes of industrial society—production and growth—take precedence over the goals of the person. Whenever nonhuman objectives are valued over persons, isolation, loneliness, and alienation result. Charles Reich in his popular *Greening of America* sees the origin of these problems in "Consciousness I's" emphasis on production, only slighted amended by the social legislation stemming from what he calls "Consciousness II"—epitomized by the liberal and the New Deal. Although Con II persons try to modify the harsh production orientation of Con I, they are still fundamentally antipopulist and antidemocratic and remain caught up in power, success, status, acceptance, popularity, achievement, reward, and the rational, competent mind.[26]

According to Reich, all this has brought on a third state of consciousness that is a product of two interacting forces. The first is a promise of life made to all Americans by "our affluence, technology, liberation and ideals,"; the second is the simultaneous threat to that promise posed by "everything from neon ugliness to boring jobs." Even though we have science, technology, and affluence, life seems even less fulfilling. Our expectations have been raised by politicians and advertising only to be dashed by reality. In the very act of accumulating wealth and developing a sophisticated technology, we have lost a basic sense of achieving and contributing to something worthwhile. We have emphasized material goods and wealth more than we have the person. This tension is one of the causes of the "career crises" we hear about so often (see Chapter 3). People who are by all external standards successful drop out of highly paid managerial jobs in order to retire to a farm or work at some craft.[27] Dissatisfaction and alienation seem to be as common among successful executives as they are on the assembly line. Meaningful work is important for all those who work, whether with their hands or their minds. It is ironic that as our personal incomes and the number of material goods we possess increase, our work and our very lives seem to offer less and less satisfaction and fulfillment.

The Loss of a Sense of Community

One of the most basic human needs is to share one's joys, problems, and aspirations with others. Our deep-rooted attitudes of individualism and enlightened self-interest, although supportive of and perhaps even necessary for a free enterprise economic system, nevertheless run contrary to the need for community. Our social system, responding to peoples' material wants and the resulting needs of the economic system, has valued the person who

[26]Charles Reich, *The Greening of America* (New York: Random House, 1970).

[27]For example, "The Failure of the Successful," *The New York Times,* June 3, 1973, sec. E, p. 11.

is mobile, energetic, creative, ambitious, and willing to undertake the novel and risky in the hope of great gain. This mobile, ambitious sort of person was attracted to the New World and has thrived here in succeeding generations. We as a society, however, have rarely acknowledged the negative qualities of that same sort of person. Granted the New World gained and encouraged the energetic and the daring, it also gained more than its share of "the rootless, the unscrupulous, those who value money over relationships, and those who put self-aggrandizement ahead of love and loyalty." It is even more critical that we gained many people who, "when faced with a difficult situation, tended to chuck the whole thing and flee to a new environment."[28] The same qualities that we value so highly—mobility and willingness to risk—encourage us to flee the difficult situation, in the hope of leaving our problems behind when we begin again. We have all seen the lives and careers that have been shattered when some person walks out—whether it be on a firm, a group of friends, or a marriage. It is easy to escape long-term responsibility in the tolerant, freedom-loving United States, if one has a mind to do so.

According to the critic Philip Slater, American culture has thwarted some of the most basic human drives toward community, engagement, and dependence. Although these drives toward trust and sharing are actually secondary needs, their almost total frustration and negation in American culture results in a sharp feeling of lack. The needs then tend to take on a disproportionate focus; they become primary. When the need for community is met, we take it for granted; when it is absent, it becomes painful and disruptive for a society. Many younger people have now begun to put more emphasis on such basic needs, as we have seen earlier. Philip Slater, in recounting these new movements and values, calls the two sets of values the "old culture" and the "new culture." He sees the two as described by a large number of polarities. The old culture, says Slater,

> . . . tends to give preference to property rights over personal rights, technological requirements over human needs, competition over cooperation, violence over sexuality, concentration over distribution, the producer over the consumer, means over ends, secrecy over openness, social forms over personal expression, striving over gratification, Oedipal love over communal love.[29]

The values that are more prevalent among younger people tend to reverse these priorities, although it is also quite clear that these "new culture"

---

[28]Philip Slater, *The Pursuit of Loneliness: American Culture at the Breaking Point* (Boston: Beacon Press, 1970), p. 14. On the need for community, see also Weisskopf, *op. cit.,* pp. 16, 52-55, 190, and Anderson, *op. cit.,* pp. 6-10.

[29]*Ibid.,* p. 100.

values are held by only a small number of middle-class, educated, young Americans.

The Limits of a Finite World

In the past few years it has become increasingly apparent that economic growth is not an unmitigated good. If growth threatens a society, then it can hardly serve as that society's unqualified goal. Almost all nations now face an anguishing dilemma: the goal of economic policy is growth, yet growth cannot be sustained because of the finite resources of the world.[30]

In the early 1970s, a team of MIT systems analysts set out to investigate how present rates of development projected into the future would affect the world. They published their findings in what has become one of the most significant books of the decade, *The Limits to Growth.*[31] The team studied global development in five areas: population increase, agricultural production, depletion of nonrenewable resources, industrial output, and pollution of the environment and concluded that present rates of exponential growth cannot continue. Within a few generations the system (the world, in this case) will break down because of starvation due to lack of food for an increasing population; exhaustion of basic and essential resources such as petroleum, iron ore, and copper due to accelerating industrialization; or fatal deterioration of the environment due to increasing industrialization in all countries. It is clear that these projections are interdependent. For example, if population and industrialization continue to increase at present rates, malnutrition and exhaustion of resources and the environment will come rather quickly. If pollution and population are controlled but industrialization continues, we still face chaos when resources are gone, although it will take a bit longer.

The United States, with but 6 percent of the world's population, consumes 30 to 40 percent of most of the earth's nonrenewable resources.[32] At this rate, we strain the world's resources; moreover, if the developing nations were at our stage of development, there would not be enough resources to go around. Are we now to tell the peoples of Asia and Africa that there are not enough resources, that they had better remain at their present stage of development? Will these peoples not look to the developed countries and charge that we are using far more of the earth's goods than

[30]Hazel Henderson, "The Entropy State," *The Planning Review,* 2 (April-May 1974). See *The Wall Street Journal* editorial, "Growth and Social Progress," for a call to distinguish between "those components of the Gross National Product that indicate progress and those that simply record increased output," (March 27, 1974), p. 12.

[31]Donella H. Meadows, Dennis L. Meadows, Jorgen Randers, and William W. Behrens III, *The Limits to Growth* (New York: Signet Books, 1972).

[32]*Ibid.,* pp. 64-67.

we have a right to? The presuppositions and some details of *The Limits to Growth* model have been heatedly debated, but now almost all who have looked into the matter agree that a simplistic national goal of growth is not only unwise but self-defeating in the long run.

Benefiting from the controversy and criticism surrounding *The Limits to Growth* is *Mankind at the Turning Point: The Second Report of the Club of Rome.*[33] The more recent study refines the earlier gross predictions by geographical and developmental regions. It points out how countries like the United States use more than their share of the earth's resources, place a far heavier burden on the ecosystem, and hence bear greater responsibility for limiting growth. This is not true of the developing countries, where growth is still necessary to meet minimal needs. By treating the conditions and needs of various regions separately, this new study focuses on human needs and places human values in a more central position.

It is quite clear that we have only one earth.[34] If that earth is exhausted and polluted in our lifetime, we will have left our children little more than devastation. These new and unsettling realizations cut to the core of much of what we Americans, and American business especially, have considered essential to progress. The corporation, whether operating at home or abroad, as yet seems to be little aware of these limits on production and consumption. In contrast, increasing personal income and accumulation of material goods are now not only questioned as intelligent and worthwhile personal goals, but are even seen as goals which, without major modification, will lead to our destruction as a society and a people. Such harsh new realities cast individualism and the consumer ethic into serious doubt as values we can any longer afford to hold. The physical finiteness of the universe poses an absolute constraint on our national goals and thus also affects our personal values.

Obsolete Values

One of the major themes of this book has been the erosion of accepted values that undergird our free enterprise system: individualism, the Protestant ethic, and delayed gratification. The lack of goals in business schools is an example of this erosion. When a society's basic values dissolve, its members are left without purpose and guidelines for their lives. As we have seen, these values have not always been very clearly articulated, but they have

---

[33]Mihajlo Mesarovic and Eduard Pestel, *Mankind at the Turning Point: The Second Report of the Club of Rome* (New York: Dutton, 1975). For a summary of these issues and the literature, see Hazel Henderson, "Ecologists Versus Economists," *Harvard Business Review,* 51 (July-August 1973).

[34]See the excellent book by that title, *Only One Earth,* by Barbara Ward and Rene Dubos (New York: Norton, 1972), esp. chaps. 8 and 9.

been the foundation for marketplace activities and even for an entire way of life.

In his assessment of the values and the lack thereof that undergird the American business system, John J. Corson says that there is no longer a consensus on goals and values, and that "This crisis of values is the root cause of the insecurity, frustration, resentment, and unrest that have been painfully prevalent."[35] A large part of this difficulty stems from the inability or unwillingness of the American people to adjust and adapt their values, in spite of their vaunted flexibility and pragmatism. For whatever reason, Americans find it difficult to cast aside obsolete values and to eliminate or restructure institutions that no longer serve good purposes.

To a large extent, the current business ideology is undoubtedly firmly held because it has developed as a legitimation of personally held wealth and social class. It therefore has firm roots in social institutions and the social system; and such institutions are notoriously inflexible. Maynard Seider examined current business values and ideology by means of a content analysis of executives' speeches.[36] He then looked for the origins of these values, and argued that ideology develops in the individual through a socialization process. Business ideology is largely derived from the values of the upper class, and these in turn are handed down through "prep schools, Ivy League colleges, fraternities, and social clubs." There thus exists "one metropolitan upper class with a common cultural tradition, consciousness of kind, and 'we' feeling of solidarity." It is a nationally held set of values, developed largely to legitimate the position of the wealthy and powerful.

In a democracy we hold that the judgment of the needs and values of a society must be made by the people themselves. Even if there were a way to circumvent the disproportionate influence that powerful individuals, institutions, the media, and advertising have on us, in our society it is still difficult to carry out reforms directed toward the poor: "A society mainly motivated by financial self-interest has great difficulty carrying out altruistic measures; funds destined for the poor and disadvantaged seem to stick too easily to the fingers of those who are supposed to administer such funds."[37] Moreover, democracy based on majority rule finds itself particularly inept when faced with trying to help minorities. In the United States for the first time in history, the poor, the disadvantaged, and the segregated are in the minority. This makes their needs even more obvious, yet also more difficult for the system to address.

No amount of philosophical discussion can provide a society with its

[35]John J. Corson, Business in the Humane Society (New York: McGraw-Hill, 1971), pp. 265-74.

[36]Maynard S. Seider, "American Big Business Ideology: A Content Analysis of Executive Speeches," American Sociological Review, 39 (December 1974), 802-15.

[37]Weisskopf, op. cit., p. 15.

values; the best that theoretical discussion can do is help probe and clarify. And on a deeper level, many Americans are afraid we have been indoctrinated and manipulated to our core. They see the structures of our various institutions as interlocking and supporting one another. The schools build habits of being on time, responding to directions, and working for outside, extrinsic rewards (grades, promotions) that prepare us to fit into corporate life, whether on the assembly line or in the executive offices. Herbert Marcuse points out some of the multitude of technical devices our society has developed to indoctrinate and to blunt dissidence: "'engineers of the soul,' 'head shrinkers,' 'scientific management,' 'science of consumption.'"[38] Given the great power of the media, of advertising, and of the schools, it can be difficult or impossible for an individual to develop values that would keep a person in harmony with nature and with other men. Marcuse holds liberation and peace in high regard, and sees little opportunity for these values to develop within our present institutions.

An Unpredictable Future

In the wake of the rapid changes in values we have all experienced, the future becomes even more uncertain. Americans have been characteristically optimistic; we have looked to the future with a certainty that things will get better. For large numbers of people, this is now no longer true. Both personal and national self-confidence stem from a conviction of purpose and goals. Those concrete goals are no longer so clear. Change has come so rapidly that it is impossible for any one of us to know what sort of lives our children's children will have. We don't know where or how they will live or what sort of careers they will have. In more stable societies, a child's future was pretty well determined by the role of the parents in that society. This sort of continuity gives individuals and society equilibrium, security, and self-esteem.

Most of the larger problems facing American society (pollution, dwindling resources, unequal distribution of goods, population growth) are problems that affect the entire world. When society is stable, it is far easier to understand "the common good."[39] When the larger society is changing rapidly, coupled with the fact that individuals and nations are increasingly interdependent, it is far more difficult to cast a steady look at society in order to probe basic problems and make policy changes. Working and sacrificing for the "common good" and for future generations is far more difficult when I have only a vague idea of the type of society that will exist twenty-five years from now. The rapidity of change is evident even in

---

[38]Marcuse, *op. cit.,* pp. 6, 234.
[39]See "Central Influences on American Life," *The Wall Street Journal,* April 4, 1972, 8.

the once visionary works of Charles Reich and Theodore Roszak, which were hailed just a few years ago as being in the forefront of new currents of thought. A rereading today shows us that in many respects they are already out of date.

The problem of diminishing resources places further constraints on our notions of goals and "the good life." Petroleum, copper, and other resources are just not available in sufficient quantities to enable us to hold out as a goal for developing countries the standards of living that we enjoy. Furthermore, the finiteness of these resources forces us to reassess our own goals of unlimited growth. Like it or not, we are at an end of the "cowboy economy"—rapid growth coupled with much waste. The earth we live on is finite, and we cannot afford to pollute it or destroy it. Regardless of our uncertainty about the future, we can predict that if we do not alter our course, we will undoubtedly leave to future generations a legacy of capital earned from investments, pollution, used-up resources, and tottering institutions.

To delay gratification is what some call an "old culture" virtue. Eyes on the future, we save for children or for a rainy day. We know our forebears knew that if they saved and invested today, they would reap much greater benefits tomorrow. This is the postponed life: the tendency not to look for present satisfaction, but to plan for it in the future. Being future-centered is a mark of the older generation. Given the rapid change and the fact that it seems increasingly difficult to anticipate or plan for the future, it is not surprising that young people are more concerned with now. They look to present job and life satisfactions. They are impatient with those who tell them to work hard now for the sake of a cloudy and uncertain future.

The malaise and pessimism of present-day America is perhaps best articulated in Robert Heilbroner's new book, *The Human Prospect*.[40] Heilbroner describes himself as a liberal and an optimist by nature, yet he has serious doubts about the ability of mankind to survive for most of the reasons we have discussed—urban decay and distrust, world food shortages, pollution, dwindling resources, nuclear holocaust. In his view, present attitudes and trends indicate that civilization is rapidly heading for chaos and its own destruction. He also sees that neither of the two major socioeconomic systems, capitalism and socialism, are capable of addressing the problems and altering the direction toward suicide. He suggests that the road ahead calls for stronger leadership, and thus more authoritarian governments. In the future, he sees the prospect of convulsive change: wars, starvation, and environmental disasters, all coming because of man's inability to cope with his own world. Heilbroner feels that if there is any possibility for man to survive, it will be by living a very different kind of life based on new values and goals.

[40]Robert Heilbroner, *The Human Prospect* (New York: Norton, 1974).

PATCHWORK AND COMPROMISE:
THE MODERATE REFORMERS

In the wake of this lessening of confidence in the corporation and its leaders, there have been a number of efforts to reform the business system in order to make it more effective and responsive. To the purist, who sees the system as intrinsically corrupting, these efforts will seem half-hearted and ineffective. But pragmatism has been and probably will continue to be the "American way"; progress comes in short, immediate, compromising steps. In this vein, organizations have been formed and books written to further the public interest.

A hero to consumer advocates and an ogre to some business people, Ralph Nader epitomizes the new movement. Nader was born in 1934, nine years after his parents emigrated to the United States from Lebanon. The Nader family lived in Winsted, Connecticut, where they made it a habit to discuss values and public issues at the dinner table,[41] and as a boy Ralph was considered peculiar because he enjoyed reading the *Congressional Record.* He graduated from Princeton Phi Beta Kappa, and then went on to obtain a Harvard law degree. He is highly critical of the latter institution, and maintains that it is designed to produce cogs for the corporate legal machinery.

Nader was a lone Don Quixote in the late 1960s; his main attack was centered on the auto industry. His impressively documented challenge to the safety of the American automobile, *Unsafe at Any Speed,*[42] had a profound influence on the auto industry and the auto-buying public, and thrust its author into national prominence. In this book Nader accused the auto industry of "over-emphasis on style, disregard for the safety of the driver and passengers, and engineering stagnation."[43] In addition, Nader testified before congressional committees. In the now well-known story, General Motors ordered an investigation of Ralph Nader to determine his credentials for judging the safety or lack of safety of automobiles that seems to have gone beyond looking into his professional qualifications. James Roche, then president of General Motors, apologized to Nader publicly before Senator Abraham Ribicoff's traffic-safety subcommittee. Nader sued General Motors for $26 million for invasion of privacy; General Motors settled out of court for $450,000. This sum gave Nader the means to enlarge his campaign for the consumer.

Nader lives a devoted and frugal life. He lives in a small and poorly

---

[41]Richard Armstrong, "The Passion That Rules Ralph Nader," *Fortune,* 83 (May 1971), 144.

[42]Ralph Nader, *Unsafe at Any Speed* (New York: Pocket Books, 1966).

[43]See S. Prakash Sethi, "General Motors' Nadir, Ralph Nader," in his *Up Against the Corporate Wall,* 2nd ed. (Englewood Cliffs, N.J.: Prentice-Hall, 1974), p. 374.

furnished apartment, and operates out of a cramped ofice. His sources of income from books, speaking fees, and contributions are all used to support his work and not himself. This famous corporate gadfly loves his work, and finds tremendous energy for it; he often works sixteen or eighteen hours a day. He sees his job as that of transferring power from the managerial suites to consumers, employees, and stockholders. This rather democratic intent is sometimes misunderstood by those who hear him when he puts it more graphically as trying "to smash corporate power."

Much of Nader's vehemence comes from his conviction that he is pressing the case of the defenseless consumer or employee. He is convinced that the crimes committed in boardrooms or managerial offices are far more serious than petty theft. Bribery, changing test data, and financial manipulation are far more serious crimes in a society that is so totally dependent on large institutions. Even though these crimes undermine the very credibility of the institutions, they most often go unpunished and even unnoticed by many of the public. Nader, like many others, feels that stiff prison sentences in place of token fines would be a more effective deterrent to unethical business practices.

Ralph Nader worked essentially alone from 1965 to 1968. In that summer he was joined by a group of law students, and this pattern has continued and expanded up to the present. The first summer group did a study of the Federal Trade Commission, and in 1969 a larger group expanded their efforts. From their Center for the Study of Responsive Law later sprang Campaign GM, Public Interest Research Group, The Center for Science in the Public Interest, and a number of other parallel organizations. The model is the same: do your homework carefully, write up the results clearly and convincingly, and get the message out to those who can do something about it. Nader's Raiders appear before congressional committees and/or release their findings to the press. Their work is generally respected because it is thorough and well documented.

Project on Corporate Responsibility

In addition to Campaign GM, the Project on Corporate Responsibility is also a Nader-inspired group pressing for corporate reform. Its vehicle is the stockholder resolution presented and voted on at the annual stockholders' meeting. Until a few years ago, annual meetings were largely a formality. Few substantive issues were ever presented to stockholders for decision, in spite of corporate theory that tells us management is responsible to the board of directors, and the board in turn is responsible to the stockholders. Even a cursory investigation shows how line management effectively controls the corporation. Management, especially the chief operating officer, generally nominates the members of the board. Since management is responsible to the board, both management and the board are thus self-perpetuating. Stockholders in large corporations are so scattered and unorganized that they rarely exert any effective control over management. So management, often with little ownership, is effectively responsible to no one but itself. In being responsible to no one, the corporation is "endocratic,"[44] and hence "these instrumentalities of tremendous power have the slenderest claim of legitimacy."[45] In attempting to bring decision-making power and hence control back to the stockholders, these activist groups are thus giving the corporation a greater claim to legitimacy.

Issues that commonly came up during 1975 stockholders' meetings were information on strip-mining activities from various mining companies, limitations on corporate political activities, minority employment, and a variety of other questions. In 1974, Gulf Oil and Minnesota Mining and Manufacturing agreed not to oppose a shareholder proposal to prohibit corporate political contributions. On the other hand, Phillips Petroleum and Goodyear Tire and Rubber, also guilty of illegal political contributions in the past, still opposed the shareholder resolutions. Church groups owning stock have been successful in encouraging various companies to release data on the number of minority and women employees. In 1974 General Motors, Xerox, Sears, Kraftco, and Polaroid released enough information that the issue was withdrawn from their stockholder proxy statements.

Activist groups feel that their efforts are successful when they provide publicity for these issues and thus bring them to the attention of top management. They feel they are doubly successful when the proposal obtains as much as 3 percent of the stockholders' votes. Most stockholders, especially pension funds, trust funds, university endowments, and other institutional investors, take the conservative path of least resistance and habitually vote with management. A failure to vote is also considered a vote for management, of course. Nevertheless, in 1973 Harvard University voted its 173,000 shares of Caterpillar Tractor stock in favor of a stockholder resolution calling for fuller information on the company's activities and employment policies in South Africa.[46] It was the third time Harvard had opposed management. Yale University also voted for the Caterpillar shareholder resolution, for a General Electric shareholder resolution calling for disclosure of details of the company's operations in South Africa, and for a

---

[44]Eugene V. Rostow, "To Whom and for What Ends Is Corporate Management Responsible," in *The Corporation in Modern Society,* ed. Edward S. Mason (Cambridge, Mass.: Harvard University Press, 1959), p. 47.

[45]A. A. Berle, *Economic Power and the Free Society* (New York: Fund for the Republic, 1957), p. 16.

[46]*Boston Globe,* April 15, 1973.

shareholder resolution asking Phillips Petroleum to terminate activities in the African states of Namibia and Angola. Yale, along with Oberlin College, voted their shares for a Xerox shareholder resolution calling for an amendment to the bylaws that would allow shareholder nominations for the board of directors, along with management's proposed slate. The Caterpillar resolution received a surprising total of 8.6 percent of the votes, and the company proceeded to publish a disclosure of their operations that has become a model for other firms. The Phillips Petroleum resolution calling for withdrawal from Namibia received a 4.2 percent affirmative vote and another 4.8 percent abstention.[47]

In response to the accusation that activists represent but a minority and are hence merely troublemakers, Philip W. Moore, the executive director of the Project on Corporate Responsibility, says that such groups survive only when they have substantial support from the larger society:

> The role of activists is to set forth options for society. Activism requires forceful and articulate presentations of these opinions for the public. Only those activist options which generate major popular support will ever have any impact.[48]

Moore acknowledges that individual shareholder resolutions will not gain a majority vote, yet he sees his work as fulfilling a vital social purpose: "We know that the specific options will not be adopted, but we also know that the options point to the direction of changes."[49] The record shows that management does take these stockholder challenges seriously. Activists are becoming more sophisticated; in 1974 they negotiated with corporate leaders to achieve the results they wanted. Moreover, they have been surprisingly successful, even in the early days. Several years ago, Campaign GM proposed that General Motors have a black person on their board of directors, and that resolution received only a small percentage of the votes. Nevertheless, the Reverend Leon Sullivan was appointed to the board shortly thereafter. Moreover, Leon Sullivan has been no token black; he has pushed for more black-owned dealerships and for better promotion opportunities for blacks, and he has been able to point to significant progress on these issues.[50]

---

[47]John G. Simon, "Yale's First Year as a Socially Responsible Stockholder," *Yale Alumni Magazine* (February 1974), pp. 17-23.

[48]"Corporate Social Reform: An Activist's Viewpoint," in *The Unstable Ground: Corporate Social Policy in a Dynamic Society,* ed. S. Prakash Sethi. (Los Angeles: Melville, 1974), p. 49.

[49]*Ibid.,* p. 50.

[50]"The Moral Power of Shareholders," *Business Week,* May 1, 1971, pp. 76-78; "Activists Step Up Their Annual Attacks," *Business Week,* March 31, 1973, pp. 76-78; "Proxy Statements Feel the Watergate Ripples," *Business Week,* April 13, 1974, p. 89.

The purpose of the firm, according to Moore, is to provide material goods and services for society. Nevertheless, and probably as important, the details of that role are also determined by the larger society. No group as significant as business firms can define themselves and their purpose apart from the larger society. Shareholder resolutions are being presented in increasing numbers at annual meetings. In 1975, shareholders in more than sixty firms found public interest issues on their proxy ballots. Institutions such as foundations and university endowments, which hold millions of dollars in stock in individual firms and hence have considerable power, found it increasingly difficult to do the necessary homework for each of these complicated issues.

In the fall of 1972 three of the major foundations (Ford, Rockefeller, and Carnegie), and some of the better-endowed private universities (Harvard, Princeton, and Stanford) established the Investor Responsibility Research Center in Washington, D. C. The purpose of the center is to investigate in depth each of the shareholder resolutions presented on the proxy statements and at the annual meetings. The center's brief background reports are written after consulting with the advocacy group and the company involved. The report presents both sides and tries to present the issues in some detail, but makes no recommendations. The center feels that its credibility with activists, companies, and institutional investors rests on its ability to treat the issues fully, honestly, and objectively. The final decision as to how to vote the stock rests with the stockholder.

General Motors: Metamorphosis of a Giant

The largest corporation in the world, General Motors, has generally been among the first targets of activist groups. GM's annual gross sales are larger than the total gross national product of countries the size of Norway, Austria, Yugoslavia, or Pakistan, so its influence is felt throughout the world. Moreover, because of its sheer size and financial power, its actions are significant for all of industry.

Not many years ago, General Motors reacted with hostility to criticisms and suggestions coming from activist groups. The confrontation with and harassment of Ralph Nader attest to this attitude. In the spring of 1971, James M. Roche, then chairman of the company, delivered a strong attack on corporate critics.[51] He accused activists of threatening the entire free enterprise system, directing doubt and disparagement toward business, business people, and America itself; and he charged them with helping to create an unfairly negative image of business. Roche said that these critics set out to sow suspicion and disharmony, and showed no appreciation of

---

[51] *The Wall Street Journal,* March 26, 1971, p. 4; also *The New York Times,* April 11, 1971, Sec. F, p. 12.

how they were adding to the cost of doing business, for each new government regulation on pollution and safety added to the cost of the
automobile. They were attempting to tell business that consumers are not
the best judges of what they want and need. Not to trust to the free choice
of the consumer, according to Roche, is to strike at the very heart of our
system.

From subsequent evidence, Roche's counterattack was the rearguard
action of a dying ideology: business's concern is with business, and it should
not be interfered with by government, consumers, or even stockholders.
Since that time, GM has instituted a policy of purchasing from
minorty-owned vendors and of disclosing figures on minority employment.
It has designated several outside members of its board to serve as a public
policy review committee, and has hired from outside the firm (GM was
becoming excessively inbred because of a policy of always promoting from
within the corporation) four vice-presidents in sensitive and crucial areas:
environment, personnel and development, research, and legal counsel. The
corporation saw the need for obtaining fresh ideas and varying perspectives.

From 1971 to 1974, General Motors sponsored an annual Conference on
Areas of Public Concern. During this entire day of talks, demonstrations,
questions and discussion, the corporation presented to representatives of
institutional investors and selected university people and activists the entire
range of what the firm was doing on public issues. The 1974 conference
featured presentations on GM's worldwide operations, new transportation
vehicles, human resources, and energy resources and conservation.[52]
Models and mockups of various power sources and safety devices were
there to be examined. During this portion of the day, the chairman,
vice-chairman, president, and vice-presidents were on hand for informal
questions and discussion. The corporate officers maintain that for them the
most profitable part of the day is the opportunity to talk informally to the
various interested parties. The two dozen top corporate officers were on
hand for the entire day for questions and discussion.

The Conference on Areas of Public Concern is a public relations effort
(the vice-president for public relations was in charge of the arrangements);
nevertheless, it involves considerable expenditure of corporate time and
money. It focuses the concern of top management on these public issues, a
concern reinforced by the interest, questions, and discussion of the outside
people at the conference. The conference is widely publicized each year, and
so tends to encourage higher expectations for performance on public issues.
It is also one of the extremely rare opportunities for top corporate officers
to have an informal dialog with people who are vitally concerned about

[52]General Motors Corporation 1974 Report on Progress in Areas of Public Concern
(Warren, Mich.: GM Technical Center, 1974).

public policy. In its very sponsorship of this conference, General Motors took the position that a business firm's concern is not exclusively with maximizing profits. Its actions demonstrate that the public indeed judges a business firm on its performance on such issues as product quality and safety, resource and energy conservation, employment and advancement of minorities and women, and the justice of its multinational operations. For the largest corporation in the world, this is a considerable change in attitudes from only a few years ago. General Motors and other large firms also publicize these new criteria when they speak of them in their annual reports and advertisements. They encourage citizens to expect more public concern from the business firm.

The National Affiliation of Concerned
Business Students

Encouraging the dialog out of which they hope will emerge a clearer and more socially acceptable understanding of the role of the business firm is the goal of the National Affiliation of Concerned Business Students, formed by a group of graduate business students at Stanford University in 1970. Since that time, groups of graduate business students have gathered at the major business schools in the United States, some forty national firms have become sponsors, national and local seminars have been held, and research and discussion has been encouraged across the country.

Located in Boston,[53] the national office facilitates planning, research, and discussion. The organization has two major objectives: (1) To promote the development of courses and research on the social role of the corporation; and (2) to contribute to the state of the art of corporate social planning and performance by research and experimentation. The many publications, research projects, symposia, dialogs, and discussions that have been held with the support of NACBS have all furthered the understanding of business people and business students on the appropriate social role of the corporation. Such research and probing discussions are clearly necessary if the actions of the corporation are to regain legitimacy and credibility.

Conferences with business people, business students, faculty, and activists have been held across the country. These conferences aided the state of the art not only by presenting new information on the environment, consumerism, and so on to the selected participants, but also by providing a relaxed forum for members of the business community and business students to speak to each other of values and goals.

---

[53]National Affiliation of Concerned Business Students, 4 Brattle Street, Room 306, Cambridge, Mass. 02138.

A Code of Ethics for Business

A detailed proposal stemming from one of the most carefully done empirical studies of business ethics to date calls for a code of ethics for business. Raymond Baumhart's inquiries of almost two thousand business people revealed that more than two-thirds of them thought a code of ethics would raise the ethical level of business practice. More than three-fourths thought that a code would be welcomed by the business community as a help in defining the limits of acceptable conduct, although an even greater number conceded that such a code would not be easy to enforce.[54] What emerged from Baumhart's study is that most of these business people would like a code of ethics to help them clarify their own ethical values and standards. In many instances, they do not *know* what is ethical, and so feel they need help. More recent cases of illegal political campaign gifts (American Airlines, Phillips Petroleum), using priviledged information for private gain (Texas Gulf Sulfur, Penn-Central Railroad), deducting vacation expenses from expense accounts so as to pay no tax, and so on, have made the problem even more pointed.[55]

Economist Kenneth Arrow has recently also opted for ethical codes. He readily acknowledges that "there are a number of circumstances under which the economic agent should forego profit or other benefits to himself in order to achieve some social goal, especially to avoid a disservice to other individuals."[56] Arrow examines the economic system's social effects and some of its defects: (1) competition is not always sufficiently vigorous; (2) the distribution of income that results from unrestrained profit maximization is very unequal; and (3) it tends to discourage the expression of altruistic motives. More specifically, Arrow assesses various strategies for encouraging more socially responsible behavior: legal regulation, taxes, legal liability, and finally, an ethical code. Arrow argues for a code, especially in cases where the knowledge of seller and buyer is very unequal, such as in purchases of complicated equipment or drugs. He gives a cautious but carefully reasoned and convincing argument for ethical codes for business.

An ethical code is, of course, no substitute for ethical individuals. A code is merely a guideline for those who already possess a basic moral sense. It can help to define and explicate the practical, specific, and detailed implications of this basic morality. But the prior and more important issue

[54]Raymond C. Baumhart, S.J., "How Ethical Are Businessmen?" *Harvard Business Review,* 39 (July-August, 1961), 166-71. See also his *Ethics in Business* (New York: Holt, Rinehart and Winston, 1968).

[55]For additional examples, see "Stiffer Rules for Business Ethics," *Business Week,* March 30, 1974, pp. 87-92.

[56]Kenneth J. Arrow, "Social Responsibility and Economic Efficiency," *Public Policy,* 23 (Summer 1973), 303-17.

remains: the need for additional personal and group reflection on ethical values and principles.

Blocks to Reform: Apathy and Cynicism

In spite of evidence of greater sensitivity and responsiveness on the part of the business firm, there is concurrent evidence of public apathy and even cynicism. The lessened confidence in leaders and institutions; the shortage of food, petroleum, and other natural resources; the growing threat of pollution; the danger of a final nuclear holocaust; and the other more immediate dangers of urban decay, street crime, hijackings, assassinations, and kidnappings have all cast a pall over American optimism. There is a growing feeling that these problems are too big to be solved. For many, the best "solution" seems to be to move to a location where they can isolate themselves from as many of these threats as possible. Although historically there has always been a great deal of apathy in America toward government and other institutions, the present crises have sown added fright and disinterest. The supposed landslide by which Richard Nixon was elected in 1972 was not much more than a third of the electorate, because so many did not bother to vote. In contrast, participation rates in elections in Western Europe "approach and sometimes exceed ninety per cent."[57]

Enlightened self-interest, when faced by seemingly insurmountable challenges, can result in retreat and protecting what one already has. Even groups designed to represent large numbers of citizens in fact represent only a fraction. Gunnar Myrdal charges labor unions with organizing only about one-fourth of all employees. John Gardner's Common Cause and Ralph Nader's Public Citizens Movement are supported mostly by the upper and upper middle classes. There is little broad-based support, especially among blue collar families, for public interest movements or efforts to make our institutions more flexible and responsive. Although the United States is the oldest modern democracy, it also in many ways is quite backward: "In America the nonparticipation of the masses is an inherited and persistent trait. Americans find that natural and, therefore, do not inquire why it is so, how it has come to be so, or how it could be changed."[58] Paradoxically, this lack of participation is even more pronounced with regard to local issues and local elections. The group that would ordinarily be expected to show the greatest communality of interest shows even less participation. The bastion of democracy, the United States, evidences little grass roots interest in reform or even governance.

[57]Gunnar Myrdal, "Mass Passivity in America," *The Center Magazine*, 7, 2 (March-April 1974), p. 72.

[58]*Ibid.*, p. 74.

Perhaps this apathy, and now cynicism, is an unfortunate by-product of an old and weary democracy. Perhaps Americans have tranquilized themselves into an unreal sense of security; we are the wealthiest, strongest, the most creative. The "let George do it" mentality is widespread. Our theory of enlightened self-interest lulls us into thinking that if there is a need, *someone* will see it and take care of it. It is probably someone else's responsibility, so why should I take it upon myself to do it? Such apathy and cynicism on the part of so many Americans is a serious roadblock to rediscovering values and renewing institutions. Most models for renewal are people-centered and focus on the local community. Nevertheless, even in the face of this general apathy, there are still encouraging new attitudes and movements emerging. These will be considered in the last chapter.

CORPORATE RESPONSES TO NEW CHALLENGES

In the face of the mounting criticism and lessening credibility of the last few years, business people and corporations have taken several alternate stances. These options might be classified as follows:

1. *Ignore the challenges.* Criticisms, upheavals, and questioning of major institutions, including the corporation, have taken place previously, and the institutions have always survived. The challenges are temporary. College campuses have already quieted down; there is no longer widespread protest. Society needs these institutions, and it would only detract from more important goals to become engrossed in tangential issues.

2. *Sell capitalism and free enterprise.* Acknowledging that these challenges are profound, gaining wide sympathy, and potentially disruptive, it is best to counterattack. Therefore it is the duty of business to educate people to the great benefits that flow from our free enterprise economic system and to refute charges that other socioeconomic values are in some way superior.

3. *Integrate new values into corporate goals and policy.* Search to find the positive values in the criticisms being leveled, and in the traditional American pragmatic fashion, try to adapt corporate policies and goals to meet the new needs.

Many business people, especially middle managers and entrepreneurs, fall into the first category and choose to ignore the challenges. Although they find the criticisms and lessened credibility unsettling, they quickly dismiss them. They see the attacks as coming from a small group of radicals and intellectuals who have no understanding of how the real world works. The critics do not understand economics, free markets, or business, and hence their criticisms need not be taken seriously.

Misinformation and overstatement does characterize much of what we see on television and read in newspapers about business. Media people tend to have a background in writing and the humanities, rather than in business and the professions.[59] It is also true that business has not been adept in getting its own story told. Moreover, business people who choose to ignore the criticisms do not tend to be reflective people. Their education in, for example, engineering, accounting, or finance has encouraged an objective, analytical examination of their own narrowly conceived task, but has provided them with neither the inclination to look to larger issues nor the tools with which to pursue that inclination.

The option of disregarding the challenges leaves those who take it without new information with which to update their own attitudes and company policies. Furthermore, they are thus ill-equipped to separate the worthwhile from the peripheral in the barrage of criticism coming their way. They are left with static, ossified mental attitudes, with lessened ability to plan ahead and adapt to future needs.

Free Enterprise Education

The second option, selling capitalism and free enterprise, proposes a counterattack. It recognizes the misinformation and overstatement of the media and critics and sets about trying to right the balance. A few years ago, James Roche, then chairman of the board of General Motors, personified this stance when he said that Ralph Nader's accusations against the automakers were undermining the free enterprise system. The classic statement of this position is contained in the memorandum of Lewis F. Powell, Jr., "Attack on the American Free Enterprise System," to the United States Chamber of Commerce.[60] Done at the request of the chamber, this memorandum was originally confidential. Powell wrote it in August 1971, just two months before he was appointed to the Supreme Court.

Powell maintained that the assault on the free enterprise system is broadly based and consistently pursued. In spotlighting the sources of the attack, Powell was not so much concerned with Communists, the New Left, and other extremists as he was disturbed by the criticism coming from "perfectly respectable elements of society: from the college campus, the pulpit, the media, the intellectual and literary journals, the arts and sciences and the politicians." The critics are often articulate and prolific, and the media give their criticisms a wide audience. Ralph Nader, Charles Reich, and others are antagonists who assault "our government, our system of justice and the free enterprise system."

---

[59]See Chet Huntley's comments to this effect in his "Media Antipathy Toward Business," *The Wall Street Journal,* August 7, 1973, p. 10.

[60]"The Powell Memorandum," The United States Chamber of Commerce, Code No. 2900. The memorandum is now available to anyone who writes to the Chamber:

What baffles Powell is "the extent to which the enterprise system tolerates, if not participates, in its own destruction." The campuses and the media are supported by funds generated, via taxes, contributions, or ads, by the business system itself. Powell chastizes executives, boards of directors, and business people who "have responded—if at all—by appeasement, ineptitude and ignoring the problem." He concedes that business people are not well equipped to respond. They have "shown little stomach for hard-nose contest with their critics, and little skill in effective intellectual and philosophical debate."

Powell feels it is a primary responsibility of business executives to defend the free enterprise system, and he proceeds to outline a program of action for these executives. He asks that each firm appoint an executive vice-president in charge of this effort. He urges firms not to contribute funds to universities or programs that tolerate undue criticism of the business system, but rather to give to staffs of scholars, programs, lecture bureaus, and. the preparation of textbooks that will provide a "balance" of views. He asks that firms provide information to a variety of sources, especially the schools. He prods the United States Chamber of Commerce to request specific courses in graduate schools of business to prepare future executives to defend the free enterprise system.

Powell's call to business to defend free enterprise in a planned, systematic way has not gone unheeded. Eaton Corporation has trained 105 executives to tell various public groups the business side of the story.[61] They speak to school classes, clubs, or whatever group invites them on "Business, People and Profits." Recognizing that public confidence in business has dropped dramatically, these Eaton executives try to point out how important it is that a business return an adequate profit. It is an attempt to teach classical economics; the talk, colored placards, and the speakers have all been prepared by public relations people. In a vein seemingly inspired by the Powell memorandum, David Packard, founder of Hewlett-Packard, received wide attention when he called for the dropping of unrestricted gifts to universities.[62] He urged corporations to contribute only to business and professional schools and to scholars and programs sympathetic to American free enterprise, and to withdraw support from those institutions and programs that give haven to critics.

Adherents of this position urge industrialists to make clear to all who will listen the great advantages of our capitalistic system: growing gross national product, higher family and personal incomes, more food and bigger (until recently) autos, and generally more comfort. Critics of free enterprise are to be taken seriously, and to be met with counterarguments and an effective job

[61] *The Wall Street Journal,* June 12, 1973, p. 1.
[62] *Chronicle of Higher Education,* November 11, 1973.

of "selling" capitalism. The fact that this same defensive posture was taken almost twenty years ago by business when similar basic criticisms arose and did not work (as described by William H. White in his book, *Is Anybody Listening?*)[63] seems not to deter its proponents. Public relations experts, who have done everything from electing a President to selling the Pentagon, are called in again in the vital task of "selling" capitalism. The fact that public relations people are hired to present a one-sided view, and that they do not have the ability, the tools, or the inclination to initiate two-way communication, and hence are going to convince very few, seems hardly to have occurred to such people as Powell and Eaton Corporation. Widespread use of public relations seems only to be widening the credibility gap.

Conditions have changed; the new challenges are real. Ignoring them or trying to paper them over will not work. The final option of trying to integrate the new values into corporate goals and policy is the most realistic response. It is in the American pragmatic tradition of incremental change in response to felt needs. However, the new responses that are required are more fundamental and profound than most Americans would like to believe. The direction, content, and depth of the new values, upon which must be built economic and corporate policies for the future, will be the subject of the last chapter.

SUMMARY AND CONCLUSIONS

Only a small minority of Americans now have confidence in business and business leadership. Enlightened self-interest continues to be clung to as the business ideology even though its effects are undermining the very institutions it is designed to preserve. Complacency and a certain Puritan self-righteousness characterizes many business leaders, as evidenced in the one-way "selling of free enterprise" stance of the United States Chamber of Commerce and some major corporations. A failure to recognize and to deal intelligently with their eroding legitimacy can bring about an even more serious lack of trust in business and business leadership in the future.

The American promise of jobs, equality, peace, and basic comforts and happiness for all remains an unfulfilled, perhaps an unattainable, dream. The resulting disappointment and malaise that has settled over American society has also profoundly affected business and business leadership. The expectations may be too great, but business and government have encouraged them. The gap between expectations and reality causes frustration, and then despair and apathy. This frustration and distrust is even more apparent when the large corporation is viewed from the perspective of the

---

[63]William H. White, *Is Anybody Listening?* (New York: Simon & Schuster, 1950).

poor and disadvantaged, whether within the United States or in Asian, African, or Latin American countries.

Large organizations, division of labor, and impersonal relationships leave people feeling alienated, powerless, and often angry. Even though pay is high and goods are available, pollution is rising and natural resources are running out. Meanwhile, Americans use five to eight times their share of the world's resources. Individualism and the Protestant ethic carried Americans fast and far in development, but now delayed gratification has given way to the consumer ethic of "buy now; pay later." Individualism encourages various legitimate and illegitimate "get rich quick" schemes, not always to the benefit of society.

In the traditional American pragmatic fashion of incremental change, there are signs of hope. Various public interest groups have been successful in urging firms to elect more blacks, women, and representatives of the public interest to their boards of directors. Firms such as General Motors have shown new signs of being sensitive to public issues. Students have begun a dialog with corporate executives to the considerable benefit of both. Institutional stockholders are beginning to exercise their ownership responsibilities and vote their shares in a socially responsive fashion. Although they are as yet only a small minority of shareholders, they may encourage a form of industrial democracy.

The changes in and challenges from the larger society—locally, nationally, and internationally—continue. Some managers and firms have begun to acknowledge these new conditions of life and work. Nevertheless, there remain fundamental, often unacknowledged, and generally unanswered questions.

CHAPTER SIX

Corporate Values
for the Future

No man is an island, entire to itself; every man is a piece of the continent, a
part of the main; . . . any man's death diminishes me, because I am involved
in mankind, and therefore never send to know for whom the bell tolls; it
tolls for thee.

John Donne

It is a straightforward task to chart the past development of American
business and economic values. The books, speeches, and cases are there to be
woven into an intelligible fabric. It is more difficult and perhaps presumptuous to try to indicate the direction of future change. This last chapter
will undertake just that: building on history and current challenges, it will attempt to point out the direction of change in future business values and goals.

THE PAST AS A BEGINNING

The accomplishments of the American business system are obvious to even
the most casual observer; its efficiency and productivity are legendary. In
spite of its faults, an objective observer must acknowledge that the material
successes of that business and economic system are staggering. No society is
as wealthy and has as high a standard of living. Free markets, competition,
and potentially large financial rewards, personally and for the firm, have
encouraged innovation and dedication to the task on the part of some of the
most talented people of our society. Many of the most intelligent, energetic,
and capable people have devoted themselves to supplying the goods and
services we now so often take for granted.

Compared with the status given the business person in other cultures, the
American manager has been accorded high prestige. Undoubtedly the
prestige given the business person has been one of the factors drawing these
talented, creative, and energetic people into business. Completing the
supporting cycle, this prestige has rested at least in part on the incomparable
success of business.

Values That Undergird Success

As has been pointed out consistently by those who have examined business values, the most salient and precious of these is freedom: free markets, free competition, free movement of men and capital—and, most especially, freedom of the individual. Antitrust legislation, however effective it may be, is an attempt to preserve the free market. Recent years have seen attempts to aid small business, again in order to maintain freedom of entry into business.

Important as personal freedom is in our society, it is not unlimited. An individualism that is not conscious of other people leads only to mistrust, frustration, and ultimately chaos. Using a familiar example, one does not have the freedom to shout "Fire!" in a crowded theater. Traffic lights introduce coercion that was undoubtedly objected to by early libertarians. A business firm does not have the freedom to mislead in its product advertising or to dump its waste in an adjoining lake. As people live closer together and become more dependent on one another, freedom must be constrained by both internal and external checks. In fact, some argue that real freedom emerges only when a people have formed internal constraints: ". . . freedom is endangered if a free society's shared values are no longer sufficiently vigorous to preserve the moral cohesion on which the discipline of free men rests."[1] Although it may seem a paradox to the individualist, activities limited by a consideration of others, such as the traffic lights or truth in advertising, introduce an even greater freedom for all.

One of the strengths of American business ideology has been its pragmatism: how to get the job done without much concern for inconsistencies. Simply put, pragmatism says that which works is by that fact good and true. Daniel Bell puts it bluntly:

> . . . the ideology of American business in the postwar years became its ability to perform. The justification of the corporation no longer lay primarily in the natural right of private property, but in its role as an instrument for providing more and more goods to the people.[2]

Pragmatism has thus led to flexibility and innovation in the search for a better way of providing those goods. On the other hand, it has led us to accept values and goals simply because they seem to work, and often regardless of inequities and undesirable by-products. While Americans proclaim freedom of economic opportunity, the enterprise system leads to inequalities in the distribution of wealth; moreover, that wealth can be passed on to one's descendants even though those children and grandchildren did absolutely no-

---

[1]Peter Viereck, *Shame and Glory of the Intellectuals* (Boston: Beacon, 1953), p. 196.
[2]Daniel Bell, *The Coming of Post-Industrial Society* (New York: Basic Books, 1973), p. 272.

thing to deserve it. Freedom of opportunity is not always so keenly felt today. In spite of our oft-proclaimed freedom, few sense it in the economic sphere. As has been pointed out earlier, the perception of alienation and powerlessness is increasing.

Any substantive defense of the values of the business and economic system cannot rest merely on the values of efficiency and freedom, for the obvious questions arise: Productivity for what? Freedom for what? These values and the business system they support are therefore not ultimate ends in their own right, but are good insofar as they allow a person to pursue other more valuable goals in life. Higher productivity allows a society to produce the goods and services it needs with less effort, and thus allows its citizens time to pursue these other goals. This is no small benefit.

Weaknesses of Enterprise Values

The American political system is democratic; the economic system is aristocratic. Politically, every person has but one vote, but some people earn more than a hundred times the average annual income; this gives them one hundred times the economic "voting power" of others. They may then spend their income on personal Lear jets, yachts, gaudy entertainment, or even political influence, while others who work just as hard or harder find it difficult to pay the rent and the grocery bill. While we say that wealth is the reward for hard work, we also know that good fortune—especially in the way of birth and resulting opportunities—is even more important. Those who inherit wealth have a most comfortable life; there is little relationship between the work they do and the income they receive. Inheritance and progressive income taxes have attempted to reduce this inequity. But recent "tax reform programs" have placed an upper limit on income taxes: no person now pays more than 50 percent of his earned income in taxes. The income of the wealthy is thus better protected than that of the poor.

The Protestant ethic encouraged people to save, thus aiding in the accumulation of wealth. Yet the value of saving and planning for the future are now largely dissolved in the consumer ethic: "buy now, pay later." In the popular culture, under the influence of advertising, inflation, and a short time perspective, the emphasis is on consumption; and indeed business does need customers and new markets. For a variety of reasons, motivations have shifted from delayed to immediate gratification. A more profound and far-reaching weakness of free enterprise values is the constant encouragement of what are ultimately selfish activities. Free markets, competition, and flexibility—all guided by Adam Smith's "invisible hand"—supposedly result in the most economic use of resources. Or as the seventeenth-century British pamphleteer Mandeville put it, "Private vices make public benefit."

He showed how blind and greedy profit seeking contributes to the public good.[3]

Making consumer sovereignty a central value is convenient because it distributes responsibility. Who is responsible for the many problems that we have drifted into in the past two decades (use of nonrenewable resources, aerosol danger to the ozone layer in the atmosphere, solid waste disposal)? Consumer sovereignty implies undirected, promiscuous economic growth. Coupled with the free market, it is also a convenient principle for economists who proclaim a "value-free" economics. It thus presumably enables them to dodge value questions. But such an approach in fact values the individual over the community, encourages self-seeking behavior, and leads to other personal and societal impasses. Consumer sovereignty enables its proponents to refuse to discuss value and goal questions—until flexibility is gone, options have been narrowed, and crises are upon us.

In fact, capitalism does reward the selfish. Furthermore, it provides a rationalization that promotes and blesses self-seeking, ego-centered behavior. Its ideology maintains that selfish activities are good for all. Pierre Teilhard de Chardin, the famous Jesuit paleontologist, finds this unacceptable:

> The egocentric ideal of a future reserved for those who have managed to attain egoistically the extremity of "everyone for himself" is false and against nature. No element could move and grow except with and by all the others with itself.

Teilhard then gives his own projection of the future:

> The outcome of the world, the gates of the future, the entry into the super-human—these are not thrown open to a few of the privileged nor to one chosen people to the exclusion of all others. They will open to an advance of *all together,* in a direction in which *all together* can join and find completion in a spiritual renovation of the earth.[4]

His widely respected, optimistic world view sees people cooperating and uniting more in the future, a position in clear contrast to that of Adam Smith and the modern-day proponent of enlightened selfishness, Ayn Rand.

Nineteenth-century capitalism in the United States was built on rugged individualism and enlightened self-interest. Huge fortunes were amassed before much social legislation was enacted. The little person, whether worker or producer, was often hurt by the robber barons. Nevertheless, these same

---

[3]See Peter Drucker, *Management: Tasks, Responsibilities, Practices* (New York: Harper & Row, 1973), p. 809.

[4]Pierre Teilhard de Chardin, *The Phenomenon of Man* (New York: Harper & Row, 1959), p. 244.

wealthy individuals eventually used much of their fortunes to benefit the public. Indeed, Andrew Carnegie's defense of wealth was based on the ability of the rich man to better use those funds for public purposes (see Chapter 2). John D. Rockefeller funded and built the University of Chicago, Carnegie built libraries all across the United States, and Huntington built a superb rapid transit system for Los Angeles (which was dismantled in the 1950s, to the chagrin of present city planners and residents). The various foundations—Ford, Rockefeller, Carnegie, Mellon—are all set up to serve the public purpose, and they have been instrumental in funding valuable new planning and programs.

There has been an obvious lack of such visionary planning in the past two decades. There have been few new libraries, museums, or parks. Suburbs have sprawled haphazardly, paving over areas that would have been set aside as parkland or rapid transit rights-of-way twenty-five years ago. It takes vision and planning to make a city livable, and we seem to have run out of both. Perhaps we have been too busy building new homes, expressways, and shopping centers to worry about beauty, community, and long-term benefits. Our cities are deteriorating because so many of our parks, libraries, and public transit facilities were planned and built before World War II, and some before World War I. In a nation that prides itself on progress, this neglect now comes as a shock. Each individual pursuing his or her own self-interest does not always work out to the best interests of the entire community.

On the international level, enlightened self-interest is leading nations into a scramble for resources. As, for example, petroleum, tin, and copper become scarce, conflicts will arise between the resource-producing nations (who are often poor) and the resource-consuming countries (who are generally wealthy). It will take military power and international pressures to offset the power of the producers; and conflicts and even wars are predictable as tensions mount.

Because of competition and the nature of the free enterprise system, some now argue that business can do nothing substantial to solve society's ills.[5] According to this point of view, capitalism makes maximization of profit and growth inevitable. Government regulation is not successful in removing the undesirable by-products of the competitive corporation. If we acknowledge the many strengths and the now more obvious weaknesses of the American business system, this brings us to the core question: How does that system go about adapting to change? How are inefficiencies and inequities repaired? What means does the economic and business system have at its disposal that will enable it to meet the future with confidence?

Change is accomplished in the political process primarily through voting

[5]Neil W. Chamberlain, *The Limits of Corporate Responsibility* (New York: Basic Books, 1974).

and the legislatures. There is no such instrument in the business sphere that can detect changing needs of *all* citizens, and thus help the system to adapt. On public interest issues Americans are generally committed to an open system and to consensus. This process often works slowly, but it does bring about changes in law and thus in life. On the other hand, when it comes to the inadequacies of the business system, we often need a good swat from a baseball bat to wake us up. It took the urban race riots to force us to realize the extent and injustice of job discrimination. Lake Erie died before we began to realize the dangers of pollution. In spite of predictions of serious long-term shortages, it took the energy crisis to awaken us to the dimensions of the problem, and many today still shrug off the possibility of any serious long-term energy shortage. Bank of America executives now acknowledge that it took the bombing and burning of a branch bank in Isle Vista, California, to force them to be more responsive to the needs of the larger society.[6]

A democratic people act when they personally feel a need. Hence a democracy works slowly, and generally requires a crisis to awaken its citizens to new public needs. Many of the needs now facing Americans are serious (dwindling resources, urban decay, nuclear disaster, pollution). If a crisis must affect each one of us before we understand the seriousness of each of these problems, there will be no time or flexibility left to find solutions.

A Summary of Inadequacies

American industrial society has managed prodigious feats of production and growth. In spite of this, it is also characterized by inadequacies in its values:

1. Acquisitive materialism is encouraged by a system that provides a rationalization for self-interest and selfishness.
2. Freedom and productivity are dominant values, with less attention paid to how this freedom and productivity will be used.
3. Because of large organizations and the division of labor, individuals seldom feel a sense of human participation.
4. Traditional unbounded faith in scientific, technological, and industrial progress is increasingly questioned.
5. There is an inequality in the distribution of income and wealth, domestically and internationally.
6. Individual decisons based on self-interest increasingly fail to add up to acceptable and humane policy for society as a whole.
7. The cumbersome machinery of majority rule may not leave us sufficient time to solve the serious problems that face us.

[6]See Louis B. Lundborg, *Future Without Shock* (New York: Norton, 1974). Lundborg was chairman and is still a director of Bank of America.

John D. Rockefeller, III, a conservative and a Republican, explains why he titled his book *The Second American Revolution*. After quoting the Declaration of Independence, he says:

> America once again has reached the point where the causes are no longer light and transient and where people are no longer disposed to suffer inequality and deprivation. Men and women have begun to act. They are of two groups: those who feel oppressed and those who sympathize with them.[7]

Several questions emerge: Is a second revolution really taking place? How basic is it? What are these revolutionary changes? How will these changes affect business and the economic system? The rest of the chapter will attempt to answer these questions.

THE IMPORTANCE OF A BUSINESS CREED FOR THE FUTURE

The social dynamics and resulting rationale that supported the capitalism of the nineteenth and early twentieth centuries were clear, concise, and compelling. More important, they were effective right up through the period immediately following World War II. In the 1950s the explicit values and ideology of free enterprise were still based on private property, individual freedom, and delayed gratification. Yet even earlier the centrality of private property had given way to absentee ownership and stockholders without effective power to control. Individual freedoms during this period were successively prescribed by expectations of neighbors and social class, time spent in transportation to and from school and stores, and so on. Finally, within the last decade delayed gratification has given way to the "buy now, pay later" ethic.

The old rationale of capitalism was no longer appropriate, yet during this happy, innocent period just two decades ago, the American economy performed prodigious feats of production. The rationale and undergirding values became less consistent and more pragmatic: the economy performed well, and this gave the system a new legitimacy.[8] The criticisms of the 1930s subsided because the economy now seemed to be working so well. Even though the new legitimacy of business and the corporation was based largely on its superior performance in getting goods into the hands of citizens, most

---

[7]John D. Rockefeller, III, *The Second American Revolution* (New York: Harper & Row, 1973), p. 17.
[8]Bell, *op. cit.,* esp. chap. 4, pp. 269-98.

business spokespeople still looked to the old rationale whenever they defended free enterprise. We have seen earlier in this book, especially in this and the previous chapter, how business people generally base their case for free enterprise on the old values of private property, individualism, and saving and planning ahead.

The basis for the legitimacy and acceptance that business and the corporation possessed in the last generation was more its ability to perform than the traditional virtues of the Protestant ethic. This shift took place gradually and almost imperceptibly, and it left the firm open to the pragmatic test of performance for its very acceptance and legitimacy. The current indictment of the corporation is precisely on the criteria of performance, although it is performance in a wider arena. Performance now is measured not only by return on investment and increase in productivity, but also by satisfying jobs, clean air and water, and safe, durable products. If a firm is a sweatshop, makes a city or its surroundings dirtier, uglier, more hectic and more polluted, it can hardly be said to perform well, no matter what its profit or productivity.

Post-Industrial Society

Business and industry have been extremely successful in the last century, especially as judged by their own measuring rods: productivity, growth of capital, gross national product, and more material goods. Until recently these standards were also those of society. Broader criteria of performance, and forcing firms to pay more of the costs of operation (or internalizing their externalities, as the economists put it) will demonstrate to all that air, water, and people are not "free goods" but must be paid for. Paying for what was once taken as free will increase costs and perhaps slow down economic growth. But even with the necessity of paying the full costs of operation, the business firm will probably still be able to provide more goods and services in the future and continue to increase productivity. This success is parallel to the success of farming in the last few generations. Farms produce more food than ever before, but, because of increased productivity, do so with fewer man-hours and fewer workers. Just a few generations ago, farmers and ranchers dominated the legislatures and the American scene in general; now they have far less influence. They are a victim of their own success. Agricultural workers are now fewer in number (only 5 percent of total labor force), and hence do not set the pace of needs, styles, and attitudes as they once did.

Much the same evolution is taking place within industry and the corporation. The business firm has been remarkably successful in meeting society's material needs. The proportion of people working in manufacturing has been steadily decreasing in recent decades. By 1969, only 34 percent of the labor force worked in industry.[9] Again, it does not take as many workers to produce even more goods. Thus, the corporation and business itself will probably not be dominant in American society in the future.

Business has also been a pace-setter because of the large number of very talented people going into the corporation, and because of the resulting innovations coming from the business sector. Current evidence seems to indicate that talented people are now going into government, education, and the services in greater proportion than before. Services already claim 61 percent of the work force. In the 1960s the United States became the first country to have more than half of its work force and GNP accounted for by services. Western European countries tend to have less than 10 percent of their work force in agriculture and the rest rather evenly distributed between industry and services. Developing countries generally have 50 to 75 percent of their work force in agriculture, and less than 25 percent in industry.[10]

As a result of the lessening proportion of the labor force and GNP that industry accounts for in the United States, business leaders will probably not continue to hold the same preeminent position in society. The old ideology and values of business probably will not dominate American cultural values, as has been the case in the last few generations. This will be true for two reasons: (1) business will cease to be such a dominant institution, as indicated above; and (2) the ideology and values of the business system in the future will not be as cohesive and widely held.

The fabric of the Protestant ethic has already begun to fray and unravel. An ethic that is no longer cohesive and convincing can hardly be the basis for widely held values. Many of Benjamin Franklin's exhortations are reversed now. Instead of saving for a rainy day in the future, the consumer is urged to buy now with a low down payment and pay for it over the next ten years. On a larger scale, but building on similar values, the United States government had established the policy of keeping on hand a substantial amount of various grains. This reserve was insurance against a poor crop and high prices at home; and it was available to countries where drought or some other natural disaster had struck. Very often America sent grain to people who would otherwise have starved. In the same fashion as advertising and our consumer economy urges us to spend now and let tomorrow take care of itself, the Nixon administration, which articulated the Protestant ethic virtues so often, arranged the sale of our surplus grain to Russia. On a national as well as on an individual level, saving and putting something away for harder days now

[9]*Ibid.,* pp. 16-17.
[10]*Ibid.*

seems to have little appeal. Without grain in storage, we are victims of price fluctuations at home, and droughts will bring starvation in poorer nations. Yet there seems to be less inclination to look to the future and to plan ahead.

Perhaps the dire consequences of this reversal will force us to reinstate some modified form of planning and saving. Our cities have suffered from forty years of sprawl and lack of planning; and the immense problems that face us require a longer time horizon, if we are ever to meet them successfully.

The Protestant ethic took hold primarily in the northern European countries—in England, Holland, Belgium, and Germany, where people have worked hard and become comparatively affluent. According to Max Weber's thesis, the peoples of Spain, Italy, and southern France are not as energetic, and hence not as affluent. Weber attributed this to religious roots, but others have pointed out that climate may have had much to do with it. People in the northern countries were forced to plan ahead. Harvests came only during the summer months. It would be a long, cold, and hungry winter if one were unprepared for it. The changing seasons, and especially the long winter, literally forced these people to think about tomorrow. The countries of southern Europe—Spain, France, and Italy—are better known, on the other hand, for their leisurely and more human life. People spill out into the streets, have close personal relationships, and seem to have time for visiting and enjoying each other.

If it is true that men and women planned ahead primarily as a defense against a fairly hostile environment they could not control, then it may follow that as people can exert more influence over their environment, they do not feel the same need. In the United States most homes and work places have central heating. Food is available, even during the winter, although it may be a bit more expensive. Social security and unemployment insurance reinforce the notion that there is less need to plan ahead.

This trend toward living for today seems to have two results, one beneficial, the other a burden. The disadvantages of lack of vision and planning are obvious in many of the problems that face us, but it may at the same time enable us to relax more and enjoy the sort of leisurely, human, person-centered life that so many, young and old, have been seeking.

Is it possible for a person to enjoy this fuller human life, and at the same time look to the future and plan for it? There seems to be no choice but to answer yes, although it will demand substantial shifts in values and attitudes.

Business: Mover or Moved

Society's expectations with regard to business have expanded over the years. Recently the community has been asking that business look to employing minorities and women, try to keep the air and water clean, and contribute in other ways to the life of citizens. The question to be asked now is this: Although the changing expectations come from society as a whole, do actual changes in corporate policy come about because of government leadership and legislation, or because the firm itself sees these needs and responds to them on its own initiative?

Historically we have seen how most social innovations in business operations have come about through the prodding of the government and legislation (minimum wage, security and exchange regulations, environmental protection). The business sector seems to need a push. Furthermore, it also helps the formulation of new rules of the game, so that no one firm is at a disadvantage in introducing a socially desirable product or program at some cost in a highly competitive market.

Is the government therefore the sole agency for determining social priorities, and setting up programs and ground rules for acting? Government consultant and Harvard Business School professor George C. Lodge would answer yes: that is precisely the role of government.[11] Business can be effective in mobilizing its resources for whatever ends government decides, as it did in producing for World War II or the space program. In fact, Lodge maintains that business works best in a structured setting to meet objectives made explicit by outside elements. The more amorphous those needs and goals are, the less efficient and effective is business in addressing them.

In the late 1960s, after the civil disturbances, President Lyndon Johnson turned to business leaders and said: "Government has failed; now it is your turn to try to save the cities." Lodge finds both the request and the attempted response futile and unworkable. Business is not equipped to set social priorities or to solve social problems. Most members of the New Left agree and would not want business to set social priorities; they do not trust business to look to the best interests of society. Business by nature looks to its own advantage; it is expected to and structured to do so. It is therefore incapable of effectively determining needs and priorities for society as a whole.

Reacting to Johnson's statement, Lodge paraphrased the hoped-for response of the business person to a president, mayor, or cabinet officer who asks business to transform the cities:

> No, my friend. That is your job; we can only help you when you have decided what will be the direction, the speed, and the design—the ideological basis of the transformation. You are the politician; you are the elected ruler of the community; you are the sovereign state; you speak for the people. We serve you.[12]

It would therefore seem to him that business can respond to the prods and constraints of government direction and legislation, but is not able to initiate

---

[11]George Cabot Lodge, "Top Priority: Renovating Our Ideology," *Harvard Business Review,* 48 (September-October 1970), 51.

[12]*Ibid.*

action on social problems. What is badly needed in any case, says Lodge, is a new ideology for business; the old pragmatic values are obsolete and no longer of any use.

There is a strong case here for separate, defined sectors and roles for business and government institutions. It is true that the business community has traditionally abhorred the interference of government in its affairs. Over the years, the Chamber of Commerce and business people themselves have taken the position that laws and regulations are intrusions that tend to hinder the free market, and so make the productive process less efficient. Moreover, it is true that every restriction and regulation tends to narrow the number of possible responses. Innovation will be hindered if all larger policy questions that stem from the expectations of society are turned over to government, with business given no choice but to follow along or object. Perhaps this is a solution, but it is one that will adversely affect flexibility and innovation within the firm, and as a result in society as well.

There is, however, another solution, and one that is probably more consonant with the latent desires of both business and government. Executives themselves are calling on their peers to be more sensitive to the expectations of society *without* waiting for legislation. It is true that, in highly competitive industries (autos, steel, rubber), a costly but socially desirable innovation (safety, pollution controls) will require legislation. The experience of Ford in trying to introduce the seat belt and General Motors' more recent attempt to sell the air bag as an option show that safety features, desirable as they may be, will often not be purchased. The firm that tries to absorb these costs is at a competitive disadvantage. Consumers want other motorists not to pollute, but would individually refuse to pay the costs of the necessary devices themselves. To bring about equal employment opportunity required legislation, primarily to ensure something approaching fair and equal application of new policies and to avoid an individual firm's foot dragging.

On other issues, such as job enrichment, product quality, and even plant location and relation to the surrounding community, it is more difficult to formulate legislation. It is harder to specify policy and to apply measurements. Furthermore, legislation in these areas would severely constrain freedom of action and operation, and this in turn would undoubtedly affect efficiency and flexibility. In these areas, it is probably better if the firm takes the lead and does not wait for law. The government is therefore not the sole agency for determining social priorities, and hence policies and programs. Business firms and executives may appropriately take initiatives that will leave them more in charge of their own future direction. Executives are thus less constrained and regulated, but in turn take a broader view of the role of the firm and its purposes.

In this model, the government continues to oversee, regulate, and facilitate participation in the economic as well as the political sphere. But more grass roots initiative is expected from every segment of business, for the sake of the entire society. This grass roots participation is prodded, encouraged, and even policed by the various new activist groups—the consumer advocates, the equal rights proponents, and the shareholder activists. There is a danger that the stridency of their charges and the lack of real attention on both sides may cause lessened confidence in institutions and leaders. Nevertheless, their record of successes is quite remarkable, and they do represent a "third sector"[13] that has developed between public and private institutions to perform a watchdog function and help keep institutions and their leaders honest and sensitive to the needs of society.

Economic Planning

Economic planning is essential as industrial activities become more complex and interdependent. Because of the intricate demands of technology, capital, and markets, larger firms have long resorted to planning. The aggregate planning universally done by large firms in the private sector Galbraith calls "the planning system." The existence of a multiplicity of free, competitive, individualistic producers is a myth; a private planning system is the reality.[14] Moreover, such private-sector planning focuses on the growth and security of the individual firm, and is only secondarily concerned with the public welfare. It thus works to the best interests of the already powerful.

Economic planning for the public welfare is therefore even more essential. A major goal of public economic planning is to bring the goals and activities of private enterprise into better alignment with the overall goals of society. Adam Smith's "invisible hand" or the Physiocrats' "pre-established harmonies" no longer provide assurance that the pursuit of private gain will automatically work to the benefit of society.[15] Americans long ago decided that the free market was not a good indicator of what should be spent on such public goods as national security, fire protection, and parks. In the last two chapters of this book, we have specified many other areas, such as the environment and the use of resources, in which the free market has not only not solved the problem, but has contributed to it.

The United States Congress, too, has recognized the necessity for economic planning and the anticipation of unforeseen and undesirable consequences of gross industrial growth. Beneath every tax, subsidy, and government regulation lie value judgments as to what sort of economic

[13]Theodore Levitt, *The Third Sector* (New York: Amacom, 1973).

[14]John Kenneth Galbraith, *Economics and the Public Purpose* (Boston: Houghton Mifflin, 1973), esp. pp. 55-175.

[15]George F. Rohrlich, "The Challenge of Social Economics," in *Social Economics for the 1970's,* ed. George F. Rohrlich (New York: Dunellen, 1970), pp. 3-5.

activities should be encouraged. Sometimes, unfortunately, these judgments are more influenced by special interest pressures than the public welfare. To look into these problems, Congress has recently established its own Office of Technology Assessment, through which it intends to review recent and proposed technological and industrial activities and innovations in order to examine all side effects—especially the otherwise unforeseen "downstream" effects.

But if we agree that free markets and competition generally do provide greater economic efficiency and also encourage self-reliance, a second question arises: Under what conditions and in what fashion can the strengths of free enterprise be retained? To put the matter differently, how can individual microdecisions be more effective in contributing to better macro-decisions with resulting benefit to society as a whole? It seems clear that long-term, global criteria such as job satisfaction, the use of finite resources, poverty, and hunger must increasingly become elements that enter into corporate decisions. These considerations can become part of corporate decision making either because of government-imposed constraints (tax incentives, regulations, subsidies) or because of the social responsiveness of the firms themselves. Incentives can be changed so that it will be to the best interest of the private firm to take into account public needs. Tax credits for recycling metals and for new, small enterprises, or additional taxes on excessive energy use would be examples.

Economic planning for the public welfare will therefore be carried out in two ways. First, those public goods that can best be provided by government directly (parks, police, urban public transportation) will continue to be so provided. Moreover, this segment of the economy may even grow. Second, on the basis of its long-term, global policies, government will encourage the private sector to also serve the public good through such incentives as new regulations and changes in the tax laws. For these initiatives to be successful will require the wholesale reexamination and restatement of economic and public policy.

Which Comes First, Ideology or Activity?

Position in society, work, neighbors, and friends all help to mold an individual's values and ideology. Clearly no person springs into society with goals and values already formulated. There is a reciprocal relationship between a person's life and values; they influence one another.

Contemporary Americans are no more inclined to reflect on their own goals and values than were their predecessors. Americans are pragmatic and even anti-intellectual. Business is judged effective and adequate because it works, not because its values are praiseworthy or consistent with society's.[16] There is an advantage in this sort of pragmatic stance: people do not become distracted by arguing over theoretical, airy minutiae. There is also a considerable disadvantage: problems are not recognized until they show up in the nuts and bolts inadequacies, which may be much too late. Perhaps it requires crises to bring changes in American democratic institutions, but that is a heavy price to pay.

Policy decisions affecting lives, careers, neighborhoods, and cities are made daily in boardrooms across the country. Using the narrow criteria of "does it work" (that is, work for the benefit of this firm) often leads to short-sighted, antisocial behavior. Spelling out values and trying to project into the future with goals, plans, and programs enables the firm and society to be more in charge of the future. Waiting to react to problems and crises leaves one a victim of his surroundings. As conditions and society change at an increasingly faster rate, it becomes even more important to look to the future. Waiting too long eliminates many of the options that might otherwise have been taken. Crises leave no time for reflection and experimentation; by that time, actions that might have been helpful are inadequate or even counterproductive. The more the firm or society fails to look to the future, the more it will lack freedom and be involuntarily channeled into certain patterns of action. Its choices and options will have vanished in its effort to survive.

Consensus or Pluralism?

For generations, those who reflected on the goals of the business firm agreed that its purpose was long-run profit maximization. A consensus emerged that, whatever else the firm did, it first had to maintain a high return on investment. Although short-run payoffs could be gained, a reputable firm would be conscious of its standing in the community. If the profits were consistently made at the serious expense of some other party, the firm's reputation could be hurt in the long run. Thus conscientious executives added "long term" to profit maximizing as the purpose of the firm.

As we have seen throughout the latter half of this book, new statements of the purpose of business enterprise are being offered, almost all of them containing something about the corporation as a citizen of the community. Most contemporary executives would maintain that even though a firm may maximize profits—even in the long run—it can still be a failure. If that firm fails to respond to the new needs and demands of citizens, it is not successful.

[16]For a discussion of anti-intellectualism among businessmen, see Robert Chatov, "The Role of Ideology in the American Corporation," in Dow Votaw and S. Prakash Sethi, *The Corporate Dilemma* (Englewood Cliffs, N.J.: Prentice-Hall, 1973), p. 59.

But there is little agreement on a new statement of purpose for the business firm. And although there has been a consensus in the past on business ideology and the goals of the firm, it is likely that there will be no such consensus in the future.[17]

This loss of consensus will bring both difficulties and benefits. The difficulties will include the problems of individual executives and firms formulating their own goals, policies, and practices. In addition, it will be even more difficult for the rest of society to arrive at any clear understanding of the goals and role of business, which may lead to confusion, misunderstanding, and additional lessening of confidence in business institutions.

On the other hand, this confusion and lack of consensus will force more reflection on purposes, values, and ideology. American business people are pragmatic, and they probably will not begin to reflect on their own values and ideology until their current ideology no longer works and the "conventional wisdom" crumbles in their hands. Inconsistencies and inadequacies in that old ideology will become increasingly apparent. For example, we have already seen how each person's pursuing his or her own self-interest can and often does severely damage the public interest.

The Lack of Clear Values

The director of a research institute[18] reported a few years ago that young people were quite critical of the beliefs of their parents and adults in general. They were not critical of *what* they believed, but of what seemed to be a *lack* of beliefs and convictions. Their elders' values seemed to be largely inherited and absorbed passively from the surrounding culture; they had very little in the way of thought-out, internalized goals and values of their own.

Confusion and a lack of clear goals and values on the part of the young puts an even greater burden on their elders to reflect on their own values. If adults in a society, those who have traditionally been looked to as being experienced and wise, do not have some considered notion of their own life goals and aspirations, there would seem to be little hope for young people. It is especially important that individuals have fairly clearly articulated values in a time of rapid change. Otherwise, these persons are left with no rudder, pushed from one job or neighborhood to another by events. Without values and goals, they are not in control of their own careers, lives, or destinies. Opportunities, challenges, and crises now come rapidly, and individuals who have never reflected on what they do and why are unable to meet these events so that they, their families, and others may profit and grow. Rather, such

[17]The author is indebted to Prof. Raymond A. Bauer for this insight.
[18]Leo Cherne, "The Campus Viewpoint: An Analysis," *General Electric Forum,* 12 (Spring 1969), 5.

people will be less fulfilled, their families confused and frustrated, and others hurt.

One of the functions of education is to enable and encourage students to reflect on their own values and make them explicit, so that they may then be able to grow and make clear life choices. Alvin Toffler, in analyzing precisely this problem, has harsh words for the schools:

> . . . students are seldom encouraged to analyze their own values and those of their teachers and peers. Millions pass through the education system without once having been forced to search out the contradictions in their own value systems, to probe their own life goals deeply, or even to discuss these matters candidly with adults and peers. . . .
>
> Nothing could be better calculated to produce people uncertain of their goals, people incapable of effective decision-making under conditions of overchoice.[19]

The need for individuals to search out and make explicit their own values and goals is underscored in a period of rapid change, and a primary vehicle for this sort of examination and evaluation is the school—yet the American school, from kindergarten to university, has failed in this respect. Educators maintain that education should be "objective," and that values are too controversial a field for a public institution.

When either an individual or an institution plans for the future, values and goals are essential for setting a direction, charting a course, and being in control of that future. Looking to the future is then not a frightening, debilitating experience, but one filled with opportunities for growth and satisfaction. Clearly stated goals and values are essential for another reason: From these building blocks come a value structure—an ideology. Out of living, planning, acting, plus reflection on those actions—out of a reciprocal relationship between action and reflection—come personal and institutional values and goals.

CLUES TO THE FUTURE

The problems and inadequacies of the American business system are no secret: many press on us from all sides; the more subtle ones are apparent to a discerning observer. These difficulties make the system unstable. It simply cannot continue as it is. Sharp shifts in attitudes have already taken place, and changes will continue, probably at an accelerating rate. The question then becomes, what is the direction and the substance of those changes?

[19]Alvin Toffler, *Future Shock* (New York: Random House, 1970), p. 370.

Future attitudes and policies will be affected by each of us, as citizens, consumers, and managers. It is imperative that we understand present needs and future trends, both for our own sakes and for that of the society in which we live.

In this final section of the book, we will review the changes that are taking place and make some predictions of the future business environment. We will then try to assess their impact on American business values. We will try to identify emerging values that will have a significant impact on the American business system of the future and on the ideology that supports it. We will try to avoid the charge of wishful thinking by adhering to what seem to be valid projections. The major values are these:

1. Central role of the person
2. Participation in decision making
3. Corporation as servant of society
4. New measures of business success
5. Harmony with environment
6. Necessity of new legitimacy for the corporation
7. Interdependence of people, institutions, and nations
8. Vision and hope
9. Concern for others

Each of these major projections will be taken up in turn and analyzed for its effect on the business system.

Central Role of the Person

A constant theme running through American life and thought is the importance of the individual person. Individualism, democracy, the free market, and the courts all have that principle as a foundation. As the average level of education rises and people's expectations also rise, they become less willing to suffer uninteresting work and being treated, along with capital, as merely one of the inputs into the production process. Business executives often proclaim "people are our most important asset." Psychologist Rensis Likert has attempted to prove that assertion, and has suggested a method for measuring human resources.[20]

In spite of rhetoric and research, however, many now feel that the central role of the individual person is but another of the unfulfilled promises of the American Dream. Ivan Illich goes further to maintain that our developed society and its institutions, especially the corporation, have made us more

---

[20]Rensis Likert, *The Human Organization: Its Management and Value* (New York: McGraw-Hill, 1967).

dependent and hence less free: "Our present institutions abridge basic human freedom for the sake of providing people with more institutional outputs."[21] Although a New Yorker for many years, Illich now lives in Mexico, and his primary concern is for the peoples of developing nations. Nevertheless, the problems he finds in our growth patterns apply to people on every rung of the development ladder.

Illich maintains that every tool (in the broad sense) should be designed and used to bring men and women closer together so as to live fuller and happier lives. Yet he finds many tools divisive and disruptive, no matter who uses them:

> Networks or multilane highways, long-range, wide-band-width trans-mitters, strip mines, or compulsory school systems are such tools. Destructive tools must inevitably increase regimentation, dependence, exploitation, or impotence, and rob not only the rich but also the poor of convivality which is the primary treasure in many so-called under-developed countries.[22]

He challenges the notions that progress means more elaborate tools in the hands of a highly trained elite, thus making each individual more and more dependent and helpless. On some new model automobiles, it is now almost impossible for a driver to change a tire. For example, it takes an engineer to decipher the operating instructions for the new screw-style jack in the Ford Maverick, and the wrench provided is too flimsy and small even to loosen the wheel nuts. What used to be a simple ten-minute job now requires calling a garage man in a wrecker.

In a General Electric report distributed to its own management, *Our Future Business Environment: Developing Trends and Changing Institutions,* several of the main findings point to the growing importance of the individual person. The study predicts a rising tide of education: more persons completing more years of schooling. Such a person "will have more self-respect, will want to be treated more as an individual; will be far less tolerant of authoritarianism and organizational restraints; will have different and higher expectations of what he wants to put into a job and what he wants to get out of it."[23] Higher expectations will also bring an erosion of the traditional work ethic. The attitude that hard, unpleasant, and unrewarding work is to be tolerated because there is no way of avoiding it will be held by fewer and fewer persons. Where people have any choice at all, they will tend to

---

[21]Ivan Illich, *Tools For Conviviality* (New York: Harper & Row, 1973), p. 12.

[22]*Ibid.,* p. 28.

[23]Ian Wilson, "Our Future Business Environment: Developing Trends and Changing Institutions," summary later published in *The Futurist* (February 1969), p. 17.

search out work that is satisfying and rewarding. They will often be willing to work more hours and for less pay, if that work is fulfilling.

The business firm will find that, in order to compete, it must begin to see that the development of its people is as important an objective as providing goods and services. Without a work environment in which the individual is challenged, able to grow, and fulfilled, the firm will be at a severe disadvantage. This is, of course, especially true of the more talented and achievement-oriented white collar and blue collar workers. Although research indicates that there is a substantial minority of assembly-line workers who are happy with repetitive, undemanding work (for they can then escape into their personal daydreams), nevertheless the majority will want more challenging work.

In the early 1970s the young workers at the new General Motors assembly plant at Lordstown, Ohio, made national news with their unhappiness with the rapid speed of the assembly line and the unchallenging work. The Lordstown workers did what social critics for years had been predicting they would do. They revolted against being treated as machines, demanded more meaningful work, work designed so that they could grow as persons, and some share in the decision making.[24] The events at the Lordstown plant were undoubtedly an early warning of attitudes that will become quite common across the land. One of the principal tenets of the Protestant ethic, that *any* sort of work has dignity and meaning, is being rejected. People do want to work, but they look for work that has significance for them. They expect the work to be worthwhile, and they hope to receive some positive recognition from that work.[25] For a business firm that produces a worthwhile product or service, it seems imperative and not impossible to structure its work in such a fashion that men and women can be satisfied with what they are doing. The idea that any work had value came close to making people a means, something to be used for the sake of the production process. They were urged to work hard and to forget the fact that their work was repetitive, superficial, unchallenging, and even demeaning. This sort of traditional attitude places more importance on efficiency and the production process than it does on the individual person.

One of the essential elements in the growth and development of the individual person is self-knowledge. Without self-knowledge in depth, we are unaware of our own needs and what moves us. We act without being aware of why we act. Without self-knowledge we find it more difficult to build on our

---

[24]For well-documented, though varying, views on these issues, see Harold L. Sheppard and Neal Q. Herrick, *Where Have All the Robots Gone? Worker Dissatisfaction in the 70s* (New York: Free Press, 1972); also Sar A. Levitan and William B. Johnston, *Work Is Here To Stay, Alas* (Salt Lake City: Olympus, 1974).

[25]See the documented human account of 133 workers by Studs Terkel, *Working* (New York: Pantheon, 1974).

strengths and to compensate for our weaknesses. Without self-knowledge we do not have adults, but only children grown old, armed with computers, television sets, and intercontinental ballistics missles, none of which they really understand. A person obtains self-knowledge from reflection and feedback from others. Often enough, our business life leaves little room for either. What positive or negative feedback, what sense of accomplishment comes from repeatedly bolting a lug on a frame? When a job is repetitive and unchallenging and when a person's relation to his or her superior is impersonal and distant, there is no human relationship and little meaningful feedback. This is not the environment in which a person is able to grow.

A work environment that provides flexibility, that challenges the multitude of talents a person possesses, one in which co-workers and superiors relate and provide each other feedback on their efforts, is one in which an individual may grow as a person. On the other hand, persons fail to develop when they are so socialized by their schools, their firms, and their neighbors that they seek to be like other men and women—losing their individuality. Workers are increasingly asking for some sort of fulfillment from their jobs. Various attempts at job enlargement and organization development have been tried. Volvo assembles its automobiles in teams, rather than using the assembly line. General Motors and the other auto firms have experimented with other types of more challenging work arrangements. Some of these experiments have not been successful, but they do indicate the direction in which large firms realize they must go in order to provide a more humanly satisfying work environment.

Participation in Decision Making

In addition to job enlargement, many workers are also asking for a greater say in major decisions that are made in the plant.[26] Various schemes have been worked out in the United States, Sweden, Yugoslavia, and in other countries to obtain worker input and even to share the responsibility for these decisions with workers. Decisions being made through consensus at the grass roots among workers (industrial democracy), as opposed to decisions being made exclusively at the top and handed down through the hierarchy, is a model now being used in many countries and in some plants in the United States[27] It undoubtedly points in the direction industrial firms will move in coming decades.

Over a longer time span, most people find that an essential element in a satisfying job is being able to enjoy the people with whom one works. If co-

[26]For a collection of articles on this movement, see Gerry Hunnius et al., *Worker's Control* (New York: Random House, 1973).

[27]Ichak Adizes and Elisabeth M. Borgese, eds., *Self-Management: New Dimensions in Democracy* (Santa Barbara, Calif.: Clio, 1975).

workers are unfriendly, insular, and uncooperative, it is difficult to enjoy a job. On the other hand, if co-workers are helpful, friendly, and provide feedback—on job-related and other items—work can be satisfying and even something one looks forward to. Large national and international firms, which formerly would transfer talented, high-potential managers almost on schedule every few years, now recognize the need people have for establishing friendships and some stability, so as to be better able to contribute to job, neighborhood, and their children's development. Life on the job and in the suburbs has often been alienating, and what friendships there are, shallow and superficial. It is too great a risk to get to know people very well, be transferred, and thus be forced to go through the pain of leaving real friends. It is simpler and less painful not to get involved.[28] Recognition of these human needs has caused major firms not to demand the same number of periodic moves of their achievement-oriented executives. They are now more apt to recognize and respect the basic human need for friends, roots, and the resulting beneficial feedback. This, in turn, enables managers to increase their own self-esteem and confidence.

On the job itself, most job-enlargement attempts to make the work more attractive involve forming work teams. These teams work together, performing the job and distributing the work, breaks, and so on, in a fashion that is agreeable to the team. Where these work teams have been formed, job satisfaction generally increases, although efficiency and cost-per-unit sometimes suffer. The advantages and the problems in encouraging cooperation in the work place are fairly clear. The assembly line is the extreme of division of labor and mechanization: small, segmented jobs done by an individual in relative isolation. Although the efficiency of the assembly line cannot be denied, neither can its negative effects on job satisfaction. Much research and experimentation is being carried on by firms in an attempt to make that work more satisfying and rewarding to the individual. Employees are also coming to value leisure time more. Not many years ago, skilled workers or middle managers would work as many hours as they were asked to by their supervisors, knowing that they would receive overtime or be more readily considered for promotion. There now seems to be far less willingness on the part of any employee to work longer hours. Especially if the work is not that attractive, the individual views it as a means and not as an end in itself.

An individual without interest in her or his work can readily become frustrated and alienated. Withdrawal from an active personal involvement then often follows, leading to the mass passivity that Gunnar Myrdal laments.[29] If

---

[28]See the William H. Whyte, Jr., classic, *The Organization Man* (Garden City, N.Y.: Doubleday Anchor, 1956), pp. 295-435; plus the more recent George W. Pierson, *The Moving Americans* (New York: Knopf, 1973); and Vance Packard, *A Nation of Strangers* (New York: McKay, 1973).

[29]Gunnar Myrdal, "Mass Passivity in America," *The Center Magazine,* 7 (March-April, 1974), pp. 72-75.

only a fraction of a person is alive and operating at the work place, it is clear that both the person and the employer are the losers—especially in the long run. Creativity, effort, innovation, and dedication to the task will decline, and hence productivity and the health of the firm will suffer. Passivity at the work place and away from it does seem to be increasing. On the other hand, many of the leading firms, General Electric and General Motors among them, have extensive research and experimental programs that are attempting to increase job satisfaction.

Passivity may stem from our affluence. What more is there to be had? This lack of concern, if allowed to go unchecked, can lead to the rigidity and eventual decay of all our institutions, as well as to the frustration and alienation of people. Individual self-reliance and small group activities are vitally important. Productive partnerships, and the growing interest in handicrafts, sewing, baking, gardening, and local community organizations can all contribute to the needs of an industrial society and its people. Many problems (littered streets, food supplies, alienation) can be addressed by a neighborhood. As an example of what one group has already done, the six-block Adams-Morgan neighborhood in Washington, D.C., has organized and encouraged citizens for self-help. They already elect a neighborhood government, gather and store solar energy, grow vegetables on rooftops, spawn and grow trout in basement tanks, and are planning many more productive, saving, and community-building activities. It is individual initiative and self-reliance that brought the many public interest groups into being and sustains their effectiveness. That portion of the traditional American spirit can perhaps be encouraged to new life.

Mature, confident, generous people who are alert to opportunities, to life, and to what goes on around them are the major asset of any society. It is clearly to the long-term benefit of the firm and society if activities are structured so that in doing them an individual is able to contribute, grow and develop as a person, and finally, to enjoy it all.

The Corporation as a Servant of Society

The free market model of business and economics supports the view that the corporation is individual, isolated and competing with other firms to survive and grow. Success is measured in dollar terms. Those who hold this capitalist model would acknowledge that the purpose of the firm is to produce the goods and services society needs. Nevertheless, the firm is judged successful whether it makes short-lived, trivial, luxuries perhaps even at the cost of low-paid workers and pollution of a neighborhood, or whether it makes durable, high-quality, basic necessities. As long as a firm shows a profit and grows, Wall Street and *Barron's* will dub it a success. But it is becoming apparent that these criteria of success are much too narrow. The business firm, especially the corporation, is a servant of society. It is chartered by the state to provide for the needs of citizens. It is not an autonomous institution, intent exclusively on its *own* profit and growth.

In contrast to the "cowboy economy" out of which we have recently moved, in which production and consumption are the measures of success, the newer "spaceship economy" has as a measure of economic success "the nature, extent, quality, and complexity of the total capital stock, including in this the state of human bodies and minds included in the system."[30] This is a totally new concept for economists and business people who have been obsessed with production, consumption, profits, and growth. The notion of "more is better" is clearly myopic, and has very many undesirable consequences: pollution; intrusive advertising; long hours of debilitating work to produce unnecessary and fragile gadgets; disruption of urban and rural areas by ugly and unplanned asphalt, concrete, and factories; heart attacks and nervous strain stemming from obsessive competition and "keeping ahead of the Joneses"; and families uprooted because of job transfer. If human needs and desires could be met with less production and consumption, heretical as it sounds, the economy would actually be performing in a superior fashion. In short, additional production and consumption are not only not goals in themselves, but exclusive emphasis on them works to the detriment of people. This is a hard conclusion for economists and business people to accept. Their models and ideology work best for an economy of gross, indiscriminate production and consumption. There is a residual resistance to such a basic shift, since it would require rethinking goals and criteria of performance.

The decreasing relative importance of economic efficiency in production and distribution was also one of the conclusions of the General Electric report on the future business environment cited earlier. Efficiency is considered an organizational value, so that when the organization performs successfully, its importance will diminish. Then the more human values of "justice, equality, individual dignity" will become more important. In the final analysis, organizations exist to serve the needs of the citizens of the larger society, not vice versa.

Organizations tend to take on a life and purpose of their own. They are not likely to phase themselves out of existence once their initial purpose has been met. Organizations and institutions, whether government agencies, voluntary groups, schools, or business firms, seek to perpetuate themselves and to find or create new needs to which they can direct themselves. This is one of the characteristics of the bureaucratic organization.[31] Business firms are no different in this respect, and thus generally require more than a gentle shove in order to rethink their objectives and structures.

---

[30]Kenneth E. Boulding, "The Economics of the Coming Spaceship Earth," in *The Futurists,* ed. Alvin Toffler (New York: Random House, 1972), p. 237; see also Kenneth J. Arrow, "Social Responsibility and Economic Efficiency," *Public Policy,* 23 (Summer 1973), 303-17.

[31]Warren Bennis, *Beyond Bureaucracy* (New York: McGraw-Hill, 1966).

One of the major criteria of the worth of any work or handcraft up to the time of the Industrial Revolution was the relative value of the good or service to society. As we have seen, with the growth of cities, industry, and especially the division of labor, an ideology developed that bestowed value on any work, regardless of its outcome. Various undesirable tasks had to be performed, so the new ideology found these tasks valuable and worthwhile. A growing number of men and women are now questioning the value of some work, no matter how well paid it may be. For example, these individuals claim that they would not work for a strip mining firm, a cosmetic manufacturer, or a hard-line advertiser. They are thereby reintroducing criteria that had been pushed aside in the last few generations: the value of work is judged both by the contribution that the product or service makes to society, and by the contribution of the individual to that product or service.[32] Some sort of individual transportation vehicles are clearly necessary, and thus the work of the auto worker takes on an importance beyond his paycheck and benefits. Whether the present noisy, gasoline-powered, two-ton steel vehicle is able to win job satisfaction for its makers is questionable, however.

Does it make any difference whether the manager or the worker is helping to make canned foods, jet fighters, cigarettes, or throw-away bottles? All goods are not of equal value, and it is possible for individuals to make judgments on the relative value of these goods. In a small, primitive economy these questions do not arise, since there are only resources and effort available to provide the necessities. In an affluent society, luxuries are possible; and this forces such value questions. If resources are limited and people are not willing to work long hours, what goods are more valuable to society? The values we are addressing here should help us to provide these criteria. Perhaps goods and services could be judged insofar as they support life, build community, give freedom, and provide joy and happiness. These values are very general, but they may provide a beginning in hammering out new criteria.

New Measures of Success

The issues that have been discussed all point to one basic question: How do we measure the success of an economic system? These considerations indicate that priority is gradually shifting from efficiency and productivity to justice, equality, and providing the means for a humane life for all. Once a people attain a certain level of affluence, they find that their needs for material goods have been met. Hence, as "education induces a greater regard for self-development, materialism progressively loses much of its appeal as a prime motivating force."[33]

[32]See the challenges to the work ethic described earlier in Chapter 5.
[33]Ian Wilson, "How Our Values Are Changing," *The Futurist* (February 1970), p. 7.

As more people find that the material goods they need are rather readily available, the *quality* of their lives becomes more important. However, agreeing on and measuring success with these more all-embracing criteria are still in infant stages. Not only do one person's notions of a better quality of life differ from another's but any sort of measurement of success in reaching those goals is also difficult. In contrast, the criteria of success in reaching the traditional business goals of greater efficiency and productivity are readily agreed upon. These criteria are constructed in such a way that they are also easily measurable and hence manageable. Determining quality of life goals, and also some criteria by which to measure success in achieving them, again underscores the point that ". . . the search for a new sense of meaning and purpose in life will become a matter of real importance."[34] We are again faced with basic questions: What sort of life do we want? What sort of society do we want for ourselves and for our children?

Recognition of the need for establishing some criteria of successful performance on larger quality of life issues has spurred a movement to develop some sort of "social indicators."[35] Both government and private agencies have attempted to outline social goals in the areas of health, learning and culture, income and poverty, justice, public order, housing, transportation, and the physical environment. In each of these areas, it is often difficult to agree on the purpose of the activity, to say nothing of arriving at a method of measuring progress toward the goal. Nevertheless, the growing social indicator movement shows that many are not only convinced of the need for a clearer statement of goals, but are already moving beyond that in an attempt to measure progress toward the attainment of those goals.

Parallel to the attempt to develop social indicators for society has been the search for a viable social audit for the corporation itself.[36] Several large companies, including Bank of America and American Telephone and Telegraph, have attempted various systems of measuring their performance in activities that affect the society around them. The more exact attempts, such as those of the management consultants of Abt Associates, try to measure the total dollar value of the firm's social contribution, and also the dollar costs to the larger society of the firm's operations, such as the pollution caused. It is exceedingly difficult to obtain accurate dollar figures on many of these less tangible items. Moreover, trying to obtain them might skew social efforts

[34]*Ibid.* See also Herman Kahn and B. Bruce-Briggs, *Things to Come: Thinking About the Seventies and Eighties* (New York: Macmillan, 1972), esp. pp. 162-231.

[35]See the more detailed discussion of social indicators and corporate appraisal criteria in another book in this series, Lee E. Preston and James E. Post, *Private Management and Public Policy* (Englewood Cliffs, N.J.: Prentice-Hall, 1974), pp. 130-41.

[36]Raymond A. Bauer and Dan H. Fenn, Jr., *The Corporate Social Audit* (New York: Russell Sage Foundation, 1972); also by the same authors, "What *Is* a Corporate Social Audit?" *Harvard Business Review,* 51 (January-February 1973), 37-48.

toward those that can be measured. Hence most firms are attempting a less accounting-like audit.

The social audits that firms such as General Electric, General Motors, and CNA Financial have embarked upon involve a careful listing of all corporate activities that have social impact, plus a reporting of the effects of and a systematic assessment of the successes of those activities. Equal employment opportunity activities at these firms, and at most others, have been so organized for some time; the federal government has required accurate reporting, and in this area clear targets and measurable results are more easy to come by. But no social audit or report can be attempted until the business firm sets forth clear policy as to what sort of social response it intends to make. So prior to social reporting comes a series of decisions, many of which are based on value judgments. Social auditing, just like any response by a firm to new social needs, demands that the goals of the firm and its impact on society be rethought and publicly restated. These new social concerns and successes of the firm are being stated not only in social audits, but also in annual reports (Ford, IBM, Xerox) and executive speeches and advertisements (Exxon, Gulf).

There are other indications that the new social concerns, involving a broader definition of corporate goals, are becoming institutionalized. As indicated in the last chapter, stockholder proposals to the major corporations on social issues (disclosure of equal employment data, political contributions, strip mining) are becoming a regular part of annual meetings. If any sort of "shareholder democracy" is to become a reality, stockholders need some help in making these decisions. The Washington-based Investor Responsibility Research Center has begun to investigate each of the issues appearing on a major firm's agenda and to write up the background, so as to enable the stockholder to make an intelligent decision on how to vote.

Another proposal for making the firm more sensitive to the needs of the larger society is through public representatives on the board of directors. Recognizing that even conscientious outside board members give only part of their time to the firm and are totally dependent for information on line management, both Arthur Goldberg and Robert Townsend have advocated a few public directors on every board who would be full-time and empowered to gather their own independent information.[37] The public interest could thus be represented by these relatively independent directors. If, for example, the corporation were planning on shutting down an inefficient innercity plant in order to move the operation to a rural area, the public director could take it on him or herself to investigate the economic and social impact on the com-

[37]Arthur J. Goldberg, "Debate on Outside Directors," *The New York Times,* October 29, 1972, Sec. F, p. 1; also Robert Townsend, "Let's Install Public Directors," and Donald E. Schwartz, "Reforming the Corporation from Within," *Business and Society Review,* 1 (Spring 1972), 63-70.

munity. Thus the public director might argue for building a new plant within the same community. That director could argue the case directly at the board meeting, and if there were no response in cases that warrant it, he or she might even release the facts to the public at a press conference.

Arthur Goldberg, former associate justice of the Supreme Court and United States ambassador to the United Nations, while a director of Trans World Airlines (TWA), wanted independent outside directors. He proposed that the outside directors have a separate staff for information gathering and that they meet independently on issues. His request was turned down, and so he resigned from TWA's board. Goldberg's proposal was worthwhile, and TWA would have benefited in the long run if it had taken the leadership on this issue. Since his proposal, a number of firms have appointed representatives of the public and have also established public policy committees among their outside board members.

Business firms that are serious about their social responsiveness have begun to restructure their internal policies, procedures, and reward systems.[38] Fine-sounding speeches and policy announcements may be a good beginning, but unless they are implemented within the firm in some hard-headed fashion, they remain words. After the policy is clearly stated, generally a staff specialist is appointed to see that it is carried out. Clear goals are specified, and it is made clear to all management personnel that performance on social policy is one of the factors considered along with other more traditional criteria for salary increase and promotion. It is only when managers are rewarded on the basis of their social performance that they realize the policy is serious and not merely public relations.

Harmony with the Environment

In addition to meeting citizens' real needs, in the future the corporation will be constrained to operate in greater equilibrium with the natural environment. Scarcity of resources, pollution, and undesirable by-products all place limits on the direction and pace of economic and business growth. These physical constraints will become more obvious, and citizens' expectations of the firm living in harmony with them will become more pronounced.

When speaking of life as a whole, many opt for simplification. At present, for example, a great deal of time and energy is wasted in transportation. Much of the time that was saved in cutting down the hours of the work day is now absorbed in getting to and from work, stores, schools, and so on. This is not only a waste of human time and energy, but also a waste of petroleum and other natural resources. Similarly, time is wasted in filling out forms such as

---

[38] Robert W. Ackerman, "How Companies Respond to Social Demands," *Harvard Business Review,* 51 (July-August 1973), p. 91. Also, "Making Minority Policies Effective," in Theodore V. Purcell and Gerald F. Cavanagh, *Blacks in the Industrial World* (New York: Free Press, 1972), pp. 223-32.

income tax returns, insurance applications, and questionnaires, and in listening to advertisements. In speaking of these same issues in the concluding paragraph of his book *Alienation and Economics,* Walter Weisskopf urges, "Wherever there is a choice between making more money and simplifying life, the latter road should be taken." He goes on to spell out the details:

> . . . abandonment of the purely activistic way of life, of getting and doing more and more for the sake of power over and control of the external world including our fellow beings; taking seriously the Kantian maxim that men should never be used as means but always as "ends"; putting more stress on being than on doing by cultivating receptivity to nature, to others, to art, to feelings; more listening rather than talking, also in relation to one's inner life; taking seriously intuition and insight by trying to resurrect what is valid in mysticism and religion; recovering the art of faith by breaking through the value-relativism of technical reason and cultivating the inner powers on which faith rests.[39]

Most of these new attitudes are already observable among many segments of our society, and they seem to be spreading.

These new human aspirations are going to have a significant impact on the firm and its activities. The successful firm will respond to these constraints, insofar as it is its prerogative to do so, either because of its own management's responsiveness to these issues, or because of government regulation. Neil Chamberlain argues persuasively that there is no way in which the free pursuit of individual greed can benefit society as a whole.[40] In any large economy where business institutions narrowly seek their own profit and growth, there will inevitably be serious undesirable side effects. To the extent that one accepts Chamberlain's skillfully argued thesis, additional government regulation seems inevitable. Business executives, on the other hand, consistently deplore government regulation. It is true that regulation takes flexibility out of the system, and the efficiency and effectiveness of government regulatory agencies are not exemplary. In fact, some socially conscious actions have been undertaken by firms at least in part to forestall regulation.

Business management is now seen to be responsible not only for product, financing, and work force, but also for any pollution or undesirable side effects their operations bring about. As Peter Drucker puts it, "Managements of all institutions are responsible for their by-products, that is, the impacts of their legitimate activities on people and on the physical and social environment."[41] It is clear that the first responsibility lies with business managers themselves.

---

[39]Walter A. Weisskopf, *Alienation and Economics* (New York: Dutton, 1971), p. 192.
[40]Chamberlain, *op. cit.*
[41]Peter Drucker confirms this in his *Management: Tasks, Responsibilities and Practices,* p. 312.

Economic and social power is so concentrated in most industries (steel, auto, rubber, oil, chemical, and computer) that there is in reality no free market. Further centralization, mergers, and concentration of power militate against pluralism and the free market. Although many of these large firms are socially conscious, many others are not known for that virtue. Since concentration further limits flexibility and the free market, perhaps there could be enacted a graduated income tax on corporate profits. Presently this tax is 48 percent, regardless of the amount of profits. Until recently—when "tax reform" came to mean giving higher-income individuals a break—Americans had come to expect the graduated personal income tax. Perhaps in the same fashion, smaller firms could be given a tax advantage so as to encourage innovation, flexibility, and new ventures.

Necessity of a New Legitimacy for the Corporation

The legitimacy of any institution depends on the extent to which that institution can justify to its constituency and the larger society its right to exist. It is a political necessity that those who wield power in a society must establish their right to do so. In any society, whether democratic or not, a group or institution that seeks legitimacy must identify itself with some principle that is acceptable to the community as a whole.[42] If an institution does not possess the support and confidence of the majority of the people in a society, it will lose legitimacy, and its future is threatened. We already know from discussion in Chapter 5 that in recent years only about one-fourth of the American people have confidence in business and business leadership. It is but a short step from this lack of confidence to a questioning of the very role, purpose, and existence of the corporation.

This problem is especially acute in a democratic society, where citizens at least theoretically have the political power formally to initiate or dispose of institutions. A corporation exists at the pleasure of society; it is granted a charter by the state to serve the larger needs of society. It is expected, therefore, that the corporation will contribute to the good of society. In the past this contribution was in providing goods and services at a profit. Adam Smith's "invisible hand" was thought to guide this individual, self-interested pursuit of profit to the ultimate benefit of society, through the most efficient use of resources and lower prices. The low esteem with which Americans presently hold business and the corporation is an indication that the "invisible hand" is no longer thought to guide the economy to society's best interest. This constitutes an erosion of legitimacy.

Americans have always had ambivalent attitudes toward business and business people. In addition, citizens have recently come to expect the cor-

[42] John G. Maurer, *Readings in Organization Theory* (New York: Random House, 1971), p. 361.

poration to be more sensitive to the larger problems of society. If these expectations are not met, confidence and hence legitimacy will be further eroded. Peter Drucker entitles the last section of his recent book, *Management*, "The Need for Legitimacy."[43] In reacquiring legitimacy, Drucker rejects the enlightened self-interest model as automatically benefiting society: "This, by the way, is why the rhetoric of 'profit maximization' and 'profit motive' are not only antisocial. They are immoral." The strength of the model in the past has been the efficiency it encouraged; its weakness is its inadequacy in addressing vitally important social problems.

Even though we reject profit maximization as the goal of a corporation because it is narrow and self-defeating in the long run, it is still possible to use the same methodologies in determining profit and acknowledge it as a constraint. That is, a business in the free market must be profitable to stay in operation. Its norm of success is surely not an exclusive, myopic profit maximization, but the extent to which the firm can satisfy the needs of society. Excess of income over expense provides the large parameters within which the firm is expected to operate. Within those parameters, management has considerable discretion. And within that area of discretion, its actions need not always be a "knee-jerk" reaction to maximize profits; it can have the firm act as a responsive citizen of society.

If this qualified profit maximization is accepted as the purpose of the corporation, it must be acknowledged that management is now often without the technical information, the skills, and the attitudes to pursue the larger goal. This leaves the corporation in an immense void. As we have seen above, many firms are moving rapidly to develop new policies and new reward systems to implement the new policies. In addition, this need has been recognized in the better business schools in their newly designed courses in social policy. Managers who have been exposed to these new issues and have reflected on them are able to grasp the new needs and act on them without defensiveness. These new policies and the resulting corporate activities may restore badly needed confidence and legitimacy to the corporation.

Interdependence of People, Institutions, Nations

In a world of more people, more elaborate tools and life styles, and quicker transportation and communication, peoples and institutions are becoming more interdependent. A military coup in Latin America or Asia is in our living room in a matter of hours via television. Malnutrition and starvation in Africa are brought home to us quickly, along with the fact that our use of lawn fertilizar, dog food, and even meat may play a role in depriving those Africans of life-giving grain. When suburbanites try to flee the problems of the city, they find that their affluent sons and daughters, without parks,

[43]Drucker, *op. cit.,* p. 810.

libraries, and corner stores within walking or bus distance, find little to do and become bored. Many then go on drugs, drop out of school, and run away from home. International policies that may have worked for England or France in the last century must be discarded for the United States today; the United States, powerful as she is, can no longer assume that what is good for the United States is therefore good for the world.

The immense problems that face us face all nations: population, deteriorating environment, malnutrition, nuclear power and threat of nuclear warfare, balance of payments, dwindling resources, and inflation. No single nation, in spite of the threats and bravado of some who speak of "project independence," can face these problems alone. Some nations, such as Japan and England, are more dependent than others on outside sources of raw materials, but ultimately all peoples will depend more and more on each other. Looking on this extremely complicated interdependence tempts many social commentators to see the problems as immense and almost unsolvable.[44] Since peoples and nations seem unwilling to limit their own individuality, sovereignty, and greed, they are convinced that there is no hope for mankind.

Sociologist of religion Robert Bellah sees America's failure in its emphasis on the atomistic self and rational self-interest, and its break with the basic understandings of the Founding Fathers. In early American documents and times there was a strong social, collective emphasis: a consideration of citizens together as responsible for the state. Bellah demonstrates how this comes from the biblical covenant between God and his people, and from the gospel notion of a loving community based on brotherly charity and membership in one common body. Bellah is convinced that the economic system of contemporary industrial America has broken with and cannot be reconciled with the early American rationale of economic interdependence as the basis of political order.[45]

Perhaps these early ideals can be recaptured. In any case, the urgency and vital importance of the many problems that jointly face the nations of the world may force their leaders to work pragmatically to determine and carry out public policy together. The continued survival and well-being of all men and women may force nations to overcome nationalism, insularity, and greed in a way that ideals and altruism could not accomplish.

Religious Roots of a New Business Creed

Personal and societal goals for Americans have been heavily influenced by religion, especially Christianity and Judaism. The Protestant ethic stemmed

[44]See, for example, Robert Heilbroner, *The Human Prospect* (New York: Norton, 1974).

[45]Robert N. Bellah, *The Broken Covenant: American Civil Religion in Time of Trial* (New York: Seabury, 1975).

from Christianity, and particularly Calvinist Christianity. Although it soon became very much a part of secular ideals and values, its religious roots are unmistakable—as indicated in its very name. Since religious values have had such a profound influence on business and economic life in the past, it is not inappropriate to ask whether religious ideals might have a significant impact in the future. Even more important, if religion does have an impact on business and our very way of life, what will that impact be?

In spite of the current fashionable and tired cynicism, there has always been a strong streak of moralism in American culture. Our history is replete with idealistic public reaction to problems and issues—so much so that many Europeans and Asians think of us as naive. In the last century the antislavery (abolition) and anti-big business (muckraking) movements were moralistic endeavors, and many of those involved received inspiration from the Gospels (as, also, did many of the defenders of slavery and big business trusts!). Ralph Nader comes from a religious family with high ideals, and John Gardner's Common Cause appeals to the generosity and moralism in Americans. The shocked American reaction to the Watergate coverup and the abuse of Presidential power also showed high moral expectations in the public forum.

The civil rights movement in the United States was led by Martin Luther King, Jr., a Baptist minister. He preached "love for the oppressor," and espoused a specific, nonviolent technique to gain social justice for blacks. The record shows how effective the movement and his leadership was. Among those protesting the war in Vietnam was a group of Catholic peace activists, led and inspired by Daniel Berrigan, S.J. This group opposed the war early, and used a confronting though nonviolent strategy in presenting their case. Whether one agrees with the group's tactics or not, it is still working for world peace and justice and release of political prisoners in Vietnam, Brazil, Chile, and around the world. More important, Berrigan as their leader is deeply contemplative and inspired by the Gospels and the life of Jesus. A man who was an inspiration to both King and Berrigan was Mahatma Gandhi, who was also inspired by the Gospels and the life of Christ. Moreover, as history testifies, his nonviolent approach to gaining independence for India from England was successful. The theme motivating all these gospel-inspired leaders and movements is liberation: freedom of the poor, ordinary citizen from the colonial oppressor; liberation of the black from white racist bigotry; self-determination for people around the world.

Calvinistic Christianity contributed to an ideology that focused on a building up of the earth's cities and standard of living. It was perhaps necessary during the past two centuries to concentrate on new frontiers, and on building railroads and industry. This need remains, but for the developed nations at least, it is now not quite so paramount. Increased emphasis on humanistic and spiritual values among certain elite groups, such as students and corporate executives, are shown in surveys. Along with a new concern for nature, sharing, feeling, and intuition is also "a greatly increased interest in, and tolerance for, the transcendental, religious, mystical and spiritual views."[46] Religion is thus a growing influence, especially insofar as it is built upon some personal experience. Institutional religions are wrestling with the questions of how to measure the validity of this experience, and how to provide an environment that will encourage it.

In any case, interest in the mystical and in deeper experiences, along with a concern for self-knowledge and sensitivity to self and the world around one, are all gaining ground. The person is thus seen as more than rational and organized; he or she is also deeply human and spiritual. This new recognition and emphasis is already having an effect on attitudes toward other persons, the environment, the city, and so on. From it will surely come attitudes that will also alter our business values.

Theology of Liberation

Theology is almost a dirty word in American society. It connotes airy, idealistic speculation on one hand, and coercion on the other. A theology, however, is merely an attempt to understand one's self, one's life, one's society, and one's God in the light of religious values, especially as experienced and presented in scripture. Liberation of peoples from bonds that constrain and oppress them is the theme of a new theology that is gaining widespread attention throughout the world. It began in Peru, Uruguay, Chile, and other Latin American countries,[47] where the gap between the few extremely wealthy landowners and industrialists and the poverty-stricken average citizen is intolerably wide. New right-wing military dictatorships have intensified the demand for liberation, for self-determination, for individual control over jobs, cities, nations, and lives. Liberation theology insists on beginning with an examination of people's actual condition in a given society. Thus one of the principal inputs is the experience of the struggle for liberation and self-determination for all men. Liberation theology is built on the social conditions in which people find themselves.

In short, if religious values influenced economic life in the past, there is every reason to suspect that they will do so in the future. One of the spreading new movements is one of liberation, whether it be women's liberation, liberation of minorities, or liberation of all men and women. The growth and success of the "theology of liberation" suggests that it may be an influence on

---

[46]Willis W. Harman, "Humanistic Capitalism: Another Alternative," *Journal of Humanistic Psychology,* 14 (Winter 1974), 21.

[47]See Gustavo Gutierrez, *A Theology of Liberation* (Maryknoll, N.Y.: Orbis Books, 1973); Phillip E. Berryman, "Latin American Liberation Theology," *Theological Studies,* 34 (September 1973), 357-95.

men's and women's attitudes and ideals in the future. If so, this will mean a demand for self-determination, whether at work, at home, or in the city. Such self-determination is not the old-fashioned individualistic sort of demand, but one that is hammered out with others, in a community of men and women who look for their own and their society's fulfillment. It is only fair here to point out that liberation theology takes a harsh and critical view of capitalism. These theologians and the movements they inspire feel that capitalism, profit maximization, and foreign ownership leads to exploitation of the poor. They opt for various forms of participation, and for worker control in the case of industry. No matter how the plant is structured, they would have some significant worker input into all decisions, whether short or long range.

It is undoubtedly a healthy characteristic for American society to have streaks of utopianism, moralism, and even righteousness. The latter can be arrogant and unbending, but it can also provide the inspiration and motivation for a people to continue to have hope and demand the best from themselves, their society, and their institutions. Perhaps it is on the basis of this sort of idealistic desire for the best for ourselves and for all that a new sort of cultural superego could be built. One of the human necessities of the future will be, according to Daniel Callahan,[48] a series of new cultural "thou shalt nots." He maintains that mankind will not be able to survive without a new set of accommodated appetites, a habitual willingness to conserve and preserve, and a general conscientious concern for others. Admitting that this is an almost impossible task, he concludes that it is nevertheless absolutely necessary if we are not to descend to starvation and chaos.

The alternatives presented by most of the social commentators who are looking at the future are stark: disruption, decay, and chaos, or developing new spiritual and human values and making them a habitual part of everyday personal life and institutional decision making. On this shrinking planet, economic and political planning must increasingly consider such larger issues. Paradoxically, it is "old fashioned" religion that has traditionally urged the viewpoint of concern for *others,* especially the poor, people in other nations, and future generations.

Concern for Others

Self-centeredness and insularity are the vices of the child. As a person, loved and cared for, matures, that same person tends to be less defensive and turned in on the self. He or she begins to move out toward others and to love. Love is a basic, human virtue. It is the act of a parent or a peer; it is an act of giving, often without hope of return. This sort of altruistic love is possible for any person, although it is more readily achieved by the person who has been loved. Self-giving love is essential for the growth of persons, families, and

[48]See Daniel Callahan, *The Tyranny of Survival* (New York: Macmillan, 1974).

society, yet it is sometimes difficult. Speaking of this sort of love, economist Kenneth Boulding says:

> It always builds up, it never tears down, and it does not merely establish islands of order in a society at the cost of disorder elsewhere. It is hard for us, however, to learn to love, and the teaching of love is something at which we are still very inept.[49]

Much of the energy of the very poor is spent on obtaining the necessities of life. Once an individual's basic needs are reasonably satisfied, that person more readily has the time and the inclination to be concerned with the needs of the larger society. Affluence can put a person in a position where he or she is no longer totally dependent, with all energies consumed in obtaining the next meal. Greater availability of food and shelter provides a physical and psychological security that can enable people to reach out beyond themselves and their own concerns. A certain amount of material security can be the foundation for loving and self-giving. The problems of human life, development of the person, and interdependence of persons and institutions can be far more readily approached. There is evidence that such attitudes are growing, as has been indicated earlier in this chapter and in Chapter 5. Western society is uniquely ready for greater love and concern for others, and the problems we face together could be better solved given such an attitude.

Vision and Hope

Some of the most widely read current social commentaries[50] find that the problems we face are so immense as to be almost unsolvable. These commentators, many of whom are veterns of research and policymaking themselves, find that our obsession with economic growth has blinded us to human needs. Although we profess democracy, people have control over their own lives and futures only very indirectly, if at all.

Many of the problems underscored by these commentators have been discussed in this book. They are very serious problems, and it would be myopic—even foolhardy and suicidal—to refuse to address them. Nevertheless, the question becomes: Do we have the resources and the motivation to change the institutions that so much affect our lives and our values? Can we alter our institutions so that we are able to approach equal rights for all men and women? Can the values, structures, and institutions necessary for peace and justice throughout the world be built?

---

[49]Kenneth E. Boulding, *The Meaning of the Twentieth Century* (New York: Harper & Row, 1964), p. 146.

[50]See for example, Donella Meadows et al., *The Limits to Growth* (New York: Signet Books, 1972); Heilbroner, *op. cit.;* and Richard C. Goodwin, *The American Condition* (Garden City, N.Y.: Doubleday, 1974).

Vision and hope have always been characteristically American virtues. Ever since the days of the frontier, we have never had patience with defeatists or fatalists. It would be foolish to be naive about the enormity of the tasks before us, but it would also ensure failure if we were to give up before we have even tried to make our values, institutions, and society more human.

SUMMARY AND CONCLUSIONS

The American business system has achieved unprecedented efficiency, productivity, and growth. It has provided more material goods and a higher standard of living for more people than any other business system in history. In spite of these measurable successes, however, this business system has also failed in many now painfully obvious ways. Gross, indiscriminate economic growth is currently being questioned as an adequate measure of success. Often enough, a firm that adds to the gross national product adds nothing to beauty, health, and personal happiness. Furthermore, its products or production process may pollute, use up nonrenewable resources, or destroy the ozone layer that protects us from cancer-producing rays of the sun.

Affluence, crumbling confidence in institutions in general, and the "post-industrial" society have all left business and the corporation in a precarious, unstable position. In addition, the current ideology of the business system—self-interest and individualism—rewards selfishness and rationalizes self-seeking behavior. Economic instability, the constraints of non-renewable resources, and new personal attitudes are bringing on a "second American Revolution." New business values are emerging.

Clues to the values that are being included in the new ideology have been with us for some time. On the macro scale, citizens are demanding that individual business decisions better contribute to the overall goals of society. A large business firm is no longer merely seen as a wholly private, self-interest-oriented enterprise; its role is to serve the needs of society. If such business firms are unable or do not choose to act responsibly, it will be necessary to enact legislation (similar to antitrust or tax incentives) to encourage social and discourage antisocial corporate behavior.

Americans are seeking greater self-activity and self-reliance, even in the face of the dehumanizing factors of modern life. In spite of encompassing institutions, whether government or corporate, individuals still prefer autonomy, personal responsibility, and the ability to share decisions. Institutions and corporations can be better structured to encourage such self-reliance and responsibility.

Self-reliance, individual responsibility, and initiative give dignity and satisfaction to the individual, in addition to generally bringing about a more efficient organization. We have found to our chagrin, however, that these motivations do not always automatically provide the best total society. Hence, it is necessary to clarify goals and to construct legislative and cultural inducements so that individual activities may better contribute to producing a more humane society.

Religion has in the past, and probably will in the future, provide a foundation for business ideology. True enough, traditional religious values generally run counter to self-interest, and what has come to be known as the consumer ethic. The Protestant ethic demanded a moderated, planned, and self-sacrificing life. Pollution, noise, anxiety, crime, and other current problems that accompany the operations of the impersonal, profit-maximizing bureaucratic corporation show the failure of the old ethic and the need for new values. Americans now seem ready for some sacrifice for the sake of a larger purpose. Most would gladly give up a Florida vacation or a third automobile if it meant a more satisfying job and life, better relationships, and the conviction that their own children and future generations would not inherit a nation ravaged by open-pit mines and cancer-producing chemicals in drinking water—the fruits of this generation's selfishness. Western religions have traditionally directed peoples' attention out beyond themselves. With this sort of vision, Americans might share some of their expertise and resources with the poorer peoples of the world so that these less privileged can have some of the more important and humane fruits of industry. It is precisely religion that urges discipline of self and generosity toward one's neighbor based on a reverence for God and a loving concern for others.

Clarifying and internalizing values and goals is necessary for any person as he or she grows to maturity. Especially in a period of rapid change, these values provide a firm foundation upon which to build a stable, challenging, and satisfying life and career. These personal values are also the building blocks out of which, together with society's conditions and needs, can be fashioned the future goals and policies of the business firm. In this essential process of examining and articulating new values and goals, leadership is also needed. The problems are immense, pressing, and complex. Nevertheless, business, government, educational, and religious leaders may yet be able to point out directions and to inspire confidence.

Index

A

Abegglen, James, 85
Absenteeism, 72
Achievement, 20
    as value, 60, 194
    Christian influence, 36
    major goals, 95
    measures of success, 56-57, 193-98
    need for achievement, 79-81, 190
    short-run performance, 47, 71-72
    See also Work, attitudes toward
Activity and work, 20-21
    alienation from, 110-12
    as value, 59-60, 190
    idleness, 36
    motives, 32, 178, 189-91
    rewards of, 59
    See also Work, attitudes toward
Adams, John, 4
Advertising, 119, 146, 155
Agriculture, *see* Farming
Allende, Salvador, 113
Alliance of Progress, 114
American Management Association, 100
American Medical Association, 63
Anglo-Saxons, 48
Anxiety, 88-90
Aquinas, Thomas, 34
Argyris, Chris, 75
Aristotle, 31
Arnold, Matthew, quoted, 56-57
Arrow, Kenneth, 164
Art, 80
Asch, Solomon E., 77

Assumptions, 84
Authority, 41, 97-98
    authoritarian governments, 156

B

Baumhart, Raymond, cited, 98-99, 164
Bell, Daniel, 172
Bellah, Robert, cited, 202
Benedictines, 33-36
Berle, Adolph A., quoted, 25, 65-66
Berrigan, Daniel, S.J., cited, 203
Brainwashing of prisoners of war, 87
Brazil, 148
Bureaucracy
    behavior, 70
    division of labor, 110-11
    goal displacement, 76, 194
Business creed
    American, 57
    classical, 58-59
    code of ethics, 164-65
    explanation of, 57-61
    managerial, 58-59
    qualities of, 68
    religious roots, 202-4, 208
Business education, 143-45, 163-67
    See also Education
Business people
    early Puritans, 2-3
    ethics, 98-101, 137
    graduate students, 93, 137, 144, 163
    personal values, 74, 91-92, 137
    role of, 46, 58

C

Cabet, cited, 104
Calvin, John, 37-38
Campaign, GM, 158
Capitalism
    alienation of worker, 110
    American, 58
    Christian view, 36
    and church, 37, 205
    decay of, 55-56
    and democracy, 115-16
    Marx's view, 127
    professional responsibility, 64, 65-66
    scope, 103
    social consequences, 118-20, 174, 205
    socialist influence, 130-31
Career, 92-93
Carnegie, Andrew, 52-53, 175
Cary, Frank T., quoted, 136-37
Catholicism, 39, 80, 86, 203-5
Chamberlain, Neil, cited, 199
Chamber of Commerce, 167-69, 182
Charity
    as basis for industry, 33, 35
    See also Love
Children, *see* Family
Chile, 141, 148, 204
China
    economy, 122, 130-31
    inspiration of Mao Tse-tung, 124-26
    social equality, 123-24
    social motivation, 124-26
    standard of living, 129
Christianity, *See* Catholicism; Protestantism;
    Religion
Churches, 49-51, 80, 82, 89, 99
Class
    economic, 115, 173
    social, 107-9, 121, 123
Colonial Pipeline, 139-40
Committee for Economic Development, 59
Communal living
    monastic life, 33-36
    New Harmony, 105
    Shakers, 104-5
Communism
    alienation of the worker, 110-15
    Capital, 107
    contrasted with capitalism, 56, 115
    criticism of U.S., 112
    criticisms of economic system, 106-7, 115
    distribution of wealth, 107

Communism *(cont.)*
    economy, 131
    equality of women, 124
    exploitation of the worker, 107-10
    goals, 122
    idea on ideology, 14-15
    ideology, 121
    mission, 121, 128
    private possessions, 109
    scope, 103
    theory of history, 106
Competition
    free competition, 42, 63, 99
    for human life, 11
    as value, 10-11, 42-43, 59-60, 78
    See also Capitalism, Free enterprise
Competitive behavior, 78, 98
Concentration, economic, 140-41, 200
Conference on Areas of Public Concern, 162
Confidence
    in business and business leadership, 117,
        138, 141, 169
    in institutions, 146-49, 200
    personal and national, 155
Conglomerate, 140-41
Conscience, 98
Conservatives and ideology, 17
Consumerism, 157-58, 173, 179
Consumer sovereignty, 174
Conwell, Russell (Baptist preacher), 51-52
Coolidge, Calvin, quoted, 139
Cooperation, 75, 103-6, 201-2, 205-6
Corporation
    accountability, 138, 139, 195-98
    as economic institution, 62, 74, 110, 183-84
    environmental concern, 140, 153
    goal displacement, 71, 76
    goals, 26, 70, 72-74, 83, 140, 185-86,
        193-95, 200-201
    influence, 70-71, 74
    legitimacy, 25-26, 41, 159, 163, 177-78,
        200-201
    management, *See* Management
    multinational, 147
    ownership, 109
    reputation, 83, 99, 149
    response, 166-69
    self-interest, *see* Self-interest
    size, 140
    social responsibility, 9, 25, 62, 158-61,
        180-83, 193-95, 197-98
    stock, 141
    stockholders, 62, 158-59, 197

International Telephone and Telegraph, 140-41, 146-47

International trade, 43, 113, 201-2

Investment, 109, 122
  foreign, 112-13, 146-48
  institutional investors, 162

Investor Responsibility Research Center, 161, 197

J

Jefferson, Thomas, 4-5, 68

Job satisfaction
  conflicts with jobs, 75, 149-50
  decision-making, 191-92
  dissatisfaction, 71, 72-73, 150, 190
  executive, 73
  identity crisis, 88, 150
  search for, 30, 149

Johnson, Lyndon, 181

Judaism, 202

K

Katoff, quoted, 124

Kennedy, John, cited, 6, 147

Keniston, Kenneth, cited, 110

King, Martin Luther, Jr., 203

Kolko, Gabriel, cited, 107

L

Labor, *see* Activity and work; Work, attitudes toward

Labor unions, 111-12, 165

Leadership, 136
  See also Executives; Management

Legislation, 142, 181, 183-84
  See also Government

Legitimacy, 25-26, 41, 159, 163, 177, 200-201

Lending at interest, 37

Levitt, Theodore, quoted, 143-44

Liberation theology, 204-5

Likert, Rensis, 83-84, 188

Limits to Growth, 152-53

Litton Industries, 140-41, 148

Locke, John, 40-41, 115

Lodge, George C., 143, 181-82

Love, 74, 81, 175, 205-6

Lundberg, cited, 109-10

Luther, Martin, 36-37

M

Management
  basic assumptions, 54, 84
  corporate, 26
  goals, 73, 140
  incentives, 126-27
  legitimacy, 159
  masculine, 66-67
  purpose, 184
  scientific management, 53-54
  structure, 25-26, 158-60
  "valueless," 84

Mannheim, Karl, 16-18

Manufacturing, 42-44, 45, 53-54, 178-79
  See also Corporation

Mao Tse-tung, 103, 120, 125, 132
  influence of, 125, 132
  Maoism, 123
  social incentive, 124-27

Marcuse, Herbert, 119, 146, 155

Maritain, Jacques, quoted, 10

Marx, Karl, 14-15, 72, 106-10, 120

Marxism, *see* Communism

Maslow, Abraham H., 81-84

Materialism
  American, 9-10, 23, 59-61, 72-74, 150, 176, 195
  economic goals, 71-72
  higher standard of living, 56, 60, 119

Mather, Cotton, quoted, 3

McClelland, David C., 79-81

McGregor, Douglas, 75-76, 84

McKinsey lectures, 63-65

McNamara, Robert, 149

Media, 93, 167

Merton, Robert, quoted, 71

Military-industrial complex, 114-15, 148

Mill, John Stuart, cited, 7

Miller, J. Irwin, 99

Mills, C. Wright, cited, 109

Mining, 45-47

Minority groups, 19, 160, 182, 204
  See also Equal employment opportunity; Women

Money, 72, 81, 86-87

Moore, Philip W., quoted, 160

More, Thomas, 87

Moral orientation, 16
  of businessmen, 98-99, 164-65
  business's current moral crisis, 99-101, 136-38
  ethical code, 164
  hard work, 59